# WHITE EAGLE

# White Eagle
## by
# Paul Anthony

The right of Paul Anthony to be identified as the author of this work has been asserted by him in accordance with the Copyright, Designs and Patents Act of 1988

~

First Published 2017
Copyright © Paul Anthony 2017
All Rights Reserved.
Cover Image © by Paul Scougal and Margaret Scougal

Published by
Paul Anthony Associates UK

By the same author
~

In the 'Boyd' Crime Thriller Series…
The Fragile Peace
Bushfire
The Legacy of the Ninth
Bell, Book and Candle
Threat Level One
White Eagle
*

In the 'Davies King' Crime Thriller Series…
The Conchenta Conundrum
Moonlight Shadows
Behead the Serpent
Breakwater
*

In the Suspense Thriller Series…
Nebulous
*

In Autobiography…
Strike! Strike! Strike!
*

In Poetry and Anthologies…
Sunset
Scribbles with Chocolate
Uncuffed
Coptales
Chiari Warriors
*

In Children's book (with Meg Johnston) …
Monsters, Gnomes and Fairies (In my Garden)
*

To Margaret - Thank you, for never doubting me.
To Paul, Barrie and Vikki - You only get one chance at life. Live it well, live it in peace, and live it with love for one another.
To my special friends - Thank you, you are special.

...... Paul Anthony

~

With thanks to
Margaret Scougal and Pauline Livingstone
for editing, consulting, and advising on my work.

~

This is a story about terrorism.
It's about those who believe in that ideology,
and those charged with the protection of the public.
In the end, you might ask
Who wins? Who loses? And why?
...Paul Anthony

The Metropolitan Police Anti-Terrorist
Hotline
0800 789321

~

Crimestoppers
0800 555111

~

Don't let them get away with it…

~

# PROLOGUE

~

The Quandil Mountains
Iraqi Kurdistan
Fifteen years ago

There was a loud splash when a boulder was thrown into the stream and landed close to a dam under construction. Darius, a thirteen years old villager, waded into the water and manipulated the rock into a better place, stood back slightly to critique his work, and then rammed it tighter into the makeshift barrier.

'Ilya,' he shouted. 'Do you see what I have done?'

His younger brother stood on the bank and replied, 'You still haven't stopped the water, Darius.'

'He can't,' intervened Suz, the youngest of the trio. 'Only men can do that and Darius isn't a man yet.'

'I soon will be,' growled Darius. 'Anyway, girls shouldn't be here. You can't lift the rocks like us boys can.'

Suz looked down at the ground for a moment and then asked, 'Where does the water come from, Darius?'

'It comes from a waterfall high in the mountains and then it flows into our valley,' explained Darius. 'If it wasn't for the water and the summer sunshine, we wouldn't be able to grow things. The potatoes and apricots, for example, would not grow and there would be no tobacco fields.'

'How do you know about the waterfall?' enquired Ilya paddling into the water beside his brother.

'Father took me once,' revealed Darius. 'One day, when you are both old enough, father might take you to the waterfall too.'

Standing on the bank swinging an old cloth teddy bear, Suz asked, 'When will that be, Darius?'

'I don't know, Suz. He might not take you,' replied Darius.

'Why not?' his sister asked.

'Because you are a girl,' declared Darius. 'Mother will take you over the mountain pass one day and you'll go to the village of Wasan to buy things. You'll probably buy food and clothes for us and things to cook with. Our aunt and uncle live there so we are always welcome. They like our apricots and potatoes and usually buy some from mother. There's also a school in Wasan and it won't be long before you learn to read and write as well as cook.'

'But there's a school here in the village,' remarked Ilya.

'Yes, but the one in Wasan is a big school with proper teachers,' revealed Darius. 'Not just old people like here.'

'What good will school do?' asked Ilya. 'Suz is a girl. Mother will teach her how to cook.'

Darius shook his head and said, 'No, Ilya, there's much more to life than cooking. When you go to school they will tell you what they do with tobacco and how it is shipped to Turkey to be made into the cigarettes that the old men smoke. You will learn all about potatoes, apricots, fruits, beans – all the things we grow in the mountains.'

'Is that all?' asked Ilya.

'Oh no,' revealed Darius. 'You will learn about the telephone and electricity too.'

'Malik has a telephone,' ventured Suz.

'Yes, but that's a satellite phone,' explained Darius. 'There's a satellite in the sky that gets the messages and sends them to him.'

'I don't understand,' sighed Suz.

'Me neither,' added Ilya.

Thigh deep in water now, Darius waded to the opposite bank and gazed upstream to assess the movement of water, its direction and strength.

'More in the middle of the watercourse where the water is slightly deeper,' he decided. 'I must divide and rule the water.'

Tall for his age, the youngster selected another rock from his collection gathered on the bank and then paddled in carrying his next contribution at chest height.

'I will teach you things,' suggested Darius as he hoisted the rock as high as he could and ventured deeper into the watercourse.

'Things father told you?' asked Ilya.

'Yes,' agreed Darius. 'I learnt things at the big school in Wasan. I will be helping father in the laboratory soon. He said if I passed my school exams that I could work with him and I will be. I get paid too.'

'What did you learn at school?' enquired Ilya.

'Suz, Ilya,' remarked Darius. 'Sit down on the riverbank and I will tell you what I learnt.'

Reluctantly, Suz sat beside Ilya and asked, 'Should we pretend we are at school and you are the teacher?'

'Yes,' replied Darius dropping the rock into place. 'I'll be a good teacher. You'll see.'

'I'm listening,' said Ilya. 'I want to learn so that I can go to work with the Taliban too.'

'I know things because I am two years older than you, Ilya, and three years older than Suz,' suggested Darius. 'I will be working soon, earning money, and doing more things that are important. If I hadn't gone to school, none of this would have happened.'

'What did father tell you?' insisted Ilya.

'Well, I know we are Kurds and these mountains that surround our village are called the Kurdish Mountains. The mountains are between 3,000 and 4,500 metres above sea level.'

'What's the sea?' asked Suz.

'A big area of water where the land stops,' laughed Darius. 'One day you might visit the sea but right now I am teaching you. These mountains are part of a chain of mountains called the Zagros Mountains. They are named after the Zagarthian people. In ancient times, the Zagros Mountains were the tribal home of the Kassites, the Guti, Assyrians, Elamites and the Mitanni.'

'Oh yes,' replied Ilya. 'Sometimes we get Assyrians visiting us on horses.'

'That's right,' admitted Darius. 'They are the descendants of the Assyrians that I mentioned. They have lived in these mountains long before Muhammad, Ibrahim, Ismail, and all the other prophets of Islam. That's why these mountains are sacred to us.'

'I see,' revealed Suz. 'What's on the other side of the mountain pass apart from Wasan?'

'All kinds of things,' revealed Darius. 'But we are not very welcome there so our people will stop here if we have to. This is our home now.'

'Why don't people like us?' asked Ilya.

Darius picked up another rock for the dam and answered, 'We live in Kurdistan. It was founded at the end of the Ottoman Empire by the Treaty of Sevres in 1920. This means that when the owners of the mountains didn't own the mountains anymore they all got together in a place called Sevres and…'

'Is that near Wasan?' enquired Ilya.

'No,' replied Darius. 'Anyway, they signed a piece of paper called a treaty. That piece of paper made Kurdistan but only the Iraqi government agrees with it. That's why father and his friends have been fighting since 1984 against the Turkish state and we can't go anywhere else because people think we shouldn't have anywhere to live anymore.'

'Is the Turkish State the people who live on the other side of the mountain pass in the north?' asked Ilya.

'Yes,' replied Darius. 'Well done, Ilya. You will be good at school if you keep listening and learning.'

A low buzzing sound suddenly invaded his ears and he immediately dropped the rock in the water. Tilting his head to one side, Darius listened intently. The noise grew louder until it he recognised it as an aeroplane.

Shielding his eyes from the morning sun, he looked up and focused on the skies above.

He saw them gradually emerging from a white cloud bank. They were flying south towards his position.

Darius squinted and captured an image of a white star and white crescent on a red flag. The iconic emblem was printed on the underwing of an aircraft. Another aeroplane appeared bearing the same logo. The aircraft was accompanied by others and he counted them out loud.

'One…. Two…. Three flags…. Warplanes!' he screamed. 'Turkish warplanes!'

Struggling to the nearest bank, Darius wobbled across the dam and yelled, 'Ilya, Suz! Run! Come on!'

They sprinted towards their home in the nearby village with Darius doing his best to hurry his brother and sister along.

'Mother! Father! They're coming,' yelled Darius. 'Warplanes!'

As the three children ran towards their home, pilots above unleashed their Maverick air-to-ground tactical missiles and began their bombing campaign against the people who inhabited the disputed lands of Kurdistan.

'Ilya! Suz!' yelled Darius. 'Warplanes! Look out!'

Missiles exploded around Darius and his siblings with a savagery that electrified them. The bombs landed and burst into plummeting clouds of death and devastation. Maverick air to surface missiles found their target, exploded into scores of white hot projectiles mutilating and murdering the Kurdish villagers, and destroyed their homes and livelihoods.

Another bomb landed squarely on the school and blew the building into a thousand pieces.

Next to the schoolhouse there was a larger, more important, building where local villagers worked in collaboration with the Taliban in the illegal drug business. It was in this building that their father worked.

Darius feared for his father, and the occupants, because he knew how badly the building had been constructed. It had been cobbled together one week as a temporary structure and never completed properly. Corrugated sheets formed the roof of the breezeblock structure which boasted one entrance and no windows.

The Taliban harvested opium in Afghanistan and transported it through Iran to the Quandil Mountains where they used the building for their illicit trade. Globally, the area was known as the Golden Crescent because Afghanistan produced sixty per cent of the world's heroin supply from opium. The Golden Crescent overlapped the nations of Afghanistan, Iran, and Pakistan, whose mountainous borders defined the crescent.

Yet it was here, in the Quandil Mountains, where villagers processed the drug and arranged its transportation to Europe and the rest of the world where it was sold. It was the mainstay of the local and regional economy and an important part of the Taliban financial system.

'Perhaps this was the real target of the attack,' thought Darius but he didn't really know. He was just a youngster trying to make sense of it all.

'Mother! Father! Run for your lives,' screamed Darius.

There was a tremendous blast when two bombs simultaneously struck the drugs laboratory and blew it to kingdom come. Corrugated sheets, plaster, concrete, and masonry exploded into the atmosphere when a ton of explosives obliterated the centre and erased it from the map.

Finding a hiding place, Darius cowered beneath a rocky outcrop as the devil rent his anger on those below. Terrified, he watched the bombers pulverize his homeland. There was an explosion to his left followed by another blast to his right.

Huge clouds of rock and soil burst into the sky as the Turkish Air Force continued to blast the village whilst people ran for their lives.

Ilya fell.

Suz crashed to the ground.

Both were killed by the missiles from hell that continued to bombard the village.

A mass of rock and vegetation climbed into the air, reached a pinnacle of horror, and then crashed lethally downwards onto Darius's home. His parents were killed instantly when a direct hit destroyed their home causing death and destruction, and warping the life of Darius Yasin forever.

Across the valley, victims huddled close, prayed to their god for salvation and hid beneath any cover they could find as the bombardment continued and shell after shell rained down mercilessly from above.

For some, they were totally unprepared and set off running towards the stream and rocky outcrops that lay in the valley floor. They searched for cover to protect themselves. Others made for the caves set deep in the hillside in a frenzied attempt to escape the bloodcurdling offensive from above. Even more rushed to the thicket and dense woodlands that ordinarily might hide their presence from above. Today, the thicket offered minimal protection from the missiles from hell.

More warplanes, more missiles, more carnage and ruination followed as the Turkish Air Force pounded the Kurdish settlement and wreaked fury on the population.

A stillness eventually followed but then a lone F-16 jet fighter flew across the land and unleashed a torrent of gunfire on those fleeing the area.

Machine gun fire raked the valley floor, chased towards the caves, and then infiltrated woodland. It was like an angry snake spitting venom in its search for easy prey.

Hit in the chest, back, neck, leg, all over – they fell and died beneath the sacred mountains of Kurdistan.

Minutes later, the sky was clear and silence engulfed the mountains and valleys alike. Only thick black smoke spiralled into the sky and dared to blemish the azure blue.

A bizarre tranquillity fell over the area and was spoilt only by the occasional crack of a broken bough crashing to the ground.

With the atmosphere surreal, and black smoke rising from the buildings and clouding his judgement, Darius felt he might be hallucinating. For a while, he was somewhat disoriented as he wandered aimlessly though the debris surrounding him looking for his brother and sister.

Eventually, Darius dropped to the ground, huddled close to a tree, and began weeping. He cried and cried again. As his chest heaved uncontrollably, tears rolled down his cheeks and left black grimy rivulets where they had invaded the dust and debris from the explosions.

Fatigue invaded his eyes, warped his mind, and bent his persona. Darius fell asleep.

Later, he woke, stretched, and tried to make sense of the horror around him.

'How long have I slept?' he asked himself but he did not know because he had no timepiece to live by. 'It must be hours.'

Hungry and cold, he decided to search for warmer clothing and something to eat and drink.

Rummaging through the aftermath of the missile attack, Darius visited the ruins of the drugs laboratory to try and find the remains of his father. Here, he found an old tarpaulin cover that he threw across his shoulders for extra warmth. Continuing his search, he stumbled across a cast iron cupboard which had been dislodged from the wall.

Inside the cupboard, Darius found six bags of sugar and he helped himself to a few mouthfuls before deciding it was too sweet to eat on its own. Exploring further, he discovered several jars containing various chemicals and additives. Carefully, he separated the jars when he saw what he thought was a row of bottled water.

'Water,' he muttered to himself. 'I must have a drink to clear the smoke from my mouth and quench this thirst.'

Grabbing one of the bottles, Darius began to unscrew the top. Glancing at the other bottles in the cupboard, he noticed the word 'Poison' printed on a label fixed to the glass container.

With the top unscrewed, Darius raised the bottle to his lips but then paused. He pushed the bottle away and tilted it slightly to read the label once more. Then he set the bottle down and checked the cupboard again. Finding another five bottles of what appeared to be clear water made Darius somewhat puzzled.

'Water or poison?' he asked himself.

Lifting the opened bottle, he held it high and read the word 'Strychnine' on the label.

'Poison!' he gasped in shock before immediately replacing the bottle.

Darius continued to wander through the wreckage of the drugs laboratory searching for his father and any signs of life. His mind was temporarily displaced by circumstances beyond his control.

Shaking himself, he gradually returned to some form of reality and punched a hole in the tarpaulin to make it into a poncho. Now the tarpaulin cover flowed over his shoulders and down to his waist. Darius began to find himself again.

On the ground, thrown there by the force of the explosion, lay a hessian sack. It was like a bolt from the blue to him.

Energised, Darius knelt to find that the end of the sack was torn. He knew immediately what the contents were. His father had spoken to him of what they did inside the laboratory, and what he might do one day when it was his turn to work there.

Pulling dark brown powder from the sack, Darius allowed the heroin to flow through his fingers and be taken by the breeze. Nearby, he found another bag, and then another. By the end of his search he found another three sacks. Each hessian sack contained heroin of various colour except for one further sack which contained pure white powder.

'Of course,' he said to himself. 'Father told me there were four grades of heroin. The white powder, that looks like salt, is the purest and easily dissolved. It's what the users inject themselves with. Then there's the brown sugary one they use for smoking. Finally, the other two grades are unprocessed raw heroin.'

Darius considered the bags of sugar and strychnine.

'I remember now,' he said nodding to himself. 'They use strychnine and sugar to cut the raw heroin and break it down into finer powder. Every time it is cut, the colour of the heroin changes. So how much do I have here?'

Counting, Darius piled the bags high and realised he had recovered between forty and fifty kilograms of pure and 'first cut' heroin. He wasn't sure because he had no scales with which to weigh his find. Yet he knew, deep inside, that his discovery would be important to him in the years ahead. It would secure his wealth for the rest of his life if he could sell it to the right people. The people who lived on the other side of the mountain pass.

'Maybe I will travel further,' he thought. 'Yes, who else uses this heroin? I must find out.'

One of the bags was loose and he allowed the powder to trickle through his fingers as he spoke aloud, 'My heritage! Thank you, father. I remember you telling me that one day I would use sugar, caffeine, strychnine, talcum powder, baking flour, or other thin powders to cut the heroin in the laboratory with the other workers. The deeper the colour of additive, the deeper the colour of heroin. These various additives never fully dissolve. It is the way such things choose not to interact with each other.'

Standing, Darius surveyed his heritage.

The sacks of heroin had been placed in an area ready for collection by couriers who were scheduled to transport their lethal cargo and filter it into the world's drug supply chain. It was here, in this place, that a significant supply of pure Taliban heroin had been cut, mixed and processed, by the workers. It was now ready for despatch to Europe and beyond.

Darius knew this. His father had told him that he must never try the heroin himself. When the drug was injected into the body, it was possible that it might clog the blood vessels that lead to the lungs, kidneys or brain. This itself could lead to infection or the destruction of vital organs. Ultimately, such an injection might cause a fatality. When multiplied a million times, he was told, the potential death count was devastating.

Eventually, the couriers would deliver the drug, in its hessian sacks, to the next lower level in the supply chain. They would be individuals who worked for rich and powerful people from various organised crime syndicates who orchestrated the delivery chain. Such people lived anonymously wherever possible and employed low life to do their bidding. They would never be involved in the actual physical acquisition or movement of the drug. Unsurprisingly, they were always behind the financial and logistical support of the delivery and supply chain in its various guises. These criminals were often millionaires or billionaires unknown to those not involved in law enforcement. They enjoyed multiple bank accounts in false names across the globe.

Gradually, by a system of couriers, international dealers, national dealers, regional dealers, and street level dealers, the drug would arrive with a heroin user. By then, the drug they had purchased, or sold their body and mortality for, had probably been cut and mixed with more additives to ensure a profit for each level of the drug chain described. The hessian sacks were never the deal. The contents of the sacks were broken down, as described, into smaller sacks, then even smaller bags, until they were bagged deals that were the size of a postage stamp that could be held in the hand.

A user buying heroin on the street would probably never know the actual strength of the drug in any packet. Thus, such users were constantly at risk of an overdose.

Darius had never worked in the processing laboratory that had been destroyed but he knew enough to realise the potential before him.

Intelligently, the young teenager stacked his hessian sacks and bottles of strychnine near a rocky outcrop close to his beloved stream. Standing back to study the plot, he realised his treasure trove was hidden from the eye.

'I must leave this place before the couriers arrive and steal my find,' thought Darius. 'I must make something of this terrible day. Who shall I trust? No-one! My father told me never to trust anyone who was involved in carrying heroin across the mountain pass.'

Looking around, Darius saw a horse standing about a hundred yards away. Carefully, he approached the horse, stood close to it for a while, and gradually gained its confidence. He stroked the animal on its neck and back and then guided it into the remains of the village.

Darius found a rope and halter which he fixed to the horse. Then he loaded the sacks of heroin and the bottles of strychnine onto the horse's back.

'Where are my parents? Where will I find Ilya and Suz? I must find them,' he thought. 'It is time to move on.'

Now, in the tranquillity of the day, a solitary white eagle ventured from its nest on a far-off crag. It flew free in the wilderness above. Only the eagle, the teenager, and a horse, had survived to tell the sickening tale of war, hate, and terror.

The eagle soared above, seemingly inspected the appalling butchery below, and then descended to perch on a jagged rock near the boy.

Unafraid, Darius watched the eagle. It was the worst day of his life but nothing would make him feel any sorrier than he was already. He approached the bird with tears trickling down his cheeks, his brain in turmoil, and his body wrecked by a fear and loathing that would torment him for years to come.

Reaching out to the eagle, Darius muttered, 'You and I are all that are left. Stay with me, my friend. I have no-one.'

The bird studied the boy but did not move.

'My father used to speak of you,' revealed Darius softly. 'He once told me that the fully grown white eagle of the Qandil Mountains is a formidable bird of prey. The pure white eagle is only found in our mountains: the Quandil Mountains of Kurdistan. You are truly unique, my friend.'

The eagle's head moved proudly from left to right and then back again as it studied its surroundings.

'Oh, yes,' continued Darius. 'I agree with you. Your beak is really powerful,' continued Darius. 'One day you will use it to tear flesh from your prey so that you might fill your belly. Your legs are strong too and those talons are so powerful. You are an exceptionally magnificent creature from our glorious mountains.'

Supreme in its environment, the eagle turned its head towards the boy, moved a step closer, and then paused.

'Okay,' acknowledged Darius, 'Is there anything else I should say about you? Well, your eyesight is also beyond belief, my friend. My father told me you can see eight times better than any human being. When you are fully grown, you will weigh over a stone, reach three feet in length, and have a wingspan of almost eight feet. You are awesome. Did you know that in other places you are called the white-tailed eagle, the sea eagle, the erne grey sea eagle, or the white-tailed sea-eagle? No? Of course, you didn't know. You cannot speak but I know that your killing grounds include Iran, Iraq, and Eastern Turkey. You are not just a bird of prey. You are a warrior of the skies.'

Darius realised the eagle was a youngster like himself. Wondering if the eagle's parents had been killed in the airstrike, he reached out towards the bird and waited.

The young eagle looked at him, seemed to look around for approval, then flew to his outstretched arm and remained there for a while.

Fearless, the bird studied the youngster.

'You are heavier than I imagined for a little one,' remarked Darius. 'Yet you are young and so am I. You are the Emperor of the skies. Did you know that?'

The bird looked at him quizzically.

'Of course, you didn't,' continued Darius, shaking his head. 'I was named after the great King of Persia who died over two thousand years ago. My name means I am noble and of high class. Look around you, my friend. What happened to us? An Emperor and a teenager of high birth. Yet I see no servants. I only see the end of life as we know it. We have nothing left except each other.'

There was a flutter from the eagle's wings but the bird remained on Darius's outstretched arm.

'Did they feed you today or are you old enough to feed yourself, my friend?'

The eagle's eyes penetrated Darius as it perched quietly on the boy's arm.

Stepping towards the charred remnants of his home, the teenager flung his arm out and watched the eagle fly to the branch of a tree overlooking a row of houses that had been destroyed in the air attack.

With the stench of smouldering flesh invading his nostrils, and smoke rising eerily from a dozen or more bomb craters that surrounded him, Darius walked towards the ruin which had been his home. He stood, watching, looking, thinking, taking in the day's proceedings for he knew there would never be another day like this one.

In time, when Turkish warplanes were long gone and the buildings were just a lingering monument to an earth-shattering skirmish, the teenager found the bodies of his family.

Gathering their charred and broken bodies close to the stream, and in the tradition of Sunni Muslims, Darius bathed their remains in clear water and cried, 'Forgive me. I, Darius, have no white sheets to wrap you in. I only have a heart to love you and only my arms to hold you. I am nothing.'

With a trowel and his bare hands, Darius buried his family in the soft soil near the water course. Respecting the Prophet Muhammad, he made sure their graves were facing south towards the Holy City of Mecca, in Saudi Arabia.

As he tended to his task, bravely, almost proudly, Darius defiantly recited, 'From the earth we have created you, and into it we shall cause you to return, and from it shall we bring you forth once more.'

Washing himself in the stream, Darius continued, 'The spirit has left your bodies now. A righteous soul leaves the body with ease, while an evil soul, which resists leaving the body, is taken out harshly by the angel of death. I honour your righteous souls.'

Stepping away, his interment and religious obligations honoured to the best of his ability, the teenager turned his back on the burial site and looked further afield to the Zagros Mountains.

Standing tall, Darius scanned the mountain range which stretched almost 1,000 miles from south-eastern Turkey to the Straits of Hormuz and lay between the flatlands of Iraq and the Iranian plateau.

The day he and his father had arranged to walk some of these mountain tops would never come.

Darius tried to hold back his tears as he considered the mountains and a life destroyed.

His work done, Darius stretched out his arm and waited for the eagle to fly to him.

'Maybe the eagle will take me to places high in the mountains where my father can never again walk,' thought Darius.

The eagle ascended into the sky, circled, and then flew to him. Carefully, talons outstretched, the bird of prey landed on the boy's arm and settled with his newfound master.

Smiling for the first time since the horrendous attack, the teenager lifted his arm slightly and, in Kurmanji - the northern dialect of the Kurdish language – he introduced himself.

'My name is Darius Yasin. I shall call you White Eagle.'

The eagle flapped its wings, stretched out one of its talons, and then the other, and then flew to a nearby rock where it turned to wait for his master to move.

'There's nothing here for us now, my friend. Soon, winter will be upon us. Snow will fall and reach my waist. It's time to go.'

Walking towards the eagle, Darius announced, 'White Eagle, both the Quran and Sunnah urge me to be tolerant and forgive others, but I claim Qisas. I demand retaliation in kind, an eye for an eye, and the right to avenge my family who have been murdered. It is my entitlement under Sharia Law. You are my witness and my judge. I will avenge the death of my family and the people of Kurdistan.'

White Eagle spread his wings, screeched loudly, and flew high into the sky.

Like Darius, the eagle's past was wrecked and its future uncertain.

'Today, we have nothing,' shouted Darius as he picked up the horse's lead. 'Yet today, we shall take our heritage. One day, we will have everything. Lead me north, White Eagle. Take me to where the valleys are green, the sea is blue, and where we can make a new life.'

Screeching, the eagle circled and headed north.

Darius followed with his horse and its valuable load as he cried, 'White Eagle, guide me to my nemesis.'

The journey of Darius Yasin began.

Heading for the path out of the village, Darius walked past the apricot trees and rows of potatoes growing in a cultivated area. Then he skirted the tobacco field and journeyed through the centre of the village where so many memories invaded his mind. Reaching the thicket, he found the way to the mountain pass and climbed to the summit where he stood and turned towards the village that had been his home for thirteen years.

Looking down on the village, Darius shouted, 'I will be back Hear me! I will be back.'

Turning, he descended the path and made for the village of Wasan which was two full days walk away. On the outskirts of the village, Darius found a rocky outcrop where he hid his load of heroin and strychnine. Entering Wasan, he found his aunt and uncle, told them what had happened, and was welcomed into the family with open arms.

Above, a white eagle flew, circled the village, and made its nest on high ground close to Darius's secret lair.

In the years that followed, Darius did what most youngsters in the region did and joined the PKK – the Kurdistan Worker's Party. As a young recruit, he was never sent to the front line to wage war against the Syrians, ISIS, or anyone else.

Darius trained, and trained, and trained.

He grew strong, learnt how to use weapons and explosives, how to attack, how to evade the enemy, and how to kill.

Darius learnt much of life in the Quandil Mountains before eventually helping the villagers when they shipped their tobacco, apricots and potatoes to Turkey to sell. Living in a virtually medieval society, Darius learnt that the Kurdish people relied heavily on smuggling food and clothing into the region whilst constantly searching for new markets in which to sell their wares. Living a life based on agrarian principles, and relying on smuggling possessions in and out of the mountains, he decided it was time to move on.

Retrieving his heritage, Darius noticed that neither the strychnine or the heroin had eroded. Both substances enjoyed a long and enduring life. It was still good to sell and would be for many years to come. Using his knowledge of the tobacco shipping route, and the tobacco traders, Darius set off to Turkey. Armed with knowledge of the local tobacco industry and smuggling food in and out of the mountains, Darius added what he had learnt from his father and his uncle about the heroin trade and its couriers and dealers. In time, it was in Turkey where he would eventually exchange part of his heritage for a degree of initial wealth.

The day came when he bid his aunt and uncle goodbye.

Driving from the village, Darius watched the eagles at play in the sky. He smiled, threw a wave, and noticed how one of the eagles detached itself from the convocation to watch over him on his journey out of the mountainous area.

He drove off and relished the future.

The sale of raw heroin made Darius a very wealthy man.

As he grew older, he traded more, and grew richer.

Yet often, Darius would turn to the south, search for the snow-capped mountains, and say to himself, 'I will never forget. I will never forgive.'

\*

# Chapter One
~

Sabiha Gokcen International Airport
Istanbul
Ten Years later…

Shortly after midnight they approached from Sanyani, to the north of the airport. The intruders parked close to an area of densely populated small trees that gave them natural cover for a short time. It was sufficient to unload their mortars from the back of a Transit van and carry them closer to the perimeter fence.

Shadows crept stealthily across the tarmac and then gradually melted into the thicket. Mysterious figures took breath before creeping deeper into the copse where they could not be seen by others.

Reaching the perimeter fence, the team gathered, bent low on their haunches, and waited for their leader.

The imposing figure of Darius Yasin was last to arrive. Towering well over six feet five inches, bearded and moustachioed, Darius wore a black coverall complimented only by a black bandanna which was knotted tightly at the nape of his neck. He carried the bolt croppers across his shoulders.

Within moments, he'd snipped the wire in carefully selected places encouraging his team to gain access to the edge of the runway apron. Then he discarded his cutters and followed the trio through the fence.

Three large holdalls were heaved to the ground, opened, and their contents removed.

Darius stood tall, glanced behind him, and then scanned the car park, airport buildings and runway with his binoculars.

'All clear,' he announced. 'Security is poor.'

'Now?' queried the marksman.

'Yes, you know what to do,' replied Darius. 'One after the other as quick as you can before there is a response.'

A mortar device was quickly assembled by nimble fingers that aimed and angled it in the chosen direction. The first mortar bomb was carried towards the short-range weapon and muzzle-loaded.

Another mortar device was made ready.

Darius glanced at his colleagues and then re-engaged his binoculars scrutinizing the airport and its surroundings.

'Ready,' disclosed one of the team. 'Range?'

'Straight ahead, set for three thousand metres,' remarked Darius.

'We can't miss,' replied the marksman. 'They are all clustered together.'

'Then what are you waiting for?' snapped Darius. 'Fire!'

The lethal weapon propelled a mortar bomb in a high-arching trajectory that travelled the distance to where several aeroplanes were on their stand waiting for passengers to embark.

Reaching the zenith of its voyage, the mortar bomb plunged downwards towards it first target. Striking the main passenger compartment in the middle of the aircraft resulted in a huge explosion and a black cloud of debris that shrouded the aircraft.

'A direct hit!' remarked Darius coolly. 'Again, wipe them out. One degree left. Fire!'

Another mortar bomb was pushed down the muzzle, aimed, and fired. The bomb arched, reached the summit of it trajectory, and then pounded a second aircraft.

This time the bomb landed on the port wing, blew the engine to pieces, and caused an enormous fireball to race into the sky and illuminate the area.

More mortar devices had been assembled.

'Range?'

'Four thousand metres! Five degrees right! Fire!' ordered Darius using his binoculars.

Another bomb struck the control tower.

Panic filled the building when the roof collapsed and fell onto air traffic controllers working on their computers. Concrete slabs, ceiling attachments, and lighting, crashed downwards in a sudden unprecedented race to destroy the environment. A screen exploded, a spark streamed along a wire into a junction box, and a fire suddenly threatened to take hold amidst the confusion. Glass shards tumbled to the ground and burst into dozens of menacing tiny particles of horror. Screaming controllers tried to squeeze beneath tables whilst others, less fortunate, died where they sat oblivious to the mayhem unfolding around them.

'More! Quickly now,' ordered Darius. 'They will come after us soon.'

A further bomb hit the departure lounge and retail shopping area where pandemonium broke out. Glass and concrete flew through the air destroying, maiming, and killing in its deadly flight.

Ten more mortar bombs exploded as the attack continued. Again, and again, Darius vent his anger on the Turkish airport with a show of unimaginable lethal force.

'Three thousand five hundred feet. Left ten degrees. Fire!' he ordered. 'Four thousand feet. Left Fifteen degrees. Fire!'

On the apron, two airport workers loading baggage onto a trolley ran for their lives when the bombing started, crawled beneath a fuel wagon, and were killed instantly when a direct hit blew them to pieces. Aviation fuel flared into the sky, snuffed out a canvas walkway, and streamed along the tarmac like a fiery beast hunting for its quarry.

31

In the passenger lounge, more windows were shattered, part of the roof fell in, and another mortar bomb landed in the kitchen of a restaurant killing and maiming both customers and workers.

Chaos abounded and was rife.

Airport managers rushed to switch on emergency lighting when armed guards ran for cover and assessed the line of fire. Then, bravely, the guards ran towards the copse firing from the hip as they engaged the attackers.

Tracer bullets dominated the route to the copse when burning powder from the base of their bullets made the projectile trajectory visible to the naked eye.

Darius withdrew a submachine gun and rattled off a salvo of bullets at the guards. One fell, then another, as Darius's bullets tore the sentry patrol to pieces.

Sirens!

An emergency signal had been broadcast and local police were responding to the scene to support the airport police. Blue lights could be seen flashing from the centre of Istanbul and the indistinct sound of sirens rent the air

'We are out of mortar bombs,' shouted one of the raiders.

'Good! It's time to go,' ordered Darius. 'Leave everything!'

With his colleagues crawling back through the hole in the fence, Darius gathered their holdalls together and placed the mortars on top of them. Then he withdrew an incendiary device and placed it next to the pile. He connected a detonation cord to the device and unrolled it carefully as he checked over his shoulder. Darius came to rest about fifty yards from their original location and grounded the cord.

Darius then jogged towards the main entrance of the airport where a fountain and various statues welcomed visitors. At the water feature, he paused, removed a phial from his pocket, and poured the contents into the fountainhead.

Backing away, Darius made his way to the detonation cord, and ignited it.

The thin cord, which resembled a clothesline, contained pentaerythritol tetranitrate (PETN). Travelling at four miles per second the substance ignited the white phosphorous in Darius's device. The effect was immediate. White phosphorous exploded and destroyed the canvass holdalls before scorching the metal of the mortars and destroying any traces of fingerprints or DNA. The burning phosphorus caused a hot, white smoke - consisting mostly of phosphorus pentoxide – to dominate the area and create a dense smokescreen designed to cover their departure.

Darius clambered through the hole in the fence. Turning, he withdrew a feather from inside his clothing and weaved it in and out of the wire mesh fence. Then he made his way through the thicket and trotted towards his colleagues in the waiting van.

The driver slammed the accelerator hard to the floor when Darius climbed in and closed the passenger door behind him.

As the first police car turned into the approach road to head for the entrance, the assailants drove headlong into the cloud of phosphorous and made off towards the main highway.

All the police crew could see from their patrol car, as they arrived at the scene, was a thick white cloud of burning phosphorous resembling an impenetrable wall. Confused, they screeched to a halt, reversed, halted again, and then ran to the copse with guns drawn. They shouted orders into the unknown before reaching the fence where they discovered how the terrorists had entered the complex.

Fifteen minutes later, Darius and his crew drove casually into a lockup garage and abandoned their vehicle.

'Get changed,' ordered Darius slamming the garage door shut. 'Do just as we planned and take your time. Leave your gloves and clothing in the van and go into the Zagros Mountains. You know where. I will join you when my work is done. Remember, no phone calls or messages to anyone. Understand?'

'The mortars and our holdalls?' queried one of the team.

'Destroyed by the phosphorous. Any traces will lead them nowhere,' replied Darius. 'The items are dead but we are clean. We will be even cleaner when I have finished here.'

Agreement resulted in the men stripping naked before taking fresh clothing from a locker in the garage. Once dressed, two of the team mounted a motor bike and rode off casually in a south easterly direction. Another climbed into an old jeep and drove off in a south westerly manner. All three headed for the Zagros mountain range.

Darius waited until everyone had left before shaving his beard off. Eventually, he stripped naked and threw all their old clothes into the van. Dressing in fresh clothing, he retrieved a fuel can from the same locker. He poured petrol all over the inside of the van soaking upholstery, gloves, and clothing. Lighting an old petrol-soaked rag, Darius threw it into the van. Once the vehicle caught fire, the flames soon took hold and began licking the garage's roof.

Satisfied, Darius walked away from the building towards the centre of Istanbul.

Five minutes later, he looked back over his shoulder and saw a thick curl of black smoke stemming from the premises.

At the airport, fire personnel were engaged in rescue operations. Some of the crews were concentrating on putting fires out. Others were using hydraulic equipment to try and free people trapped beneath fallen masonry. Ambulances provided a shuttle service of casualties to local hospitals whilst investigators scoured the area for clues. Dozens of emergency vehicles dominated the scene as a team of doctors carried out triage on the those seriously injured.

Black-faced from fighting fires and battling through smoke, two firefighters pulled away from the action to change equipment. Resting near the fountain, they eased oxygen packs from their backs and dropped them to the floor for a moment.

Inhaling fresh air, one of them suddenly coughed and quickly replaced his oxygen mask.

'What's the matter?' asked his mate before coughing when he too took in a lungful of air.

'The air,' croaked the fireman. 'There's something in the air.'

A police dog handler approached restraining his dog on a short leash.

'Stay away,' shouted one of the fireman. 'There's something in the air. Something poisonous!'

The policeman stopped in his tracks about thirty yards from the firemen. He reached down to tousle his dog's neck and inadvertently snagged the leash on his cuffs. The dog stepped leisurely away, reached the fountain, and began lapping the water.

'White phosphorous smoke!' yelled the policeman. 'They exploded a phosphorous bomb. It will irritate your eyes and your nose and can burn your skin if you stay too close to the smoke for too long. Get out, get away, don't sit there. Over exposure may result in death!'

'Okay, thanks!' replied a fireman.

One of the firemen then promptly collapsed. He fell to the ground clutching his chest with his colleague coughing and spluttering nearby.

The policeman moved in, took a lungful of air, and dropped to his knees in agony.

35

Rolling over on his back, he snatched the oxygen mask from the collapsed fireman, and took in as much oxygen as he could. Standing, he dragged the fireman away from the fountain. The other fireman crawled from the fountain, made twenty yards' distance from the water, and then sank into oblivion.

Using his wireless, the policeman shouted for assistance radioing, 'The fountain! Keep away from the fountain at the entrance. There's something in the water. It's not just the phosphorous bomb! I have two down at this location. We need protective clothing! It might be a chemical warfare attack! I don't know but it's killing us. Send medics!'

There was no reply.

'Now!' screamed the policeman.

Minutes later, three casualty officers, dressed in protective clothing and wearing breathing apparatus, rushed to help as the policeman's dog lapped at the water from the fountain.

The dog stepped back, tried to turn towards his master, and promptly fell to the ground stone dead.

'My dog!' the policeman cried as he tried to rush forward to help his canine friend.

Casualty officers collared the policeman and dragged him from the area.

'Poison!' they yelled. 'Don't know what kind but someone has poisoned the fountain. Keep away.'

Throughout the night, emergency services worked to regain control. Body bags were filled, casualties taken to hospital, and rescue operations undertaken.

When dawn broke over the airport, a thin, cruel wisp of white phosphorous smoke still clung in the air. On the apron, burnt out aircraft and damaged buildings gave silent testament to the night's proceedings.

A scene of total devastation was evident.

Sorting through the debris to find evidence needed a keen eye and a high degree of expertise. Viewing CCTV and making enquiries in the area were essential but time consuming. An investigation of the highest order was required.

Elsewhere, a new dawn was breaking.

A telephone rang in an office at NATO Headquarters situated at Boulevard Leopold III, Brussels, Belgium. The NATO complex sat on the northeast perimeter of the city and was home to national delegations of member countries and to liaison offices or diplomatic missions of partner countries.

Giuseppe Mouretti answered with, 'Commander Mouretti speaking. How can I help you?'

The NATO man listened, made notes, and then lifted another phone to place a call.

'We have a hostile enemy attack in Turkey,' remarked Mouretti. 'An airport on the outskirts of Istanbul. I'm deploying staff there to bolster our nearby base. I'll let you know of any developments that may require specialist skills... Yes, leave it with me for now.'

The call ended and Mouretti moved to a coffee pot by the window.

In a cage, nearby, a bird squawked.

Mouretti raised his fingers to his lips and whispered, 'Shush, my beauty.'

Looking out across the boulevard, Mouretti wondered what the final body count would be.

Later that day, in London, 1,550 miles away, the telephones were red hot. The Turkish ambassador visited Sir Henry Fielding at the Foreign Office in King Charles Street, Whitehall.

37

On being admitted, the ambassador explained, 'Good day, Sir Henry. How does my visit find you?'

'Well, my friend. Well! Will you take tea with me?'

'But of course, Sir Henry. Why not?'

Sir Henry poured tea for two and continued, 'A chocolate digestive perhaps?'

'How nice,' smiled the ambassador helping himself to a biscuit from a plate on the coffee table between them.

Now tell me, what can Her Majesty's Government do for you today?'

The ambassador cleared his throat and replied, 'The Turkish government request assistance in investigating a raid at Sabiha Gokchen airport on the outskirts of Istanbul. I'm sure you will appreciate that as members, and partners, in NATO, we can only offer our sincere condolences to those who were killed and injured in this terrible atrocity. I must inform you, Sir Henry, that a list of British holidaymakers killed in the attack is being prepared and will be delivered to your office within the hour. Our country feels unduly threatened by this atrocity and I must particularly extend our deepest sympathies to those from your country who have suffered at the hands of these terrorists.'

'Thank you! Yes, yes, of course,' replied Sir Henry. 'It is tragic, is it not?'

'Absolutely,' replied the ambassador. 'I am instructed by my government to remind you of an intergovernmental military alliance based on the North Atlantic Treaty which was signed in 1949. The organisation constitutes a system of collective defence whereby its member states agreed to mutual defence in response to an attack by any external party. The Turkish government are concerned as to how easy it has been for a very small group of individuals to carry out a devastating attack on an airport on the outskirts of Istanbul. If it is that easy, at a civilian airport, how easy would it be to carry out a similar attack on Incirlik air base, Adana: the NATO air base which arguably gives the Alliance access to the lands of the former Soviet Union, the Middle East, and further afield?'

Sir Henry nodded politely and suggested, 'You surely have sufficient internal resources to investigate such an incident in your own back yard, ambassador? How on earth could Her Majesty's Government help?'

'It's simple,' replied the ambassador. 'The British police are the best in the world at investigating serious crime at the international level.'

Smiling softly, Sir Henry replied, 'Such kind words, and of course, we must not forget that your government has dismissed thousands of police officers over the last few months due to that coup which apparently wasn't a coup.'

The ambassador did not reply.

'I don't think we need to discuss that at length, ambassador. Yes, leave it with me,' declared Sir Henry. 'I will discuss your request with the Prime Minister and respond as soon as possible.'

'Unlike many other so-called terrorist attacks throughout the world,' explained the ambassador. 'No-one has claimed responsibility for this highly successful offensive. In any event, who is behind the intrusion, we ask? Was it Islamic State, the Taliban, Al-Qaeda, a potential enemy country probing national security at one of their primary airports, a bunch of criminals planning the downfall of the Turkish State, or a terrorist organisation yet to identify itself?'

'Indeed, a potential unsolvable mystery at all levels,' suggested Sir Henry. 'But you are right, we do have a police service with expertise in the area you mention.'

'Scotland Yard,' replied the ambassador. 'And your MI5. I believe the Special Crime Unit are amongst the best police investigators in the western world. If you could ensure…'

'But of course,' replied Sir Henry. 'But I disagree with you there.'

'Whatever do you mean?'

'The unit you refer to is not amongst the best in the world it is the best in the world,' chuckled Sir Henry. 'Or I'm not the Foreign Secretary of a country that considers Turkey to be one of our closest allies in NATO, and, of course, Europe itself.'

'I am indebted to you, Sir Henry,' ventured the ambassador. 'Quite indebted.'

'More tea?' enquired Sir Henry.

'Why not?' replied the ambassador. 'Perhaps we can discuss the arrangements to be made?'

Doors were opened and closed. Calls were made. The complex relationship between international diplomacy and associated politics came into play.

By mid-afternoon, Detective Superintendent Sandra Peel and Detective Inspector Joe Harkness, of the nation's Special Crime Unit, were headed for Heathrow and a flight to Turkey.

Known in the office as 'Sandy', the superintendent was second in command of the unit. In her mid-fifties, she had served over thirty years in various departments including Traffic, Community Support, Crime Prevention, CID, and the National Crime Squad. Noted for imposing high standards on everyone, she stood six feet tall and cut an imposing figure. Favouring a dark trouser suit and polo necked sweater, Sandy had personally selected Joe Harkness to accompany her on the investigation.

Joe was a former member of the Kent Serious and Organised Crime Unit. Trained in criminal investigation, he was also a financial investigator of some repute.

Whilst Sandy and Joe queued at the gate for the flight to Turkey, Joe bought a newspaper and read the headline…

'…Turkish airport attack. Fears across Europe raised. A new threat or ISIS on the rampage? Government send London detectives to assist in hunt for terrorists….'

'That's us, Sandy,' suggested Joe chuckling at the thought of being mentioned in the newspaper.

'I'm not sure that is good news or bad news,' suggested Sandy. 'If we make any significant inroads, Whitehall will love us to bits. If we don't get anywhere then we'll be reviled as incompetent. Damned if we do and damned if we don't.'

'What's your gut feeling?' asked Joe.

'I hate flying so my guts, as you call them, are in total turmoil, Joe. I don't know. I'll keep an open mind for now.'

A flight attendant made an announcement and Sandy continued, 'Come on, that's our flight. Turkish delight? We'll soon find out. One thing is for sure, though. If we hadn't been here we would have been training with Boyd and the army somewhere.'

Joe laughed, grabbed his suitcase and replied, 'Come on I'll race you.'

On the outskirts of Hereford, in the United Kingdom, Detective Chief Inspector Boyd, of the Special Crime Unit, looked at the instructor and queried, 'Not fast enough?'

Sergeant Mills replied, 'That's right. Not fast enough! Not for me. No! Again! Do it again only this time do it faster and cleaner, and make your shots count. There's three targets. I want to see you racing down that wall and crashing into the windows like that they do in that film 'Who Dares Wins'. Come on. Second place is first loser.'

Boyd nodded, turned to his team and ordered, 'You heard the man. Let's do it until we get it right.'

They carried their gear to the roof again, roped and secured their kit, and heard Boyd say, 'I'll go first. You should never tell someone to do something that you're not capable of doing yourself. Stand back.'

Anthea Adams, Terry Anwhari, Ricky French and the rest of the team looked on when Boyd inched himself over the edge of the roof, abseiled down three flights, and then crashed through a window as he made a covert rapid entry into a building.

The image of a man pointing an AK 47 at him appeared on an electronically controlled target screen. It was immediately followed by an image of a woman with a machine gun then a man carrying a cricket bat.

Boyd crouched low, withdrew his Glock 17, and shot all three targets cleanly.

Unexpectedly, a fourth image appeared. It was a youth firing a rifle from the hip.

Boyd failed to respond in time when a klaxon sounded.

A red light filled the room and flashed continually.

'Better!' yelled Mills. 'Much better but not yet up to the mark. Good entrance but you killed three targets when you were only supposed to shoot two. Why did you shoot the man with the cricket bat? Was it loaded? Big mistake, Boyd. You were too slow for the fourth target and he got you.'

'You said there were only three targets,' argued Boyd.

'Never believe the intelligence you are given,' declared Sergeant Mills. 'I lied. There were four. Do better next time and wait for the lights to go out when the exercise is finished. Understood?'

'Yes, got it,' nodded Boyd.

'Remember,' responded Mills. 'You must be adaptable. We shall be teaching you about explosive devices soon. They are more often referred to as bombs. We shall be showing you how much care you need to dismantle a basic device. It is a slow progress. Comparatively, if you train for rapid entry you will have the advantage over your enemy. If you shoot to kill, make sure you shoot the right target. Next! Two abreast this time please.'

Ricky and Terry stepped forward as Anthea murmured, 'I hate training with the army. I'm getting too old for this.'

'Boyd too by the looks of things,' murmured Ricky. 'Or is he just having a bad day?'

*

## Chapter Two

~

Midday
Covent Garden, The West End of London, England
The following day

'Is that him?' queried Terry Anwhari as he drove his silver coloured Saab casually down the street. 'Outside the newsagent! Is it the chap carrying a briefcase?'

Mehmet studied the man Terry was referring to before slinking low in the front passenger seat and settling a pair of sunglasses onto the bridge of his nose.

Then, deliberately turning his head away, Mehmet muttered, 'Yeah, that's him. That's Adam.'

Engaging his throat microphone, Terry radioed, 'All units! Contact outside the newsagent shop. Our man is carrying a black briefcase in his right hand. White on blue.'

Moments later, Terry's earpiece buzzed, 'Red Alpha One has him. White long-sleeved shirt, blue denim jeans, dark brown shoes, six-foot tall, broad, Asian appearance. Designated Tango One and he's entering the newsagent. We have him, Terry.'

'I have that,' replied Terry before turning to Mehmet and asking, 'Adam what?'

'I don't know his last name,' explained Mehmet. 'His real name is Adem. At least, that's what he calls himself in the mosque.'

'You're sure it's him, Mehmet?' insisted Terry. 'It's important. I need you to be sure'

'I'm sure,' snapped Mehmet, angrily. 'Where's the guvnor? You said he would be here this time?'

'He's busy at the moment,' revealed Terry.

'In that case,' pleaded Mehmet, 'Can you get me the hell out of here before Adam sees me?'

The Saab accelerated smoothly past Adam with Terry remarking, 'He hasn't seen you, Mehmet. He didn't even look at us. The man doesn't even know we're onto him.'

'It's easy for you to say that,' replied Mehmet. 'But you're not the one standing on the firing line if it all goes wrong. If I'm spotted with a copper and he gets to get know then I'm dead. I'll end up skewered inside a doner kebab somewhere.'

'Nasty,' grimaced Terry. 'I don't think you'd enjoy hanging around a kebab shop with an iron bar stuck up your arse.'

'You don't understand, do you?' snapped Mehmet. 'Adam is the real deal in our community. He's a very dangerous man. Tell your guvnor that because I'm not playing games.'

'So you keep telling me,' countered Terry. 'But we need his name and you've been on him for weeks.'

'He's the Collector,' snapped Mehmet. 'I heard someone say the Placer brought him here. That's all I know. He's the one you want. Now drop me off at the tube station. I want out of here.'

'Placer! What does that mean?' probed Terry.

'I don't really know,' replied Mehmet. 'I've heard someone places things. You know. Sorts things out, puts people in the right place. You told me to watch Adem and report, not to make him my best friend. That's all I know. He's doing the collections. That's' what you wanted to know.'

'You mean there's someone out there that arranged for him to live here so that he could make collections for the organisation?'

'Hey! You got it at last. Come on! Get me out of here.'

Newly promoted Detective Sergeant Terry Anwhari smiled, removed some twenty pound notes from the breast pocket of his shirt, and handed them to Mehmet saying, 'Here's a ton! Make him your best friend, Mehmet. Day by day, week by week. Nice and smooth just like I said. You're doing fine so far.'

'Am I really?'

'Yes! Let's hope you're right about Adam being a collector otherwise I'll be wanting this back.'

Snatching the money, Mehmet curled it in his fist and chuckled, 'You won't be disappointed, Terry. Trust me. But don't forget our arrangement. I want my family here when this is all over. That's more important than money to me.'

'I know,' responded Terry stopping outside the entrance to Leicester Square tube station. 'But we've a long way to go. Out! I'll be in touch!'

Mehmet slipped the door handle and was scurrying from the Saab and into the depths of the tube station in less than three seconds.

Selecting first gear, Terry moved away briskly and engaged his throat microphone radioing, 'Red Alpha One, Patient Lamb is on his toes. Where are you?'

'Tango One is out of the newsagent and into a red Opel,' replied Red Alpha One. 'We're heading north. He's following the signs for the M1. Make ground. You're tail-end Charlie.'

'Did he make a collection in the shop?' asked Terry.

'Not known at this stage,' replied Red Alpha One.

'I'm making ground! Out!' replied Terry.

'All copied,' radioed Detective Inspector Bannerman from the Operations Centre. 'Just a reminder, folks. We will have visitors listening in one day this week. Do a good job and keep safe.'

'Red Alpha One has that,' radioed Boyd: the surveillance commander. 'Still northbound towards the M1 motorway.'

In the operational centre of the nation's Special Crime Unit in New Scotland Yard, Detective Inspector Bannerman rattled his fingers across a computer keyboard before turning to Commander Maxwell and offering, 'They're off, Commander. Destination unknown! Outcome unknown!'

Commander Edwin Maxwell had been a policeman for most of his working life. The long-established London detective, who had served in the West End, the East End, the Anti-Terrorist Branch and Counter Terrorist Command, was both a gentleman and a legend. He had the gift of being able to charm everyone he met. The Commander was also head of the Special Crime Unit.

'Thank you!' replied Maxwell. 'It's just another normal day then. A daytrip around the boroughs, I suspect. Keep me posted, Bannerman. I need to prepare for the Commissioner's visit. He's bringing the Foreign Secretary with him.'

'A government inspection?' probed Bannerman with a smile. 'Or just passing through?'

'Having recently spent a couple of million pounds on our unit, I suspect Sir Henry – the Foreign Secretary – wants to ensure they're getting their money's worth. Apparently, this unit is now the lead police unit in 'intelligence capture'.

'Intelligence capture?' queried Bannerman.

'The latest from the spin doctors,' replied Maxwell. 'Meaning receiving information from multiple sources. I'll catch you later.'

'Very good, sir,' replied Bannerman. 'Don't worry. Boyd runs a tight ship but a good one. If the informant involved in this operation is correct, then they should follow the target and tie him to a terrorist organisation.'

47

'Good!' replied Maxwell. 'Our problem is that, despite what the government spin doctors may say, we have decided to run this operation on flimsy intelligence. We don't even know the identity of the target.'

'That's true,' said Bannerman. 'Hopefully, we'll have a lot more when the job is over. Terry Anwhari is fluent in Arabic and is of English-Pakistani origin. He's managed to recruit a good source in the Turkish community. We'll get there.'

'Yes, I'm aware of the situation, Bannerman. Terry's asset is coded Patient Lamb,' replied Maxwell. 'When our visitors make their inspection, we must remember they are here to look at our systems, not to learn of individuals we have recruited.'

'Don't worry about that, sir,' countered Bannerman rising to his full height and towering over the Commander. 'I've never met a politician that I was able to put my faith in. I'm unlikely to begin trusting one now.'

Maxwell smiled and replied, 'I'm late. We've a bad Turk in the city and a patient lamb to look after. Let's make the case.'

In the city, William Miller Boyd, a Cumbrian detective attached to the Special Crime Unit, oversaw covert operations in the unit. Tall, athletic, with broad shoulders and a finely-honed body to match, he was married to Meg: a nurse who lived on the outskirts of the Lake District. In the unit, everyone referred to him as Boyd. He was the surveillance commander and he was driving a black Porsche Cayenne: Call sign Red Alpha One.

In the passenger seat sat Detective Inspector Anthea Adams. Married to Raphael, a senior Portuguese detective based in Lisbon, Anthea was more than just Boyd's second-in-command, she was a crack shot and she did not suffer fools gladly.

As the team followed Adam through the London boroughs, Boyd's deep blue eyes and square chin seemed to know their way around and second guess the way forward. He had a way with surveillance. It was almost second nature to him.

'Hang back, team,' he radioed. 'Tango One has pulled up outside another restaurant. This appears to be the fourth collection. Stand by for full deployment.'

Glancing at Anthea, Boyd ordered, 'Let's nail it this time. Anthea, take control. It's yours.'

'I have that,' replied Anthea.

'This is Red Alpha One. Anthea has control,' instructed Boyd.

'I have control,' replied Anthea. 'Red Alpha Two has control.'

Adam locked and secured the Opel, retrieved his briefcase, looked around, and then made his way inside the restaurant.

'All units take up your positions,' radioed Anthea.

'I have that,' rattled across the airwaves as Adam disappeared into the depths of the restaurant and Boyd's eight vehicle surveillance unit began their manoeuvres.

Anthea nodded to Boyd and slipped out of the Porsche onto the street.

Ricky French moved to the fore and parked his blacked-out Nissan Qashqai about fifty yards from the restaurant. An ex flying squad officer, Ricky was studying for a masters in criminology. He was the surveillance unit's 'gizmo' man. Reaching inside the vehicle's dashboard, he pocketed a handheld device.

Detective Inspector Anthea Adams stepped towards the restaurant. Her auburn hair flowed to her shoulders, and no further, as she walked steadily forward.

Using her throat mic, Anthea radioed, 'Red Alpha Two approaching target premises. I have control. Operation Distinguish… All Units…. Go!'

A 750cc BMW motor cycle cruised past the building and turned into a nearby junction with Detective Constable Martin Duffy on board.

A former member of the Special Escort Group, Martin radioed, 'Solo One has an eyeball on the Opel, designated Victor One. I have the plot covered both ways.'

'I have the rear,' from Mick Turner.

'Holding back for a reciprocal action,' from Hazel Scott.

'I have the straight through,' radioed George Fish.

Others radioed their positions as Detective Sergeant Janice Burns, a feisty Scottish detective from Greenock, radioed, 'Coming through and going in.'

Meanwhile, Harry Nugent, was ahead of the game when he radioed, 'I'm in by the rear door. No problem.'

Driving a gun metal grey BMW series 5, Janice guided the vehicle into a vacant place and made her way on foot to the restaurant.

With the premises surrounded by officers on either foot or in their vehicles, the airwaves went quiet.

'Bannerman,' radioed Anthea. 'I have control. Stand by for live coverage.'

In the London office, Bannerman's fingers cruised across his keyboard before he turned to another screen and brought it to life.

A few seconds elapsed before Bannerman came back with, 'I'm live and ready to receive.'

Discreetly, Anthea switched on a video recording device as she entered the restaurant. Ignoring Harry Nugent, who was sat near the rear entrance, she took a seat near the front door and waited to be served.

The restaurant was busy with customers occupying most of the fifty covers that the business provided. They were all unaware of the covert live coverage emanating from a wide-angled button hole camera in Anthea's jacket.

A waiter approached Harry who ordered a coffee whilst perusing the menu. He placed his smartphone on the table top, angled it slightly, and allowed the covert camera inside to record proceedings.

Quietly, Harry radioed, 'I'm live too.'

Moments later, Janice Burns entered, made her way to the bar, and plonked her handbag down abruptly saying, 'I'd like a menu and a large coke, please, and, if you don't mind, now.'

Staff behind the counter recognised a potentially awkward customer and immediately attended to her needs as Anthea concentrated on everyone else in the room and quietly whispered, 'Red Alpha One, I'm pretty sure our man is in an office behind the bar. I have coverage. We are three inside and rolling.'

'I have that,' replied Boyd.

'Reception is good,' added Bannerman from the operational centre back in the London office.

Janice heard the comment, nudged her handbag slightly on the bar, and knew the camera hidden inside the fabric would also capture the images they wanted.

Outside on the street, Ricky walked along the pavement, found the red Opel, and radioed, 'Red Alpha One, I'm ready to deploy.'

Boyd checked the street, assessed the people walking by, and replied, 'Wait one... Anthea.'

'All clear,' radioed Anthea quietly. 'I repeat, the entrance is clear.'

'Safe to deploy,' radioed Boyd. 'Ricky, you have control.'

Ricky immediately knelt and to fasten a shoe lace. Whilst bending, he placed a tracking and audio device onto the underbelly of the Opel.

Standing up, Ricky radioed, 'I have control. I have deployed the device. Test signal and sound. Ten, nine, eight...'

In the Ops Room, Bannerman radioed, 'Seven, six, five... Audio signal good. Stand by!'

Swivelling his chair slightly, Bannerman checked a computer screen on his desk, located a mark on the image of the map displayed, and radioed, 'I have your location too. Device deployment is a success.'

'I have that,' replied Boyd. 'Operation Distinguish is live.'

Ricky gathered the collar of his jacket closer to his neck and returned to his vehicle acknowledging with, 'Good to go and I'm gone.'

'Anthea, you have control,' radioed Boyd.

'Have that,' whispered Anthea inside the premises.

Inside the restaurant, a door to an office behind the bar opened allowing Anthea to spy Adam standing beside a table. He closed the lid of his briefcase, smiled, and spoke to a man wearing a suit. Anthea presumed Adam's contact might be the owner or manager of the restaurant. It was the first good view of their target she had obtained since the operation began. Furthermore, Anthea thought she picked up the words, 'Thank you, we knew we could rely on you,' but she couldn't be sure.

Browsing a menu, Anthea pretended to ignore the two men.

Meanwhile, her buttonhole camera recorded the images of both men and relayed them back to the Ops Room in the Special Crime Unit.

Seeing the target emerge from the office, Janice noisily rattled the counter with her knuckles and shouted, 'Service! Any bloody service in this place?'

'Can I help you?' responded a barman forcing a smile.

'No, thanks,' replied Janice picking up her glass of coke.

She stepped briskly towards Adam and slammed the glass into his chest.

Adam wheezed with the impact, felt the liquid soak his shirt, and immediately grabbed the glass and put it on the bar.

Janice retrieved the glass and shouted, 'I take it you two are the owners. What the hell kind of wine is this you're selling?'

'I'm sorry,' explained Adam indicating the man standing beside him. 'I don't work here. The gentleman with me is the owner.'

'To hell with the wee man,' exploded Janice in a broad Scottish accent. Stepping forward, she yelled, 'Taste this ya bloody Sassenach!'

As the restaurant owner and his staff moved to quell Janice's outburst, Adam realised the glass was only inches from his face. He had no option but to raise his hands to shield himself.

Janice shouldered her bag, moved forward again, and persisted with, 'Go on! Try it! In fact, ma bonnie wee man, you'd best taste it before you order anything to eat here. These bloody Sassenachs couldnae run an open day at a brothel.'

Reluctantly, and with little choice from this pushy woman, Adam took hold of the glass, sniffed it, took a sip, and replied, 'It's coke, not wine.'

'Aye!' yelled Janice. 'Bloody coke!'

'It's what you asked for,' argued the barman.

Everything went silent for a moment as Janice stared into the black abyss that was her coke.

'Bollocks!' she screamed at the top of her voice. 'Coke, my arse. I asked for red wine. Châteauneuf du pip! You plonker!'

Anthea intervened, raised her voice, and offered, 'Excuse me, madam, but the barman is correct. You did ask for a coke. I heard you quite clearly ask for coke, not red wine.'

'Keep your nose out if it, you posh Sassenach cow!' yelled Janice.

'Madam,' insisted the barman. 'You really did ask for a coke and could I ask you to kindly lower your voice. We can all hear you.'

Things went quiet for a moment until Janice realised she had the restaurant's full attention.

'Oh shit!' screamed Janice handing Adam a menu. 'Here, hold this for me a minute, won't you?'

'Madam, you appear to have made a genuine mistake,' suggested the restaurant owner smoothly. 'Perhaps…'

'Did I?' replied Janice, cutting the gentleman out. 'Well, that's my fault. I'm so damned embarrassed now. I'm so sorry. What a fool I've made of myself. I'm off.'

Snatching the glass and menu, Janice stormed from the building as fast as she could.

The door crashed behind her with Adam and the restaurant owner both apparently shell-shocked at her sudden departure.

Across the restaurant, there was a low buzz of disapproval mixed with one or two audible chuckles.

'She's taken a glass and menu,' remarked the barman.

Anthea stood up with her back to the door and said, 'She probably doesn't even realise what she's done. She wanted out so quickly. What a damn fool she turned out to be, and a foul-mouthed Glaswegian too.'

The barman tried to follow Janice but, without making it obvious, Anthea had positioned herself to foil anyone from immediately following Janice into the street.

'How embarrassing for you all,' proposed Anthea rummaging for her phone. 'Do you want me to call the police? It's just a drunk with a glass and a menu but I'll ring them if you want.'

The barman glanced at the owner who revealed, 'It's an irrelevant matter. Forget it. She's gone now. What can I get you?'

'I'll just have a coffee if that's alright with you. Black! No sugar!' replied Anthea. 'The table here by the door will be fine.'

'Of course,' replied the restaurant owner clicking his fingers.

The barman responded and took Anthea's order.

'By the way,' queried the owner. 'Did you know that woman?'

'She's a Scottish nutter,' declared Anthea. 'And obviously, an embarrassed wino with a drink problem. I expect you get people like this occasionally, do you?'

'Yes, but only occasionally,' smiled the owner. 'I'm so sorry you had to witness her outburst. Your coffee will be on the house.'

'Why, thank you,' smiled Anthea sitting back down. 'How kind but most unnecessary.'

Adam tapped the owner on his shoulder and said, 'Peri, I must be going. I have much to do before the end of the day. Thank you, same time next month?'

'Of course, no problem,' replied Peri: the restaurant owner. 'Safe journey.'

As Adam walked through the front door, Janice was already driving away from the area and at the other end of the street.

In the Porsche, Boyd's mobile rang. He answered it to find Antonia Harston-Browne on the other end.

'Morning, Toni, what can I do for you today?'

'How is your operation going?' asked Antonia.

'Well, for the information of MI5, Anthea has just finished an attempt to try and identify our target,' revealed Boyd.

'Successfully?' queried Antonia.

'Janice has just walked off with the target's photograph, his fingerprints, and probably his DNA,' replied Boyd.

'I take it he didn't volunteer?'

'Not quite, Toni,' chuckled Boyd. 'What you might call a covert identification process. It's a step forward. The car he is driving is registered to an address that was demolished six months ago. I want to bottom out who he is and who his contacts are. We've got what we want. The team will just follow him now and record details of all his stops.'

'Stops?' remarked Antonia. 'Or collections?'

'The latter, I suspect,' confirmed Boyd. 'That was the fourth collection, I believe. If he keeps running around the boroughs he can easily make twenty or more in a day.'

'The surveillance log tells me he was headed for the M1 motorway.'

'That's true,' confirmed Boyd. 'He took the northern route, latched onto the ring road, and obviously uses it as a quick way to reach his customers.'

'How much is involved?' asked Antonia.

'No idea at this stage,' replied Boyd. 'But what I can say is that he's got no idea we're onto him. He's not even careful about his personal security. No gloves, no minder, no nothing. Everyone seems to trust him. It seems to me that he must have been doing this for quite a while. It's a habit. Hopefully, Adam will already be on record and we can identify him fully. If not, then we've at least made an inroad.'

'You seem pretty certain of your man,' proposed Antonia.

'I'm pretty certain of my team,' replied Boyd. 'Terry has been drilling into a dubious squad of people for a while. I think he's on to something and we're going to prove it. Anyway, you didn't ring me for this. What do you want and how can I help?'

Antonia sniggered and said, 'Oh, Billy, you never change. But you're right, I thought I'd ask how you felt about Sandy being sent to Turkey and not you?'

'I'm doing more important work here,' replied a tongue in cheek Boyd.

'Ha-ha,' replied Antonia. 'It's only a week since you were telling me you were looking at Turkey as a possible holiday destination for you, Meg, and the kids.'

'Not anymore,' revealed Boyd. 'I did fancy a holiday on the Turkish Riviera at Marmaris but it looks as if it's going to be the Marmaris barber's shop in Silloth.'

'Where?' enquired Antonia.

'Never mind,' laughed Boyd.

'Sandy's initial report should be in tomorrow,' revealed Toni. 'I know you're not flavour of the month anymore but I thought you'd like to know. Who knows, it might even impact on your minor Turkish enquiry.'

'Minor!' snapped Boyd. 'We'll see. These collections might be going all the way to Turkey to fund the war. Will it be minor then?'

'Of course,' jested Antonia. 'Sandy does all the big jobs now. You can hand your passport in.'

'If I didn't know you were winding me up, I'd cancel our dinner date at the weekend,' suggested Boyd.

'You can't do that,' replied Antonia. 'Phillip is looking forward to you and Meg joining us for the weekend.'

'Oh, we'll be there unless I get called out to help Sandy in Turkey,' joked Boyd. 'There is one thing you can do for me, though?'

'Which is?'

'Ring our friends in Legoland and ask them to activate whatever sources they have in Turkey. If our theory is right and we're chasing the collector, then there must be a receiver somewhere.'

'I'll do that,' replied Antonia making a mental note to contact the Secret Intelligence Service. 'Although they'll probably tell me to mind my own business as they're all over the middle east at the moment.'

'Thanks,' responded Boyd. 'A mention ought not to cause too much of a problem. Look, our man is on the move again. We're there. I have to go.'

'Stay safe,' replied Antonia.

The line went dead as Boyd listened to the radio and tried to figure out where the next collection might be.

By the end of the day, Boyd's surveillance team had successfully followed Adam to over thirty locations in London. These included a host of business premises in Enfield, Haringey, Islington, Hackney, Waltham Forest, and the city of Westminster.

By late afternoon, the team followed Adam to a bank on Bayswater Road where Adam was seen to present his briefcase to a bank teller.

'I have him in my sights,' radioed Detective Constable Tom Richardson. 'He's in the queue, standby.'

Tom sorted through a collection of pamphlets on display in the bank whilst using the reflection of the window to watch Adam.

'Internal CCTV operating,' revealed Tom. 'Target approaching counter.... Target presenting the briefcase.... Briefcase open... Counting in progress... Stand by.'

Moving position, Tom joined the queue at the counter, watched proceedings, and then stepped away to answer an imaginary phone call when Adam ended the procedure and walked away.

'Target leaving the premises,' whispered Tom. 'Turning left into the street.'

'Join us, Tom,' instructed Boyd on the radio. 'We'll revisit the bank following debrief. I have the target in Bayswater Road. He's returning to his car. Let's house him.'

Boyd selected a gear and casually moved off when Adam was on the move again.

'How much, Tom?' asked Boyd to his passenger.

'I'd say more than ten thousand pounds. It was all in twenties and fifties but there was obviously some tenners as well.

Difficult to say unless I was breathing down his neck, guvnor, but I can confirm a deposit was made in an unknown account.'

'Good,' replied Boyd. 'Adam is correctly codenamed The Collector by all accounts.'

'Looks that way to me,' proposed Tom.

'We'll identify the account later,' revealed Boyd. 'Right now, it would be nice to house him at his home address.'

'There's one thing for sure, guvnor,' remarked Tom.

'What's that?'

'Our man chatted to the banker as if they'd been doing business for quite a while. I reckon Adam has been collecting for ages. He's as cool as a cucumber. Nothing bothers him.'

'Yeah, I agree,' replied Boyd. 'Here we go. He's turning into a hotel car park.'

As Boyd pulled into the kerbside, Tom Richardson heaved his fourteen stone of humanity onto the pavement and made for the reception area. He would be there before Adam had parked his car.

Tom approached the reception desk, accepted a tariff for inspection, and waited in the lobby.

Boyd's surveillance operation continued with the reality dawning that they had watched a member of London's Turkish community collect a goodly amount of cash for a terrorist organisation that was probably based in Turkey.

Later, in the office, Boyd held a debriefing session.

'Tom, Janice, I'd like you to follow up on the bank account investigation, please, and seize the CCTV footage in the bank too. You'll get the timeframe we are interested in from the surveillance log. I also want to know what name Adam used to deposit the money. Was it his own or someone else's name? Into which account was the money paid and how much? When you've done this, we'll decide on the next step. We can let the account run or we can freeze the assets. I'll speak to Commander Maxwell about that one.'

The pair nodded and made notes.

'Anthea,' continued Boyd. 'Follow up on the target's identification, any criminal record, the works. I want a full profile on the subject, everything we know about him. How long has he been staying at that hotel? Has he had any visitors? Who has he telephoned. What colour are his socks? What does he eat for breakfast? Turn this barrel upside down and shake some results out.'

'Leave it with me,' replied Anthea. 'I'll set up a small enquiry team to push it faster and further.'

'Great,' agreed Boyd. 'Ricky, go with Tom and cover the hotel. I want to know everything there is to know as soon as is reasonably possible. Now then, can I remind you all that it would not be prudent for certain sections of society to learn of our covert operation. Usual protocol applies. Don't discuss our work with others outside the office. Need to know means exactly that and your mates outside don't need to know. Just a reminder.'

Nods and murmurs of approval followed before Boyd, declared, 'Finding one bad Turk does not mean that terrorists and criminals have infiltrated the capital. Who has made the donations and why? Were the donations made by people who thought they were buying tickets for a Turkish lottery, donating to charity, or supporting terrorism? Let's find out. The real problem,' argued Boyd, 'Is that we need to prove that Adam's cash is beings routed to one of three terrorist organisations operating in Turkey – Hezbollah, Al-Qaeda, or the PKK (the Kurdistan Workers Party). The next step is to ascertain which of the three organisations Adam is working for and where the money in his chosen bank account leads us. Any questions?'

There were none.

'Okay, rest, go home, sleep,' advised Boyd. 'Tomorrow we start again. You know what to do.'

'Och that sounds like good use of source intelligence,' remarked Janice as they adjourned to the canteen for coffee. 'I mean it was good operation, guvnor. We made good progress thanks to Ricky's source.'

'True,' replied Boyd. 'That, in itself, can sometimes be a problem, Janice.'

'I dinnae understand what you're driving at?' probed the Scot.

'Never, I repeat never, wholly trust a source,' suggested Boyd. 'You can get so close to them that sometimes they pull you in without you knowing it,' explained Boyd. 'Before you know it, they're running you but you don't realise it. Another thing, never take anything for granted.'

'Thanks,' replied Janice. 'I'll try and remember that.'

'There's one thing gnawing at me though,' remarked Boyd. 'The money, it's not right.'

'What do you mean by that?' asked Janice.

'Oh nothing, forget it,' replied Boyd. 'It's just occurred to me that someone somewhere must love Adam. He's on his own. Everyone trusts him.'

'They must hold him in high esteem,' proposed Janice, pushing the buttons on a coffee vending machine.

'Probably,' accepted Boyd. 'No doubt, in time, we'll find out how much Adam deposited in the bank

61

but that doesn't necessarily mean that's how much he collected.'

'You mean he's a rip off merchant and not a collector for a terrorist organisation?' queried Janice.

'I've made a presumption that our man is a collector. That's true, Janice, but we need to prove who he's collecting for. We could be on a wild goose chase for all I know. He could even be pocketing the money for his own use. At this stage, who knows?'

Later that night, Anthea rang.

'Bannerman and I have examined the still photographs and videos taken from the live operation, guvnor,' explained Anthea. 'We uploaded them to the Ticker Intelligence system. Facial recognition software has identified Adam as Adem Sidik from Istanbul. There are no criminal convictions recorded against Adem Sidik, just a photograph from a Turkish passport.'

'Good,' replied Boyd. 'We're making progress at last. At least we've something for the Commander tomorrow.'

'It will be on your desk later tonight,' revealed Anthea.

In NATO Headquarters, Brussels, Mouretti opened a cage door. Reaching inside, he offered a slice of apple to his pet with one hand whilst stroking its back with the other.

'There, my beauty,' said Mouretti praising the yellow-crested cockatoo that happily hopped onto his outstretched hand.

The bird's talon curled around Mouretti's wrist as he admired the cockatoo that continued to peck away at the apple. At a metre in length, the cockatoo tore into the food. Its feathers were brilliant white but the cockatoo's crown was a vivid display of yellow. It was a beautiful example of a wonderful bird.

'Come on,' remarked Mouretti withdrawing the bird from the cage and stepping backwards. 'You are safe here, my beauty. Stretch your wings and sit with me as I work into the night. I have so much to catch up with, didn't you know?'

The cockatoo nodded its head continually for a few seconds and then concentrated on nibbling the apple.

Mouretti guided the bird from his wrist to his shoulder, placed clean water in the cage, and then replenished the feeder with a mix of nuts, fruit and seeds.

Replacing the cockatoo in its cage, Mouretti returned to his desk, poured himself a black coffee, and continued sorting through his emails.

Mileage expense claims, meal expense claims, miscellaneous expense claims – all were dealt with as the time-served Mouretti worked through his emails. Finally, he turned to intelligence reports. He sat back, lifted his feet onto the edge of the desk, and read through the offerings.

'Sabiha Gokchen airport,' remarked Mouretti aloud. 'A quick response from my people there, my beauty. Let me see.'

Mouretti clicked into the email, savoured the report, and then downloaded the attached photographs.

The cockatoo was hungry. It squawked when its final piece of apple disappeared down its throat.

'Shush, my beauty,' advised Mouretti. 'I shall be with you in a moment.' Glancing momentarily at the bird, Mouretti added, 'I'm busy.'

Spellbound, Mouretti read a report from a NATO investigator who had visited the scene of the recent terrorist attack, liaised with local investigators, and then forward Mouretti the details.

There, before him on the screen, was the image of a white feather entwined in the wire mesh of the airport's perimeter fence.

Mouretti studied the image and then clicked the three dots situated in the top right of his internet browser. He increased the zoom capability and enabled himself to study the image of the feather much more closely than hitherto.

Examining the feather led him to scrutinise its length, the angle of the feathers from the spine, and the colouration evident in the heart of the feather. A further click drove him deeper and further into the structure of the feather.

Eventually, Mouretti, rubbed his eyes, stepped away from his desk, and approached a map of the world bolted to the wall.

Turning to the cockatoo, Mouretti said, 'My beauty, if I ignore the undoubted attraction of your yellow crest, I see only a gloriously white bird. Are you an exception in your breed? Of course, you are. Well, look at this, my beauty.'

Mouretti approached the map, laid a finger on an area of the Middle East, and said, 'My beauty, you are my best friend. You and I know that I am a keen ornithologist. We know that this feather came from here.'

Turning, Mouretti stabbed his finger into the map and said, 'The Quandil Mountains! We are ahead of the game.'

In the Special Crime Unit, in London, Anthea was also burning the midnight oil when she submitted an intelligence report which read as follows…

Target ADEM SIDIK… Preliminary Report.

… Adem Sidik, a Turkish national, has been followed for twelve hours in north, north-east, and central London. He has been observed collecting money from various business contacts, has lodged the collection at a High-Street bank in Bayswater Road, and has been housed in an apartment on the top floor of a four-star hotel in central London.

Information suggests these collections were bound for the hands of terrorists in Turkey. Further intelligence is anticipated relevant to finance, telephony, and covert enquiry in due course…

Further details in attached surveillance log.

Initial assessment: insufficient evidence at present stage for Home Office eavesdropping warrant.

Preliminary submission to surveillance commander Boyd, Wm Miller... and Maxwell, Edwin... Commander S.C.U....

Provenance: Personal involvement.

Ends... Adams, Anthea.... Det Insp. SCU. Operation Distinguish

*

## Chapter Three

~

The Special Crime Unit
New Scotland Yard
London

A computer screen flashed in a secure area of the Special Crime Unit in New Scotland Yard, London.

Nearby, Antonia Harston-Browne – Toni, as she was known in the office – noted Anthea's report, closed the buff file marked 'Secret', and moved across to read the computer screen.

Tall and slim, Antonia's long red hair flowed down her back and covered her shoulder blades. With an hour-glass figure, she wore a dark blue, two-piece, executive-style suit set off with a silver brooch worn on the lapel. The neatly tailored skirt stopped short just above the knee. Articulate, sophisticated, cultured, educated well above the national standard, and of upper middle class bearing, she carried a highly polished professional demeanour. Enjoying two honours degrees and playing a merciless game of squash, she was employed by the British Security Service at Thames House. Antonia was also the senior Intelligence Officer in the controversial Special Crime Unit at New Scotland Yard.

'Boyd,' she shouted. 'There's something on the Ticker system you might be interested in. It's an update on the Turkish airport attack.'

'I'll be there in a moment,' replied a husky male voice. 'Sandra's report by any chance?'

Toni chuckled and began interrogating her computer.

In her element with the so-called 'county set', Antonia could easily utilise airs and graces if she wished. Yet, in the oak-panelled corridors of Whitehall, she could wheel and deal with the sharpest of kids on the block. In the City, she wined and dined at expensive restaurants and wore long, flowing gowns that vitalised her sophisticated charms and discarded the facade of her other life. She was privileged, the daughter of parents since departed: parents who had left her a financial legacy that revealed her to be of comfortable private means. Antonia had connections in every corner of society that one might imagine: the good, the bad, and the ugly. She was also falling in love with Sir Phillip Nesbitt, the Director General of the Security Service.

'It most certainly is,' replied Toni. '

'What does the report say?' asked Detective Chief Inspector Boyd.

'I've asked the Commander to join us,' replied Toni. 'He'll be here any minute.'

No sooner said, there was a polite knock on the door and Commander Maxwell entered accompanied by Bannerman, Anthea, and the recently appointed Commissioner of the Metropolitan Police, Neil Atkinson. With the group was an older gentleman bearing a walking stick and dressed in a three-piece suit. He was immediately recognised as the Foreign Secretary.

'Sir Henry!' gushed Toni. 'What a surprise to see you. How are things in the Foreign Office today? I trust you and Lady Cynthia are well?'

Caught off-guard for a moment, Sir Henry flustered a little before expressing himself with, 'Goodness! Antonia! Yes! Yes, of course, I am well. We are both well, and you?'

'I am fine, thank you,' replied Toni. 'Please give Cynthia my best, won't you?'

'Yes, of course,' replied Sir Henry moving his weight from one foot to another and leaning on the walking stick.

There was a flurry of polite handshakes before Sir Henry opened proceedings with, 'So, Commander Maxwell, this is where it all happens?'

'Not really,' replied Maxwell. 'This is where we house the Ticker Intelligence system. It's a secure room equipped with various gismos to prevent bugging and hacking.'

'Ticker?' queried Neil.

'No disrespect, sir,' explained Maxwell. 'But I am aware that you are new in post. How much do you know about the Ticker system and our unit?

'Not as much as I'd like to,' replied the Commissioner. 'Your unit is all very hush-hush and seldom referred to by either the rank and file or many of my senior staff. Enlighten me, Commander, or does my security clearance not clear me?'

Commander Maxwell smiled and replied, 'The Special Crime Unit is a hand-picked team of detectives. We recruit from Counter Terrorist Command but also engage detectives from all over the British Isles as well as some hand-picked individuals from MI5 and MI6. They are all experts in some field or other.'

'Yes, Inspector Adams did mention something like that to me,' replied Neil exchanging glances with Anthea. 'Do continue, Commander Maxwell.'

Nodding, Maxwell replied, 'The unit's official remit is to police, defend, and secure the freedom of the nation and its people from serious organised crime and national and international terrorism. The unit works from a secure area within the Security Service building. My officers only have access to this area within Thames House for obvious reasons relevant to security. They need only know that which concerns them. The very latest equipment is installed to prevent cyber hacking and we call our floor The Operations Centre. This area in New Scotland Yard is replicated in the Security Service building.'

The Foreign Secretary nodded his understanding but challenged with, 'Why two bases? Isn't that a waste of money?'

'Not if one is put out of action,' contended the Commander.

'I see,' replied the visitor. 'So, you really are the sharpest tool in the box?'

'That's the plan,' ventured Maxwell. 'Detective Superintendent Peel is my second-in-command whilst Chief Inspector Boyd is Head of Covert Operations in the unit. 'Boyd's speciality is running a stand-alone response team capable of running any major investigation anywhere in the country, and if necessary elsewhere. The unit has one commander – myself - one detective superintendent, one DCI – Boyd - and 4 other wings each overseen by a detective inspector.'

'Our partners in the intelligence community from America, Canada, Australia, various parts of Europe, and elsewhere,' disclosed Boyd. 'They all contribute to the effectiveness of the system. Once an intelligence officer – from the police counter terrorist agencies, the military or intelligence services – is authorised to use the system they are up and away. It is so easy to use and each operative has password entry to the system. What we have is a worldwide collection of intelligence data being sent to the system by authorised personnel only. The people sending it don't necessarily have access to read anything on it. Various analysts have different levels of security access. The higher your security clearance the more you can read about what's on the system.'

'Everyone contributes but only a few actually know what's in the system,' revealed Anthea.

'Exactly!' admitted Antonia. 'It's computerised need to know in one way. Every ticker report lies over a comprehensive report so we can read more when we want to by just clicking on a ticker report as it passes across the screen on its way to the security data warehouse. The report then opens and takes you to a separate file. Once it gets to the data warehouse it is kept for reference and analysis before being disseminated as appropriate.'

'Interesting indeed,' commented the Foreign Secretary.

'It is the most advanced system of its kind in the world. It took years to design and cost millions to put in place across secure partner sites,' revealed the Commander. 'The most technically advanced 'secure, search and analyse' software is in position. It works in conjunction with CAST – crime analytics software for terrorism - They tell me it's impregnable due to the multi facet encryption embedded in the system.'

'Good,' intervened the Commissioner. 'However, I should tell you that I received a call from the Prime Minister today. She is concerned about the attack on an airport not too far from our NATO base in Turkey.'

'I rather presumed that was the reason for Sir Henry's visit,' remarked the Commander.

'Her Majesty's Government are mindful and very conscious of all such atrocities that impact on NATO,' stated Sir Henry. 'You will be aware that Turkey is a member of NATO, Commander. One of our primary concerns is to ensure the security of our various bases across Europe. Article five of the North Atlantic Treaty states that any attack on any one member of NATO is acknowledged as an attack on all members of the alliance. Consequently, we are anxious that you provide our government with a neutral assessment of the matters being investigated.'

'My dear, Sir Henry,' oozed Toni suddenly coming to life from her desk. 'Such complicated political speak is wonderful for the media but I have to ask you – why not ask MI6 for their assessment? Come, come, sir, you can tell us. Unlike these officers, I am not constrained by their organisational protocol and rank structure. An obvious question needs to be asked. Why us? We are on your side, Sir Henry... Commissioner... Tell us, what's the bottom line?'

Sir Henry immediately threw a sideways glance at Neil.

Momentarily taken aback, Neil eventually replied, 'Her Majesty's Government wants a fresh perspective, hence our involvement. The government want to know if this is the Russians in sheep's clothing? Or is it the work of a new terrorist grouping that we are unaware of?'

Toni nodded pensively and responded with, 'Commissioner, you and the Foreign Secretary really mean that, due to recent anti-government rallies and demonstrations in Turkey, you would prefer not to unnecessarily expose our intelligence officers and embassy officials to the changing face of their democracy. Indeed, one might argue that democracy is dying in Turkey. They seem to be arresting everyone who does not agree with the government of the day. I understand they've locked up thousands of people. That's hardly a good way to run a country and certainly seems to lack any democratic bearing.'

'It's just as well we are not Turkey,' ventured Bannerman. 'We don't have enough prisons.'

'Thank you, Antonia,' replied Sir Henry. 'We wish to remain adaptable in our diplomatic solutions but as Turkey becomes more unstable we have to take steps that we might not ordinarily take. For that reason, this unit has the job.'

'And the job is?' enquired Commander Maxwell.

'Put simply, Commander Maxwell, are the Turks telling us the truth at this stage? I want you to find out if this is Islamic State, the PKK, or a Russian covert intervention. Is that clear?'

'Oh, absolutely,' replied Commander Maxwell.

'Indeed, absolutely,' added Toni with a cheeky smile.

'Good! That's settled then,' replied Sir Henry. 'I'll leave you to it, Commander.'

'Not before a sherry in my office, perhaps?' queried the Commissioner.

'An excellent idea, Neil,' replied the Foreign Secretary 'Perhaps you will arrange for Superintendent Peel to telephone me with an update when next she touches base?'

'Of course,' replied the Commander. 'Of course.'

As the entourage left the office, Toni turned to Boyd and offered, 'Nose put out, chief inspector? It looks like you are no longer flavour of the month. Your face doesn't fit anymore.'

Boyd balled a piece of paper in his fist and threw it at Toni saying, 'Absolutely, but then I have my own Turk to sort out here in London. We need to remain adaptable to the life of would-be terrorists in this country. By the way, you didn't show them Sandy's report.'

'No, I didn't. How remiss of me,' chuckled Toni. 'I noted that Commander Maxwell knew we had received Sandy's report yet chose not to discuss it with either the Commissioner or the Foreign Secretary. I wonder why?'

'Because he's a wily old bird,' remarked Boyd. 'And the Commander likes to be one step ahead of everyone else. If he tells the Foreign Secretary everything then they'll know as much as us, and that would never do. The Commander will have his reasons, I'm sure.'

'Who is running the country?' ventured Toni. 'The Commander or our elected government?'

'The Foreign Secretary and his cronies,' suggested Boyd with a mischievous smile. 'But tell me, why didn't you raise the report with the Commissioner?'

'I thought we'd read it first,' replied Toni. 'There's no need to put Sandy into the firing line at this stage. A report for government will follow by the usual methods. Here, read this.'

Boyd took the flimsy from Toni and read it...

Preliminary Investigation into mortar attack at Sabiha Gokcen International Airport, Istanbul, Turkey. Attachments (2)

Unnamed persons, believed four in number, arrived at scene in a non-descript van, approached airport fence by exploiting natural cover, used bolt croppers to effect entry, made extensive use of mortar bombs and caused major damage and disruption to the airport. Offenders engaged in short small-arms firefight with airport security personnel before exploding white phosphorous bomb to cover escape in same van and destroy evidence. Forensic examination of remains suggests three mortars were used.

Multiple fatalities and casualties include British holidaymakers who are UK residents ---- (see attachment)

As yet, van not recovered but may be identical with one found burnt out 24 hours later in an industrial site in Istanbul. To be confirmed.

Forensic analysis reveals that a quantity of strychnine had been added to the water in the fountain of the airport named after the first female combat pilot to fly for the Turkish Air Force. Adding the poison to the water at the same time as the mortar attack suggests a two-pronged assault – one immediate, the other residual and long lasting. Two firefighters and a police officer were hospitalised because of inhaling strychnine. Fortunately, for them, there was insufficient strychnine in the water to cause death. Water had diluted the strychnine and they survived the attack. One of the firefighters was also treated for serious phosphorous burns. Dozens of casualties, from across the globe, were listed as 'fatalities', whilst scores were hospitalised with various injuries.

A police dog was also declared dead at the scene of the atrocity. Veterinary examination reveals death by strychnine poisoning.

Investigators examined CCTV and recovered burnt remnants of what appear to be three canvas holdalls, and several mortars. Shoe prints recovered from a copse near to the fence are from Adidas training shoes, sizes 11, 10, 9, and 8. This appears to confirm the presence of four attackers at the point of entry to the airport.

Also, recovered - a pair of bolt croppers, the remains of a device that had ignited a phosphorous bomb, and various miscellaneous investigative leads. No specific clues prompting further urgent investigation are immediately apparent.

A bird's feather found threaded into the mesh of a wire fence was logged and noted by investigators but regarded as irrelevant. It was assessed that it was probably put there by children playing in the area whilst waiting for a flight with their parents.

Turkish authorities have labelled the event as a terrorist related incident but are unable to ascertain whether the attack originated from Islamic State, the PKK (Kurdistan Workers Party), or an unknown anti-Turkey or anti-NATO group.

No one has claimed responsibility for the incident, which leaves the way ahead unclear. There are no primary or secondary suspects presently in the frame. A government-controlled Turkish media is playing down the incident as 'isolated' but I fear it may be the prelude to further attacks in the area. Since no terrorist group has claimed responsibility, the perpetrators may well prove to be 'state-sponsored' by a nation in opposition to the present Turkish government.

It is my belief that weapons and artillery used in the attack could only have been sourced via the military.

NB... This is the first known strychnine attack in Europe if not the world.

Strychnine ... (see attachment)

'Shall we?' asked Toni. 'Chemistry was not my favourite subject at school so I'm a little hazy as far as strychnine is concerned.'

'Absolutely,' replied Boyd. 'What does Sandy have to say about it? It's a poison, isn't it? If Sandy has highlighted it then it may have some bearing on the investigation.'

'She's gone into things with a fine-tooth comb,' suggested Toni. 'Do we really need to know who the airport is named after and about children playing with feathers?'

'Not at the moment, Toni, but you never know with these things,' advised Boyd. 'Sandy has experience in major crime enquiries. I'm sure she's trying to cover all the bases. That's all, but tell me where can you get your hands on strychnine these days?'

'No idea,' replied Toni. 'I could make a couple of phone calls and see what we can find out. Having some facts relevant to strychnine in the United Kingdom might help but I wouldn't know where to start in Istanbul. Let's see what she says.'

The attachment was opened and printed. Boyd and Toni read the flimsy....

Strychnine...

A bitter-tasting, odourless, colourless, crystalline powder, which is an extremely deadly chemical found in the seeds of a species of tropical plants called Strychnos....

The strychnine tree, strychnos nux-vomica, is the source of the poison strychnine. This tropical plant is found in India, Sri Lanka, the East Indies, and Australia.

'It's tempting to believe that the suspects might be from one of those countries?' suggested Boyd. 'But somehow I doubt it.'

'Maybe, maybe not, read on,' replied Toni. 'There's one thing for sure.'

'What's that?'

'There's no strychnine trees naturally growing in either the UK or Turkey which tends to suggest the strychnine was obtained from either a source country or a pharmacy supplier somewhere.'

'Mmm,' noted Boyd shaking the flimsy. 'Are you a detective by any chance?'

They read the flimsy.

Strychnine poisoning can be fatal to humans and other animals and can occur by inhalation, swallowing or absorption through the membranes of the nose, eyes, or mouth. For example, a person could be poisoned by inhaling strychnine powder that has been released in the air. It produces some of the most dramatic and explosive convulsions of any known toxic substance. Strychnine attacks the central nervous system and within ten minutes causes all the muscles to contract simultaneously beginning with the victim's face and neck. The shoulders, arms, and legs, follow until the victim's back finally arches continually.

Today, strychnine is used primarily as a pesticide, particularly to kill rats. Uncommonly, very minor traces of strychnine are occasionally found mixed with 'street' drugs such as LSD, heroin, and cocaine.

The slightest sound or movement will bring on fresh spasms and worsen a victim's condition. Rigor mortis begins immediately and freezes the body with its eyes wide open…

Provenance: Personal Enquiry.

Source: Istanbul Law Enforcement /Foreign Office Liaison Group

Attribution: Sender.

Time of Origin: as per report.

Ends....

Sender: Peel, Sandra – Detective Superintendent. Special Crime Unit, New Scotland Yard, London. (on temporary attachment)

Transmit... 1125 hrs...

'Nasty stuff,' stated Boyd.

'But interesting,' suggested Toni. 'No-one claimed responsibility for the act of extreme violence. A lengthy report which details the first strychnine attack on this scale but concludes the authorities have no suspects and no primary leads.'

'How unusual!' remarked Boyd. 'Islamic State or the PKK, I would say.'

'How about Russian Special Forces posing as terrorists to destroy a facility often used by NATO personnel?' argued Toni.

'Spetsnaz?' offered Boyd.

'It's possible,' suggested Toni. 'The world is a dangerous place. Nothing is sacred these days.'

'Or a gang of terrorists hiring themselves out?' proposed Boyd. 'Then again, is it Hezbollah's military wing in Lebanon on their holidays? They have the military capability.'

'Let's make some notes and draft an acknowledgement,' proposed Toni. 'The Commander will be interested in this one, that's for sure.'

Meanwhile, in an airport departure terminal in Europe, Darius folded his magazine and checked the time. Casually, he eyed those around him before making his way to a phone cubicle. Once inside, he used a mirror on the wall to watch for anyone who might be following him. Satisfied, he relaxed and turned around to face the door.

Tapping the number, he made a call.

'All is ready,' declared Darius. 'You will deliver half to me now and the other half upon completion. Once it has settled into the bank account, I will move into position. Do you understand my requirements?'

Listening, Darius scanned the faces inside the terminal building and then replied, 'Good! Thank you! White Eagle awaits your deposit before conclusion. Don't be late. I have other clients to satisfy.'

When Darius boarded his flight, Boyd, Meg, Toni, and Phillip enjoyed a meal together at a Spanish restaurant in London.

'Holidays?' enquired Sir Phillip. 'I take it Turkey is out. How about Spain or the Maldives? Perhaps Mexico or a cruise to the Caribbean islands? Any ideas yet?'

'Silloth, replied Meg. 'It's on the west coast and it's famous for being nice and peaceful.'

'The Canary Islands,' ventured Boyd. 'Silloth is famous for rain. The Canaries are famous for sunshine.'

'Those islands are named after dogs from the Latin canis, I believe,' advised Toni. 'Apparently, the Romans were amongst the first to visit the islands and were greeted by wild natives with even wilder dogs.'

'Fascinating,' replied Boyd. 'More wine?'

'Yes, good idea,' suggested Phillip nudging Toni playfully. 'It might shut the Encyclopaedia Britannica up.'

'Oy!' remarked Toni.

The evening wore on and a good time was had by all.

In London, that weekend, rain fell on the tarmac streets and gathered in pools in the gutters.

Across the English Channel, in France, the sun shone and welcomed visitors to the iconic streets of its capital.

## Chapter Four

~

Avenue des Champs-Élysées
Paris
Later.

Red!

Darius waited patiently for traffic lights to change at the roundabout at La Place de la Concorde. Eventually, the lights changed to green and he set off on his motorbike to turn right into Avenue des Champs-Elysées.

Working through the gears, he felt adrenaline surging through his body when he joined other motorists travelling towards the Arc de Triomphe. There were five lanes of traffic travelling in both directions and no-one hung about in the race to the next junction. Darius tucked in behind a bus full of tourists and steadied himself.

Trying to relax, he resettled his sunglasses and glanced at a six-man army patrol strung out across the pavement. The patrol walked towards the Paris Ferris Wheel and were armed with FAMAS 5.56mm assault rifles and Glock 17 pistols. Young, fit, and athletic, the soldiers dominated the city streets and wore the soft maroon beret of French paratroopers.

Realising he was almost at his destination, Darius reduced speed and moved towards the offside of the boulevard. He noticed a police car come into view and stop beside a bank on the opposite side of the road. A group of youths, in their mid-twenties, emerged from the bank and made their way down the street.

Darius pulled up outside a pavement café and glanced at the customers sat at various tables enjoying

79

themselves in the sunshine. He recognised the man he had been sent to Paris to find.

For a moment, a nightmare from long ago threatened to infiltrate Darius's mind as he thought back to that time in the mountains. Then a clink of glasses nudged the motorcyclist back into reality.

He shook his head free of the horrifying vision inside his brain and glanced again at the trio sat enjoying themselves. Glasses were filled with wine. A smile was offered, and returned.

There was a chink of glasses when the words, 'Á votre santé,' were heard.

Casually, Darius manipulated the handlebar mirror and took in what was happening to his rear. Firstly, he caught a glimpse of his beard and sunglasses. A slight nudge of the handlebars produced a much better view.

With the engine idling, Darius watched two officers get out of their police car and line up the youths from the bank against the building line. They began to search them. One officer patted the suspects down whilst the other stood in support with his hand curled around the butt of a holstered pistol. The officers wore the uniform of 'Police Nationale'. They were both 'Gardien de la paix' – keepers of the peace – and each wore two stripes on their epaulettes.

Darius recognised the suspects police were checking as of middle-eastern appearance. Syrian, he thought. Perhaps they are refugees but I don't know for sure.

Moving the mirror once more, he watched the paratroopers walking in the direction of the Ferris wheel and the Louvre, in the far distance. Casually, he relaxed, deliberated on traffic to his rear, and then studied people's faces as they walked along the pavement.

Am I being followed, he wondered? Or are they already here waiting for me?

The boulevard was packed with individuals and vehicles. Some drivers tooted their horns in a bizarre ritual of French road rage that was prevalent in Paris. Others lined up like lemmings and followed the vehicle immediately in front as they queued to get away from the hustle and bustle of city life. On the pavement, the café culture was as popular as ever. The heart of the capital beat healthily as it fed and watered tourists and Parisians alike beneath a score of French tricolours flying defiantly in the breeze.

This is Paris. A state of emergency exists following numerous terrorist attacks by Islamic extremists since January, 2015. Operation Sentinel is in full swing but it didn't deter the French from going about their daily affairs.

Even so, everyone was on tenterhooks.

Glancing to his right, Darius watched the three men sat at a table. They were enjoying lunch together and there was a half-consumed bottle of wine and three glasses on their table. Each man wore a light-coloured business suit and had placed their briefcases on the ground at the foot of the table.

Darius studied the three men for a moment and then turned away.

Checking the mirror, he moved his head slightly. He scrutinized the two policemen searching their suspects then looked behind and noted that the paratroopers had split up. Three were walking towards him on one pavement whilst the other half of the patrol were on the opposing street patrolling in the same direction.

One of the waiters glanced at the biker and gesticulated to him.

'What do you want?' the waiter asked.

It was time, Darius decided as he settled his sunglasses on the bridge of his nose again and thought it through. There are so many people about. Who is who? Which faces belong to normal people and which faces belong to police undercover officers? Do I abort or carry on?

'Damn these nerves,' he thought. 'Do it!'

Shaking his head, Darius looked again at his target, reached inside his leather jacket, and withdrew a submachine gun.

'I will not forget. I will not forgive,' yelled Darius.

Levelling the weapon at one of the three men, Darius pulled the trigger. A short spurt of gunfire followed, struck the victim in his chest, and ripped the man to pieces. The assailant quickly moderated his firing line slightly and pulled the trigger again. Darius shot the two other men in the same short callous manner.

The air was filled with screaming when frenzied panic gripped the area in a manner not experienced before.

Thrown backwards against his chair, the first victim had smashed into a neighbouring table and slithered unceremoniously to the ground.

Following suit, the other two victims were pounded backwards.

The waiter screeched in shock, shuddered, dropped a tray of drinks, and ran inside the building.

Pandemonium broke out with customers diving beneath tables or running inside when they realised what was happening.

Unfazed, Darius rode his motorbike onto the pavement and reached inside his jacket. Withdrawing a feather, he threw it towards his victims. As the feather floated gradually to the ground, the killer lined up a head shot and let rip another short hail of bullets that penetrated the first victim's skull and upper body.

The paratroopers reacted instantly and began running towards the scene closely followed by the two policemen who abandoned their search operation and responded to gunfire.

Open-mouthed, a taxi driver saw the drama unfold, lost concentration, and ran into the back of a Renault saloon in front of him. The driver of a BMW, following the taxi, reacted by swerving onto a pavement to avoid a collision, and promptly crashed into a lamp standard.

Coolly, Darius deliberately dropped his submachinegun on the footpath, checked over his shoulder, and twisted the bike's accelerator.

Master Corporal Xavier Dubois was the nearest paratrooper to the scene. A sturdy five feet eight inches tall, he stepped into the middle of the road and began running towards the café.

'Down! Everyone get down!' he yelled.

Raising his rifle to shoulder height, Xavier screamed at the crowds as he closed with the killer.

'Down! Hit the deck!'

'Watch your background!' shouted Hugo Durand, the first policeman to join him. 'There's too many people about.'

Darius's motorbike twitched and shook when the back wheel bounced from the pavement onto the road and he accelerated as fast as he could.

Xavier dropped onto one knee, tightened the rifle butt hard into his shoulder, and fired a round.

The portly Hugo withdrew his handgun and fired a shot.

Anticipating the contact, Darius ducked low, zigzagged between traffic, and captured the centre of the highway as he raced up the street in the middle of ten lanes of traffic.

A cacophony of car, taxi, and van horns greeted Darius as he bent low, twisted the throttle and roared up the street.

A waiter from a neighbouring café ran onto the pavement, threw an empty bottle at the fleeing assassin, and watched it smash into a dozen pieces when it missed and landed on the tarmac.

Simultaneously, Xavier's bullet zipped through the air, hit the killer's handlebar mirror, smashed the lens, and totally missed its human target.

Hugo's bullet slammed into the building line, destroyed some masonry, and embedded itself in the concrete.

Lining up another shot, Xavier fired again but to no avail.

More police, together with the remainder of the army patrol, arrived breathless at the café.

'He's getting away,' shouted Xavier taking further aim.

'He won't get far,' yelled Hugo bending down to tend to the victims. 'Radio it in,' he shouted.

Already using the radio, his colleague replied, 'I'm on it, Hugo. They'll get him at the top of the hill.'

The top of the hill was the roundabout at Place Charles de Gaulle where the Arc de Triomphe is situated. Here, another army patrol emerged from the underground tunnel on the Avenue de la Grande Armee side of the roundabout. They immediately sought out their target and ran towards the shooting.

Instantaneously, two police cars came into view and swung across the road attempting to block traffic.

The fleeing motorcyclist heaved his handlebars upwards and mounted the pavement once more. Head down, Darius bobbed and weaved through a glut of pedestrians.

People on the Avenue des Champs-Élysées parted as if it were the Red Sea. But this wasn't Moses leading the Israelites fleeing from the Egyptians. It was Darius hell bent on escape with people scattering everywhere. Only the police and army paratroopers ran towards the perpetrator.

'Target acquired,' shouted an army commander. 'Engage and neutralise!'

There was more screaming and panic when people ran to get out of the way. Dozens scampered back down the steps of the underground facility at the Arc de Triomphe whilst others hid behind the arc's pillars and tried to make themselves invisible,

More army bullets chased the assassin but none made their target.

Seconds later, Darius was gone in a growling roar with a wisp of exhaust fumes to his rear and a clear road ahead.

Determined, he swung into a side road, abandoned his vehicle, and strolled casually down the steps into an underground tube station. On route, Darius discarded his crash helmet and sunglasses in a litter bin and made for the nearest platform.

A Métro train pulled into the station. The doors opened automatically and its passengers poured onto the platform like ants covering a dying worm.

Darius threw a glance over his shoulder, edged forward through the throng, and boarded the train. Two minutes later, he was travelling on the underground, sat next to a door, and staring at discarded Playboy magazine on the floor in front of him. Continuing to avoid eye contact, he held his gaze on the front cover. It was a semi-naked leggy blonde with a huge smile, and other attributes, which did little to entice Darius in his present state.

His mind was alive, his eyes darting everywhere, and his senses at their highest peak.

The man sitting opposite Darius lowered his newspaper, glanced at Darius, and then returned to the inside pages.

Nervous now, Darius felt the sweat running down his neck. He could do without anyone looking at him and remembering his face. Standing up, he made for the doorway and peered out of the window to hide his face from other passengers.

Brick wall after brick wall blurred his vision as the train sped through the underground tunnels at high speed.

When the Métro stopped, the door opened and he stepped onto the platform. Darius bounded up the escalator and walked into the pleasant sunshine two miles from the Avenue des Champs-Élysées.

Hailing a taxi, he got into the rear passenger compartment and gave an instruction to the driver. Darius was gone from the centre of Paris within minutes of the assassination.

Back at the scene of the triple murder, the police arrived in force and cordoned off the area. Identifying and questioning witnesses began.

'What did you see?'

'How many were there?'

'Where did the motor bike come from?'

'Did he speak to anyone?'

'What did he look like?'

'Did you get the number of the bike?'

'How many people did he shoot at?'

'What was he wearing?'

'Are you sure it was a man or was it a woman?'

'He shouted before he shot them! What did he shout?'

Police diverted all traffic whilst paratroopers, with weapons drawn, scanned the entire area for anything suspicious as the questioning continued.

The adrenaline rushed, sweat poured from the skin, hearts beat faster. Police knew it was more than a domestic incident. It was a multiple murder. But they wondered if it was a terrorist attack or a gangland killing, and was it over?

Is it a lone wolf killing by one crazy individual suffering from mental health problems? Or is it a terrorist cell embarking on the first of many attacks that day? Maybe it's just a tit-for-tat killing rooted in the enigma of people smuggling, human trafficking, or the supply of drugs?

They didn't know.

As the minutes ticked by, more squadrons of armed police were deployed across Paris as every effort was made to bolster security and prevent another atrocity. The atmosphere was alive with the sound of klaxons blaring as squad after squad of police moved into position.

Trains, buses and taxis were abruptly filled by commuters determined to get out of the city centre as soon as possible.

Mouretti arrived and uplifted the ribbon cordon that sought to protect the crime scene.

Xavier and Hugo approached but before either of them could speak the smartly dressed Mouretti flashed his identity card for inspection.

Snapping to attention, Xavier saluted the plainclothes man and explained, 'Sir, we don't yet know who the victims are.'

'I do,' replied Mouretti. 'They are all senior officers in NATO.'

'How do you know that?' asked Hugo.

Mouretti bent low, gently touched the forehead of the first victim, and held the dead man's hand before revealing, 'Because this man is my father. He invited me for lunch with his colleagues. I was late, far too late, it seems.'

Stunned, Hugo stuttered, 'Oh! I am... I am so sorry for you... and your father, of course. I don't know what to say.'

'Then don't say anything,' advised Mouretti.

Studying his father's features, Mouretti kissed his father on what was left of his forehead and felt a stack of tears swelling up inside. He took a breath and then exhaled loudly before cradling the man in his arms.

'Napoli, my father!' offered Mouretti.

Tears flooded Mouretti's face as he wept.

Xavier placed a hand on Mouretti's shoulder in a consoling fashion and said, 'Sir… Sir… If there's anything we can do?'

Mouretti pursed his lips, looked down at his father, and replied, 'I will take you back to Napoli, father. I will lie you in the graveyard next to Mamma. My sisters and I will drink Chianti from your vineyard and eat olives. We will talk late into the night of the love you showed us. We will never forget you my father. Never.'

Mouretti embraced his father, held him close, and allowed the teardrops to trickle down his cheek.

Glancing across at the other two victims, Mouretti composed himself and declared, 'Gentlemen, you have three off-duty Generals from NATO dead on the streets of Paris. One from Italy, one from France, and one from Germany. May I suggest you inform your senior command as soon as possible. I do believe you may have witnessed either a killing from a hostile enemy agent or a deliberate assassination from a terrorist group opposed to NATO and the west. I'm not sure which just now but time will tell.'

'Your card, sir?' queried Hugo. 'May I see it again?'

'Off course, but why?' replied Mouretti.

'Who are you exactly?' queried Hugo.

'Just a nobody who works for NATO,' replied Mouretti as he produced his identity card once more.

This time the policemen inspected the card and turned it over to read the full content. He took in the imprinted photograph and compared it with the man before him. Then he nodded smartly, returned Mouretti's card, and stepped away to speak urgently into his radio.

Engaging the Italian closely, Hugo declared, 'Giuseppe Mouretti, why yes, of course. I have heard of you, sir. We'll get him, sir. We'll do our best. You have my word.'

'Thank you, officer! Vive La France!' replied Mouretti.

'Viva l'italia!' responded Hugo. 'Now then, sir, is there anything I can do for you?'

The Italian knelt, cradled the man who was his father, and said, 'Can I introduce you to my father? He was such a great man. His name is Tomaso Mouretti and he is a NATO General and senior officer in the NATO Italian Rapid Deployable Corps.'

Holding his father close, Mouretti let the tears fall once more. He held his father tighter and closer to his body. Life had gone from the General. He was cold and grey in his final moments. Yet his eyes were wide open.

'I wish I could turn back time, sir,' suggested Hugo.

'Don't we all,' replied Mouretti.

Giuseppe Mouretti looked towards the Arc de Triomphe and quietly whispered, 'I will avenge you, father. As God is my witness, I will have justice. It's what we stand for. You will not die in vain'

A few moments later, Hugo asked, 'I'm sorry, sir but I must ask you some questions.'

'Go ahead,' replied Mouretti.

'What type of weapon did the killer drop?' asked Hugo.

Looking at the submachine gun nearby, Mouretti replied, 'It's an Israeli made Uzi submachine gun.'

'Good!' replied Xavier. 'The killer obviously panicked. I suppose that means there's an Israeli connection in this?'

'I think the killer wants you to think that,' offered Mouretti. 'When the police interview witnesses, they might ask if the gunman dropped the gun by accident or deliberately. The assassin might want you to believe there's an Israeli connection beyond the weapon used. It's quite a common firearm in the scheme of things, you see, but not necessarily one you might expect to be used in a close quarter assassination. I think our killer might want you to believe there's a Jewish connection or something like that. It's perhaps too early to tell but the Uzi left at the scene is just not right in my eyes. Our man is trying to lay a red herring.'

'I see,' replied Xavier.

'As I understand it, sir,' delved Hugo. 'The killer rode a motorcycle to this point, stopped, and then shot the three men. I wonder if it might be a random shooting or is this a regular haunt for a trio of friends?'

'They meet here, in this place, at this time, on the last Friday of every month, officer,' explained Mouretti. 'I suspect the killer somehow knew that and arranged to be here at the precise moment he opened fire.'

Hugo nodded but then added, 'By the way, I've found this. The waiter tells me the gunman on the motorbike threw it at the bodies before he shot the first victim the second time.'

'A feather,' replied Mouretti examining the find. 'Where was it?'

'On the ground beside the bodies,' explained the policeman.

Mouretti took the feather in his hands and studied the plumage.

'Bloody pigeons,' exclaimed Xavier. 'They are everywhere. We need a cull to get rid of them. It's just fluff, that's all.'

Allowing the plumage to trickle through his fingers, Mouretti replied, 'Not a pigeon, I'm afraid. I am familiar with this particular object. Birds are a hobby of mine. This is a tail feather. It's the plumage of an eagle.'

Again, Mouretti hugged his father and swept the man's hair from his face before kissing him on the forehead.

'An eagle?' queried Hugo. 'There are no eagles in Paris, sir.'

'There is now,' replied Mouretti quietly. 'One we need to find and neutralise.'

Later that day, the flame of the unknown soldier lying in a vault beneath the Arc de Triomphe was rekindled by one of the French Veteran's Associations. The daily occurrence was witnessed in full view of a mass of tourists who were not completely aware of earlier events.

Elsewhere in Paris, Master Corporal Xavier Dupois ended his patrol and handed in his report to the duty officer of his unit - the First Parachute Hussar Regiment.

Within the hour, an accredited operator sat down at a desk and transcribed the content onto a classified computerised intelligence system which was shared by multiple intelligence agencies in various countries. Those involved in the sharing of such intelligence included the United Kingdom – The Ticker Intelligence System.

'Operation Sentinel in Paris,' replied Toni. 'A report from our contact in the 1st Parachute Hussar Regiment.'

Boyd leaned over her shoulder to read the screen and remarked, 'Crack counter-terrorist troops, aren't they?'

'Renown!' agreed Toni. 'But not good enough today, I'm afraid. There's been a shooting in the centre of Paris. Three dead and they are all NATO generals. The suspect made off on a motor bike. He has a beard and wore sunglasses apparently.'

'Is that all they've got?' asked Boyd.

'The killer left a feather on the bodies,' added Toni.

'A feather?' queried Boyd.

'That's what the report says but I don't know how relevant that might be,' replied Toni.

'The killer might work with birds, be a zoo-keeper, or sell hats for a living,' suggested Boyd.

'Ornithology,' proposed Toni. 'The study of birds.'

'Any connections we need to know about, Toni?' queried Boyd.

'Other than the victims being from NATO, then no,' replied Toni. 'There's no known connections or activity here. That said, Boyd, the Commander likes to know about these things and the UK is a member of NATO. An attack on one member of NATO is regarded as an assault on all members of NATO. Remember? I'll alert him as to the incident and then he knows. I don't think the killing of three NATO generals will pass quietly and without comment.'

'You can say that again,' agreed Boyd.

'It's terrible and it's tragic,' declared Toni. 'Every politician and newscaster in Europe will have something to say about this.'

'Thanks, replied Boyd. 'Commander Maxwell likes to be in tune with the top landing as well as the political departments. He gets upset when the Commissioner knows something that he doesn't.'

Toni pressed a button and replied, 'Well, it will be on his Ticker screen now. More importantly, are you taking me for a drink when the office closes?'

'The office closes?' queried Boyd. 'Since when did our office ever close?'

'Never,' replied Toni, 'But a drink would be nice and I'm ready for a break.'

'I take it Phillip is away?' enquired Boyd.

'Just for the weekend,' replied Toni. 'A security conference at The Hague with his European pals.'

'Ahh, the heads get together?' proposed Boyd.

'Something like that,' responded Toni with a pleasant smile. 'I can neither confirm nor deny his whereabouts.'

Smiling, Boyd replied, 'Why am I not surprised?'

Toni returned to the Ticker system and interrogated the computer.

'Paris!' cried Toni, suddenly. 'Why on earth would you leave a feather at the scene of a murder?'

'You wouldn't normally,' suggested Boyd. 'It's the middle of Paris. It probably just floated there from a passing pigeon.'

'Maybe, maybe not,' contended Toni. 'But if the murderer did deposit a feather at the scene then ask yourself why?'

'Was it dropped deliberately or left for a reason?' probed Boyd.

'Exactly,' nodded Toni. 'Mind you, the assassin also left a Uzi submachine gun at the scene — deliberately, apparently.'

'I'll guess the gun was excess baggage for his getaway,' considered Boyd. 'What kind of feather?'

Toni's fingers rattled across the keyboard as she voiced, 'A white feather!'

'The traditional symbol of cowardice,' observed Boyd.

'True,' admitted Toni. 'But spiritually, a white feather is also seen as a sign from the angel or spirit of a loved one who has passed on.'

'Really!' asked Boyd. 'I've not heard that one before.'

'That's because you've led a sheltered life,' responded Toni, cheekily. 'I remember reading about these feathers in a magazine recently. White feathers symbolize faith and protection and are most significant when found in a spot where they are not likely to be.'

'In a spot where they are not likely to be,' mused Boyd.

'Why is a white feather bouncing around inside my head?' muttered Toni. 'I've read scores of Ticker reports in recent days but why does a feather stick in my mind?'

'In a spot where they are not likely to be,' pondered Boyd again. 'Where have I heard that before? In a spot where…. Got it!'

'What?' cried Toni.

'The possibility of a signature murder,' ventured Boyd.

'Now I'm lost,' admitted Toni. 'My job is terrorists and spies, Boyd, not criminals and murderers in the way you are talking. That's your bag. What do you mean by the term signature murder?'

Stepping thoughtfully across the room, Boyd declared, 'A signature murder is a murder which exhibits characteristics personal and unique to a specific criminal.'

'Oh, that's very helpful, Boyd,' replied Toni shaking her head. 'You'll have to do better than that.'

'Okay, let me explain,' responded Boyd.

'Please do,' replied Toni, listening avidly.

'Some aspects of the quirky behaviour of a serial killer are known as signature behaviour or signature characteristics,' explained Boyd. 'You see, Toni, whereas the modus operandi concerns how a crime is committed in a particular way, signature behaviour fulfils a psychological need within the murderer and, unlike the MO, does not often change.'

'You mean it doesn't matter how someone is killed because there's always going to be a white feather left at the scene of the murder?' suggested Toni.

'Precisely,' replied Boyd slamming his fist onto the table. 'That would make the white feather particularly significant to the killer. The assassin leaves a white feather at the scene of each killing. It's his signature to the murder he's just committed. Have we got a serial killer on our hands?'

'How the hell would I know from what we've got so far?' countered Toni.

'Ticker!' recommended Boyd. 'Click into the search panel and type white feather. What does it bring up?'

Rattling the keyboard, Toni sat back, looked at the screen, and announced, 'Incidents at Sabiha Gokcen International Airport, Istanbul... and a café on the Avenue des Champs-Élysées, Paris.'

'Bingo,' yelled Boyd. 'Both are also connected to NATO in some way or other. Two murder scenes, both entirely different, but both have a feather left at the scene.'

'That's just dumb,' argued Toni. 'You've just made one crazy assertion that we're looking for a serial killer who is running around Europe handing out white feathers. What's more, you've based it on the flimsiest piece of evidence available – a feather.'

'Agreed,' replied Boyd. 'It can't be right and it won't be right if the world is full of pigeons flying in the wrong bloody place.'

In an adjoining room, a buzzer sounded and Anthea interrupted the conversation with, 'Bank robbery in progress, guvnor. It's Ricky's snout - Patient Lamb - Our asset says it's going down any time now. We're on and you're listed as tactical commander for the operation. We're up, guvnor.'

'On my way,' replied Boyd. 'Use of firearms are authorised per standard operational unit briefing. Make sure the team doesn't forget their protective vests.'

Turning to his colleague, Boyd withdrew a handgun from his shoulder holster, checked it was fully loaded, and snapped, 'Toni, do me a favour. Send Sandy a message. Ask her to recover the feather from the evidence lock-up in Istanbul and get it forensically

95

examined by someone who knows about birds. Same with our man in Paris. I want to know everything there is to know about those white feathers? I know it sounds stupid but we have two incidents so far and if there is a connection we're going to look even more stupid if we miss it.'

'I'm on it,' replied Toni.

Spinning on his heel, Boyd continued, 'Don't forget to tell Sandy about the connection. Everything might just drop into place over there. Who knows?'

'Leave it with me,' replied Toni. 'Now go!'

As Boyd and Anthea rushed into the main office, Toni returned to the Ticker system and interrogated the computer.

'Featherweight,' she muttered. 'They get the action and I get to play with feathers!'

A metal battering ram had been fixed to the front bumper bar of an open-topped dark green Land Rover.

There was the constant blip of an accelerator pedal before a voice in the driver's seat shouted, 'Now! For Kurdistan!'

A foot depressed the clutch and a hand pushed a gear stick into first gear. The vehicle lurched forward, gathered speed, sped across the highway, mounted a kerb, and smashed through the front glass doorway of the building society.

Half a ton of toughened glass, fractured, and then – as if in slow motion – crashed to the ground.

The Land Rover reversed a few yards and then sped forward again into the heart of the building.

Glass crunched under the pressure of the tyres, customers screamed, scattered, and ran for cover when two masked gunmen in the rear passenger area stood up and began firing sawn-off shotguns into the ceiling.

Plaster crashed to the floor as the vehicle slewed to one side and the two gunmen suddenly jumped over the glass partition and landed on the counter.

Turning, one of the men caught a holdall thrown from the driver's seat. Then he caught another before spinning around, hurling it towards staff, and screaming, 'Fill the bags!'

A female member of the counter staff stepped forward, grabbed a holdall, and dropped it on the floor.

Petrified, she froze.

'Fill them both,' screamed the gunman throwing a second bag at her. 'Now!'

A male staff member bent down, collected the bags, and began piling bank notes into them.

'No!' screamed the gunman. 'The woman, not you!'

Shaking, the woman began filling the bags with money.

A stop watch was inspected and a voice from the driver's seat calmly remarked, 'Thirty seconds!'

With two gunmen standing on the counter, the driver rammed the vehicle into reverse gear and began to back into the counter.

'See, he'll drive right over you. Hurry up!' screamed one of the gunmen threatening the staff. 'Get the money into the bags. As much as you can. Big denominations only, you clown.'

'One minute,' voiced from the front of the vehicle.

A grey BMW, series seven, appeared at the front of the building society. The nearside doors opened inviting the occupants of the Land Rover to get in.

'Thirty seconds left,' voiced from the driver's seat of the Land Rover. 'Our taxi has arrived.'

The driver of the BMW blipped the accelerator pedal impatiently. The getaway driver was nervous, ready to take-off at speed, and eager to go with his three fellow robbers and their swag.

The bags were filled with twenty and fifty pound notes, dragged across the counter, hoisted onto the shoulder, and carried towards the blown-away front door and a waiting BMW.

'Let's go!' yelled from the front of the Land Rover.

With the engine still running, the driver was out of the vehicle. With his back to the getaway car, he lowered a submachine gun to waist height and threatened staff.

'Stay where you are,' he shouted.

Outside, Boyd's surveillance team arrived with a mass of flashing headlights interspersed by blue lights and flashing warning lights.

The BMW driver checked his mirrors, saw the flashing lights, anticipated the arrival, and drove off at high speed with the tyres squealing and the passenger doors flapping in the wind as they abandoned the gunmen inside the building society.

'Red Alpha One has control,' radioed Boyd. 'Red blanket down! Speed is vital. Units one and two north, units three and four south, all other units engage! Strike! Strike! Strike!'

Janice, Anthea, Terry and Ricky were out of their vehicles and using car doors as cover when Boyd jumped from his Porsche, lifted a megaphone, and shouted, 'This is the police! You are surrounded. Drop your weapons. You're going nowhere.'

Anthea edged forward, took aim at the fleeing BMW and then thought better of it. Turning, she hugged the building line and crept towards the front door.

Inside the building society, the two gunmen stalled at the doorway and stole a glance outside.

The Land Rover driver shouted, 'In the back! Get in the back of the Land Rover! We'll blast our way out.'

'Throw down your weapons and come out with your hands up,' shouted Boyd through the megaphone. 'It's over. You are surrounded.'

Anthea lowered her weapon and from the side of the front door shouted, 'They're preparing to drive straight out, Boyd.'

Nodding, Boyd radioed, 'Strike units, masks.'

The team donned gas masks and waited for orders.

'Deploy stun and gas,' radioed Boyd.

There was panic on the street. People ran from the area, others stopped to stand and stare mesmerised by proceedings. Then all hell broke loose when Boyd's team hurled a mix of stun grenades and tear gas pellets into the building.

As a cacophony of noise, smoke, and gas delivered turmoil to the inside of the building, screams outside rent the air when some of the public finally realised there was a battle taking place – and the battle was right there in their own High Street.

The two gunmen emerged from the building society coughing and choking.

Taken to the ground immediately, Anthea, and her colleagues, dragged the men away from the door and quickly applied handcuffs to their prisoners.

Moving forward, Boyd held the pistol in his left hand and used the doorway and building line as a shield.

Addressing the remaining gunman inside, Boyd shouted, 'You in there! It's your choice. Come on out!'

Turning for a moment, Boyd nodded and watched Terry return to his vehicle.

The engine fired. Terry slipped the car into low gear and edged forward to park his squad car across the entrance to the building society. The way out was blocked.

'You're going nowhere,' announced Boyd on the megaphone. 'There's nowhere to go. You're finished. Throw down your weapon!'

Boyd's request was met by a hail of gunfire directed into the ceiling.

'Missed!' shouted Boyd. 'Call it a day. You're going to run out of ammunition soon. That will make our job even easier. Think about it.'

A submachine gun was slid along the floor and kicked to a safe distance by Boyd.

Inside, smoke billowed and swirled in mysterious clouds accompanied only by the sound of people sobbing and whimpering from the terror of it all.

Cautiously stepping forward, the gunman held his hands up and declared, 'I have rights. I demand a solicitor and hereby claim asylum in the name of the oppressed people of Kurdistan.'

'Turn around,' ordered Boyd. 'Now walk back slowly to me until I say stop.'

The gunman did as he was told until Boyd ordered, 'Stop! Stand perfectly still. Now get down onto both knees and put your hands behind your back.'

Once the gunman had fully complied, Boyd nodded and his team moved in to handcuff and search the third and final prisoner.

Hauled into a squad car, the three prisoners were taken to the nearest police station as Boyd and the remnants of his colleagues began to assess the damage and sort out the witnesses.

A siren sounded in the street and a uniformed superintendent stepped out of the passenger seat of a police car and shouted, 'Who is in charge here?'

'That'll be me,' replied Boyd. 'Chief Inspector Boyd, Special Crime Unit, and you are?'

'Bloody angry, you idiot! You've turned the borough into a shooting range. Have you no sense?'

'I meant your name, sir,' ventured Boyd.

'Barnes! I'm the local Commander,' barked the Superintendent angrily. 'I know you, Boyd. What a bloody mess you've made of this.'

Storming into the building society, Superintendent Barnes barged his way behind the counter, took a quick look at the scene, and then eventually reappeared at the front door coughing and spluttering from the effects of the smoke and remnants of teargas.

As witnesses and staff were led out of the building, a fleet of ambulances arrived and first aid was given.

'Carnage!' bellowed the Superintendent wiping his eyes with a handkerchief. 'You're an absolute disgrace, Boyd. You've turned the borough into a war zone, destroyed the building society, and god knows what you've done to these poor people. Look at them! They're shell-shocked.'

'They're safe now,' argued Boyd. 'And I think you'll find the Land Rover destroyed the building prior to our arrival.'

'They were safe before you bloody arrived,' screeched Barnes. 'Why wasn't I told of this operation? Who is your superior? Why didn't you give the job to my divisional personnel? You look like the SAS, not a bunch of deskbound detectives from Scotland bloody Yard. Furthermore, chief inspector, one got away so your operation was a total bloody failure.'

'Any particular order of reply, sir?' frowned Boyd.

'Don't get smart with me, Boyd,' snarled Barnes. 'I'll have your guts for garters. Just answer the questions!'

Boyd unloaded his weapon and stashed the ammunition in a leather holder whilst explaining, 'One – This is an intelligence led operation which gave us no time to plan or prepare for the job. In accordance with force orders, I ordered standard operational procedures as taught in my unit and which is part of the daily briefing. Two - In addition, I organised red blanket procedures via the control room at the Yard. On receipt, they informed all police personnel in the borough to leave the immediate area as the red blanket commander has primacy during an on-going firearms incident. Three – No disrespect intended but we train for this sort of thing, your divisional personnel do not and may well have been wiped out because they don't have that training, the equipment, or the ability to use same.'

'That's how I got to know about it,' roared Barnes. 'When someone rang to tell me that I did not have primacy on my own patch!'

'This procedure also prevents a blue on blue and my officers know they are the only police in the area,' argued Boyd. 'Four - There's no-one superior to me; my supervisor is Commander Edwin Maxwell at the Yard. Five - We're not SAS but we have been trained by Special Forces in some aspects of attack and entry. They are the best of the best. We're just good at we do. Six – Yep, someone drove off in a BMW. What a pity but we'll see what can be done about that in due course. As far as deskbound detectives are concerned, my desk awaits me. Now, if you'll excuse me, sir. I'll be gone from your streets. My DI will relinquish control when she is ready and not before.'

Boyd holstered his empty weapon and stepped away towards his Porsche.

Turning he offered, 'Sorry, sir, but that's the way it is with us. We train for stuff like this. It's not easy and there's a hundred different ways to resolve an armed incident. Realistically, the perpetrators tend to boss the incident until we turn up. Then it's all about timing, luck, and being in the right place at the right time. Some crooks stand and fight; others see the writing on the wall and take the easy way out. These ones chose the latter and I'm pleased they did.'

'Are you really?' challenged Superintendent Barnes. 'You look like a bunch of gun toting cowboys looking for trouble if you ask me, Boyd.'

'I wasn't asking you, sir,' replied Boyd. 'By the way, not one round was fired from our weapons. We deployed CS gas pellets and non-lethal stun grenades to disorientate our targets. Unfortunately, innocent people are often caught up in this and suffer from shock and smoke inhalation. The alternatives are a gun fight or a kidnap-hostage situation inside the building society. We avoided both. That's my statement to you and anyone who wants to investigate my leadership capabilities. I suggest you make a complaint to senior command. My complaint would be that no-one taught me how to be perfect and please everyone every time. That's never going to happen. I learnt years ago, that people like me, and units like mine, can never take pole position in the opinion stakes. My job is to win and that's what counts. I'll inform Commander Maxwell you are displeased.'

Boyd fired the Porsche and said, 'I'm off to the nick to arrange interviews and build the case. Anything else, sir?'

Dumbfounded for a moment, Superintendent Barnes stood with his arms on his hips speechless.

'Then I'll be gone,' replied Boyd. 'My deputy, Detective Inspector Anthea Adams will preserve the scene and gather all the evidence here. No worries.'

Suddenly the Porsche was gone from the street with one senior police officer angry, exasperated, and at his wits end.

Anthea sidled up to Superintendent Barnes and advised, 'Step away from the building, sir.'

'What? This is my patch!' replied Barnes. 'Don't you start. I'll take it from here.'

'No, you won't, sir,' insisted Anthea. 'And, for your information, you're contaminating my crime scene and disrupting our witnesses. Now if you don't mind, sir.'

Aghast, Barnes replied, 'Do you know who I am?'

'Yes,' confirmed Anthea. 'But the quicker you get out of the way the quicker we'll get the job done. I need to preserve the scene for forensics. I'll need your shoes before you go.'

'Shoes! Why do you want my shoes?' enquired Barnes.

'Because you've traipsed right across all the debris and entered the heart of the building. If you go back to the nick wearing those shoes you have the potential to contaminate the evidence if you go anywhere near those prisoners.'

'It's my police station.'

'And I'm the major crime scene commander,' barked Anthea. 'It's my neck on the line. Your shoes, now, sir. It's a preventative action, nothing personal.'

Reluctantly, Superintendent Barnes removed his shoes, handed them to an exhibits officer, and replied, 'You're finished. You know that, don't you? Finished!'

'Thank you,' remarked Anthea. 'Watch your feet on the way out. There's a lot of glass and debris on the floor and you're finished here.'

Boyd made the police station and parked in the yard close to the back door. His mobile rang and he answered it with, 'Boyd!'

'Are you free to speak?' queried Toni.

'I am now,' replied Boyd.

'Good!' responded Toni eagerly. 'You're onto something. Sandy reports that the feather recovered in Istanbul is from a white eagle. The police in Paris also confirm that the feather from the café on the Champs-Élysées is also from a white eagle.'

'Wow!' replied Boyd. 'That's a turn-up for the book. Bash that Ticker system, Toni. Interrogate as many concoctions of white, bird, eagle, ornithology, or whatever you can. See what else you can find out.'

'I've already started,' replied Toni. 'I'm running a global search but there's one thing I can tell you already.'

'Which is?'

'If the feather is from a totally white eagle then the bird – and therefore presumably the feather - originated in the Quandil Mountains.'

'Where on earth are the Quandil Mountains?' asked Boyd.

'Kurdistan, on the Iraqi – Iranian border with Turkey,' revealed Toni.

'You mean we're looking for a Turk?'

'To be precise, Boyd,' explained Toni. 'We could be looking for a Turkish Kurd.'

'Kurdish!' remarked Boyd.

'Yes,' replied Toni. 'Tall, with a beard, and wears sunglasses.'

'Sunglasses and a beard?' queried Boyd. 'Wow! That narrows the field down. Let's hope he never takes them off.'

'Sorry,' offered Toni, giggling. 'It's just that I'm reading straight from my computer screen. That's the entire description we have of the suspect.'

Getting out of his Porsche, Boyd watched their three handcuffed prisoners being escorted into the police station.

'If that's the case, what the hell do we have here?'

'You mean...'

'I do, Toni,' indicated Boyd. 'Our source, Patient Lamb, just came up trumps big style. Our problem is we've got three prisoners who have tried to rob a building society. One of them shouted, 'For Kurdistan', before they bulldozed the building and went in with all guns blazing.'

105

'Is everyone okay?' asked a concerned Toni.

'No casualties other than a few shocked and traumatised civilians,' explained Boyd. 'And a distraught local borough commander but I wonder if the man Sandy is looking for is amongst these three? If not, do they know who is responsible for the airport job or the Paris job? Probably not but I'm thinking if the proceeds of this robbery were bound for Kurdistan, then by what means? Have they got the right connections? What's their access to those who control the finances? We've got work to do, Toni, and it's not going to be easy.'

'The Collector,' remarked Toni. 'Operation Distinguish was about following and identifying the Collector. Terry's source of intelligence led you to these robbers.'

'That's right,' agreed Boyd. 'But Patient Lamb also told us that the Collector placed people. Maybe we should have called him the Placer. We're just scraping the surface at the moment. Who placed The Collector? Who placed the white eagle feathers? Do you know, Toni, because I don't?'

\*

## Chapter Five
~

The Serpentine, Hyde Park
London
Three days later

It was a glorious day. A ray of sunlight danced on the lake as the ducks bathed in the glory of it all. Meanwhile, nearby, London's traffic chugged by polluting the capital and providing a poor accompaniment to proceedings.

Ricky stood by the lakeside feeding the ducks from a bag of breadcrumbs he'd brought with him. Kneeling, he teased one of the drakes to come closer before flicking a crust into the water and watching it move in to snatch it away from the competition gathering nearby.

Stretching now, Ricky stood and waited for Mehmet to arrive.

On a bench, about thirty yards away, Terry Anwhari sat reading a magazine.

He glanced at his wristwatch. Patient Lamb was late.

'I see him coming. He's two o'clock on you, Ricky,' radioed Terry. 'He's approaching the lake. He's on his own.'

'He's yours,' replied Ricky. 'I'm watching your back. Come! You are clean!'

A few minutes later, Mehmet approached the bench and sat beside Terry. Both men ignored each other.

'Wait,' radioed Janice. 'The guvnor is on the move.'

Boyd appeared some fifty or so yards behind Mehmet, nodded the all clear to Janice, and made casually for the bench where Terry and Patient Lamb were sat.

'Clear this end,' radioed Janice.

Strolling along the waterside, Ricky dug deep into his coat pocket and removed another bag of bread crusts. He broke them into smaller pieces, knelt, and fed the ducks once more.

Simultaneously, Ricky's eyes looked out for others who might have been following Mehmet and Boyd. He scanned the area but only saw people he was happy with – families, children, teenagers, people behaving normally and as if they belonged with each other.

Engaging his throat mic, Ricky radioed, 'All units, report.'

'All clear,' from Janice.

'Clear,' from Anthea.

'Likewise,' from Martin.

'I have that,' replied Bannerman.

Putting both hands in his pockets, Ricky set off walking. Passing Terry, Boyd, and Mehmet on the bench, Ricky removed his hands, ignored the trio, and turned his collar up.

It was the signal Terry had been waiting for. The sign that meant Patient Lamb was in the clear. No-one had followed him to the rendezvous on a park bench beside the Serpentine Lake. It was safe to talk.

Terry closed his magazine and said, 'You made it then. Is everything okay with you?'

Mehmet nodded and replied, 'So far but I need to know how the search for the BMW is going. Are the police any nearer to finding the driver?'

'No,' replied Terry looking straight ahead. 'It seems like the car was on false plates and hasn't been seen since.'

'And the driver?' enquired Mehmet.

'No sign,' voiced Terry. 'He wore sunglasses and a hat like he was told to and disappeared into the darkness without a care in the world.'

Mehmet stared down at his feet, took a sideways glance at Boyd, fidgeted, and said, 'I looked in the mirror and saw a woman taking aim at me. I thought she was going to shoot me as I drove away from the building society.'

'She was never going to shoot you, Mehmet,' advised Boyd standing up to face Mehmet. 'But I'm glad she gave you the impression she was going to pull the trigger because everyone else in the street thought she was going to do exactly that and shoot at the car. The detective got away with it because there was a lot of people in the street.'

There was silence for a moment before Boyd continued, 'The airport at Istanbul, Mehmet? Who do you know there that we might be interested in?'

'The airport attack?' queried Mehmet.

'Yes, that's the one,' replied Boyd.

'There's plenty in the community, and from the mosque, that used to live there. Some of them still have friends and family in Istanbul but I've never heard any word about who might be responsible.'

'And Paris?'

'No,' answered Mehmet. 'Never been mentioned.'

'You mean no-one is interested in what is happening in Turkey?' asked Terry.

'No, not like that,' explained Mehmet. 'They're always talking about the Turkish government, politics, and stuff like that, but there's no talk of who bombed the airport or who might have done it. And Paris! No-one is interested in Paris'

'You're sure?' asked Boyd.

'I'm sure,' replied Mehmet.

'Maybe you can drop a few remarks in next time Istanbul is mentioned,' suggested Boyd. 'You know, something that stimulates conversation about the bombing there?'

'Yes, I'll see what I can do,' answered Mehmet.

'Okay,' intervened Terry. 'Do you know who is behind the others we locked up at the building society? Who placed the job and where was the money bound for?'

'No, I don't. It was just a job put together by themselves as far as I know,' argued Mehmet.

'Are you sure?'

'As sure as I can be,' confirmed Mehmet.

'And the airport at Istanbul?' challenged the detective. 'Paris? Are you sure there is no talk about these jobs, Mehmet?'

'Not a sniff but what about the other three at the building society,' queried Mehmet. 'Did they name me as the driver of the getaway car and drop me in it?'

'No,' confirmed Terry. 'As expected they said nothing. We had them bang to rights so the case was sewn up at an early stage. They're all tight-lipped.'

'My time working for you people is running out. They'll know it's me when they get together and talk about it,' ventured Mehmet. 'You might have caught them but they're not stupid. They've got long memories and good contacts.'

'By the time they realise it was you that leaked the information, you'll be long gone from these shores and settled with your family in a place of your choice,' advised Terry.

'Are you sure?' queried Mehmet.

'I'm sure,' acknowledged Terry. 'It will be ratified when the case comes to court and they get sent down. Relax, give it time, keep working, listening, and doing your best for us.'

'Then what happens?'

'One day we'll meet. You'll get a new passport, a new name, and a nice bank account.'

'Is that all?'

'You'll no longer exist,' revealed Terry. 'You'll have no past, just a quiet future with your family in a place where you can live a normal life.'

'Is the guvnor okay with this?' enquired Mehmet looking up at Boyd. 'I was part of the robbery team and you let me off it.'

'You were never going to do the robbery, Mehmet,' disclosed Boyd looking around. 'You were hired as the driver. You didn't plan it. They didn't have a driver and you stepped in.'

'It still seems wrong,' said Mehmet shaking his head.

'I suggested you need to disappear when this is all over,' replied Boyd. 'Some things are done for what we call the Greater Good. You know what we're doing, Mehmet. We're chasing down people who spend their life plotting the death and downfall of others. Istanbul… Paris. Any place where evil operates. It's not a game we're playing. It's a quiet war that Mister General Public has no idea of. In the scheme of things, we need to get to where we want to be and if that means things get a little awkward then so be it. It's our problem and we'll look after you. Just remember, it never happened, did it?'

'No, guvnor,' nodded Mehmet. 'No, it didn't happen, did it? I was never there.'

'For the Greater Good,' stated Boyd. 'Keep in touch. You know the drill.'

Boyd turned his collar up, nodded at the two men, and walked away.

Terry and Mehmet sat for a while before Terry asked, 'You okay with things?'

'I'm fine,' replied Mehmet. 'No problems but I think I might be running out of time and your guvnor tells me what I want to know. Can I trust him?'

'Do you trust me?' asked Terry.

'I don't know,' replied Mehmet quietly.

Watching the ducks on the lake, Terry explained, 'When the guvnor was talking about the Greater Good, you didn't quite get it, did you?'

Mehmet stroked his chin and said, 'Not completely.'

'When we chase most normal murderers,' revealed Terry, 'If there is such a thing as a normal murderer - We're generally looking for someone who has either killed someone in the heat of the moment or has taken a relatively short time to plan how to kill a particular individual. When we chase terrorists, we know that such a person, and the organisation they are associated with, live and breathe their beliefs. The terrorists we chase might spend months or years planning a multiple murder and take out dozens or hundreds of people in one foul blow. There's a difference between the two.'

Mehmet nodded.

'The Greater Good just might be applied to terrorist investigations, my friend. Okay?'

Mehmet smiled and nodded.

Sliding his magazine closer to Mehmet, Terry stood up and volunteered, 'Centre pages!'

As Detective Sergeant Anwhari walked away in the opposite direction of Boyd, Mehmet's hand dropped to the magazine. He picked it up and casually turned to the centrefold before pocketing a bundle of twenty pound notes folded inside.

Two drakes paddled ferociously towards a piece of crust that floating on the lakes surface. There was a splash and a chatter from both birds when one succeeded in claiming the prize and the other paddled away with nothing.

Anthea pulled her squad car into the nearside, allowed Boyd and Terry to get in, and then drove off.

'You in a rush?' enquired Boyd.

'Not really,' replied Anthea. 'But the monthly meeting is scheduled for this afternoon and I don't want to be late. Maybe we'll have time to bag a sandwich and a tea before we start?'

'Coffee!' suggested Boyd. 'I prefer coffee. Anyway, what's on the agenda this afternoon?'

'Sandy is back from Turkey with nothing to declare apparently,' revealed Anthea.

'Straight through the green channel at arrivals?' chuckled Boyd.

'Looks like it,' said Anthea. 'The problem for us is that I suspect the Foreign Secretary will be displeased and the Commissioner will be unhappy. It might be a bad afternoon.'

'In that case, cancel the tea and the coffee,' ventured Boyd. 'Brandy is the answer.'

'If only,' chuckled Anthea pulling out to overtake another car.

'Reputations and careers are at stake,' declared Boyd. 'Things can't get any worse – can they?'

'We are about to find out,' suggested Anthea.

Boyd's mobile sounded and he answered the call.

Moments later, he turned to his colleagues, and revealed, 'That was Toni. She's got the latest electronic trawl from GCHQ. There's a ton of telephone data to go through. It's a good job we've got that CAST software otherwise it would take forever.'

'Let's hope we get lucky,' quipped Anthea.

'Yeah, we need all the luck in the world,' admitted Boyd. 'So far, we're behind in the game.'

*

## Chapter Six
~

Europol Headquarters
The Hague, Netherlands
One week later

Kurt Baumann was an unlikely member of the Europol Cyber Intelligence Team. Standing six feet six inches tall, and weighing over eighteen stones, his physique was more in keeping with that of an Olympic weightlifter, rather than a man who spent much of his time at the forefront of Europe's cyber war.

His blond hair was cut close to his skull whilst his face was chiselled uniquely to a square chin. Blue eyes complimented his looks and, not unsurprisingly, he was considered by his female colleagues to be an extremely handsome man. Yet Kurt was gay and made no attempt to disguise his sexuality.

On route to a monthly conference at Europol Headquarters, Kurt strode out clutching his briefcase and checking his wristwatch to ensure he was on time.

The walk from the railway station had been short and without problems. Traffic was light despite the time of day and he anticipated arriving in time for a coffee before business began.

As he approached a junction about three hundred yards from the building, another gentleman joined him, nodded, and walked beside him with a smile.

Kurt glanced at the man by his side. He was well dressed wearing a dark suit, tan shoes, and a brown trilby. Indeed, Kurt took another look and wondered if his new-found companion was also gay. Was it a chance encounter, considered Kurt? Or was it just someone from the same building accompanying him to work? Whoever he was, he certainly had one hell of a smile.

Sporting a neatly cut moustache and beard, and carrying an umbrella, Kurt's newly acquired colleague winked and remarked, 'Nearly there,' as he pointed his umbrella enthusiastically towards the Europol building.

'Another dollar, another day, as they say,' chuckled the stranger. 'I hope the lift is working today. I had problems yesterday morning and nearly had to take the stairs. I hate it when the lifts go down and we have to use the stairs. How about you?'

'Yes,' replied Kurt politely. 'The lifts are always a problem we can do without. Yes, indeed, but tell me, which floor are you working on?'

'I couldn't possibly answer that,' replied the stranger. 'Not outside the building. You know the drill surely.'

The two men walked on with Kurt somewhat surprised at the stranger's response.

'You are with the team, yes?' queried Kurt.

The man returned a huge grin and replied, 'Oh yes, for some years now. I quite enjoy the work but it's rather stressful at times. Don't you think?'

'Quite!' replied Kurt. 'But you get used to it and it's worth it when you get a good result.'

'Of course, it is,' replied Kurt's new friend.

The two walked on with Kurt's colleague whistling happily before asking, 'How do you like my new umbrella? It's brand new, you know. I've never had to use it before today.'

'It's not raining' remarked Kurt.

'I don't need rain to use the umbrella,' revealed the stranger.

'I'm sorry,' offered Kurt, 'But I can't place you at all, sir.'

'You mean you don't remember me?' queried the man.

Kurt came to a standstill, looked quizzically at his associate, and said, 'No, I'm afraid not. Indeed, sir, you have the better of me.'

Thrusting the point of his umbrella into the back of Kurt's knee, the assailant pulled a short trigger on the umbrella handle and injected poison into the German's body saying, 'You should never forget. I never forget and I never forgive.'

Kurt gasped and felt the point of the umbrella penetrate his skin.

'Yes, my friend, I do have the better of you,' replied Kurt's new-found friend as he continued to plunge the point of the umbrella into Kurt's knee.

'Argh!' squealed Kurt dropping his briefcase and clutching his lower limb with both hands. 'What have you done?'

'It's called revenge, my friend,' replied the assailant. 'Nothing personal but you are what they call a soft target.'

Kurt's face turned a deathly shade of white when the aggressor thrust the umbrella further into the back of his knee and twisted it violently.

With one limb weakening immediately, Kurt rocked, began to lose his balance, and agonised, 'Revenge? What have I done?'

The attacker released the trigger mechanism and withdrew the umbrella point as he replied, 'You are who you are and you have done far too much, my friend. Far too much! You've hurt so many of my people over the years.'

Falling to the ground, Kurt's eyes began to water and lose focus. Pleading into the eyes of the man, he saw the killer withdraw a white feather from the band of his trilby and offer it to him.

'This is for you,' announced the man.

Reaching out, Kurt grasped the feather, and then fell backwards onto the pavement. He rolled painfully onto his side and looked at the feather lying next to him on the footpath.

Confused, bewildered, he had no other choice but to study the feather and reach out to it.

'What does the feather mean?'

'You'll never know,' replied the aggressor.

'Where am I? What's happening to me?'

Slowly but surely, the poison infiltrated Kurt's body as his brain began to turn off.

Gasping in pain again, the cyber intelligence agent closed his eyes as he tried to shut out the agony.

Smirking now, Kurt's attacker looked down on his prey and stabbed him again. Driving the point of his umbrella into the chest area, he forced traces of poison into Kurt's body once more.

Helpless, open-mouthed, Kurt had no words left. Thin fingers nervously brushed the feather as if it were an iconic flag. The mind was going places it had never ventured before as his brain tumbled into a dark abyss when his assailant walked away without a care in the world.

'Bye,' remarked the assailant as he faded from Kurt's view.

Moments later, a passing police car stopped and its occupants rushed to Kurt's side trying to help him.

Ten minutes later, Kurt's muscles begin to spasm. It started with the head and neck and then spread to every muscle in the body. Kurt began to convulse continuously. The convulsions worsened and increased in intensity and frequency until his backbone arched continually.

The police were shocked, and helpless.

'What do we do?'

'I don't know. It's an epileptic fit, isn't it?'

'I've never seen anyone have a fit before.'

'Me neither!'

A presumption that a man lying on a pavement had suffered from an epileptic fit quickly disappeared. Yet neither of the officers knew what was wrong with him.

'Hospital?'

'Yeah, get the back doors open.'

Deciding the man needed immediate urgent attention, they loaded Kurt into the rear of their patrol car and set off at high speed towards the nearest hospital.

There was a blare of lights, the sound of a klaxon, and the ignoring of traffic lights as the police car sped to the hospital.

On arrival at the emergency entrance to the hospital, asphyxiation, caused by paralysis of the neural pathways that control breathing, set in. Kurt died two hours after being injected, poisoned by an unknown assailant with an umbrella close to the Europol Headquarters.

An accident and emergency consultant arrived and pronounced death. He examined the body with assistance from a trauma consultant. Both agreed the man had been injected in the back of the knee and the chest with a poisonous substance.

'Injected?' queried one of the policeman. 'What with?'

'It will depend on the autopsy,' replied one of the consultants. 'But if it helps your initial enquiry then I can tell you that my knowledge base suggests death might have been caused by strychnine poisoning.'

'Strychnine?' agonised the policeman.

'Yes, I'm afraid that might be the case, officer,' ventured the consultant. 'But as I say, my theory cannot be confirmed until an autopsy has taken place and bodily fluids examined. You see, the subject died following acute convulsions witnessed by your two selves. Listening to your description of when you found the man, I fear he suffered asphyxia and rather severe pain prior to his death. These are some of the symptoms of strychnine poisoning.'

'If you are right,' suggested the policeman, 'Then the man was murdered. I mean, it's not a sudden unexpected death we're dealing with. It's murder not an epileptic fit like we first thought.'

'Correct!' confirmed the consultant. 'You have a murder to deal with.'

Later, at the scene of the crime, investigators cordoned off the footpath, began a fingertip search of the immediate area, and recovered a white feather from the footpath. They also recovered CCTV images of a smartly dressed man with a beard and moustache. His proximity to the deceased suggested he needed to be ruled out at the very least. For the moment, the man with the beard was the prime suspect.

The cyber intelligence team had lost one of their best operators who had been responsible for penetrating the online activities of numerous political and terrorist factions in the middle east.

In the Special Crime Unit at New Scotland Yard, that night, an intelligence report streamed across the Ticker intelligence system and was read by Detective Inspector Anthea Adams.

Anthea lifted the phone, dialled a number, and said, 'Chief Inspector Boyd please.... Guvnor, there's been an umbrella poisoning in the Netherlands.'

'Ricin poison?' queried Boyd.

'Strychnine, guvnor,' replied Anthea. 'As far as I know there's never been a strychnine poisoning by this method in Europe. It's a new one.'

'Suspects?' queried Boyd.

'A smartly dressed male in his mid-thirties who left a white feather at the scene. No sunglasses this time, just a beard and moustache but they have CCTV images of the suspect. They're not brilliant apparently. I suggested it might be from one of those CCTV tapes that has been used so many times that the image isn't as good as it should be.'

'A tape used so many times that the product has become virtually worthless?' suggested Boyd.

'Possibly,' agreed Anthea. 'Put it this way, when I mooted the possibility of a bad tape I didn't get a reply.'

'Typical,' remarked Boyd. 'When will people realise that technology only works if you look after it and run these systems properly?'

'I know what you mean,' replied Anthea. 'It's like our Ticker system. If we don't pay the electric bill, will it work on fresh air?'

'Nope! Definitely not,' chuckled Boyd.

'Guvnor, can you understand this thing with the white feather? What's all that about?' enquired Anthea. 'Is the man we're looking for a feather addict of some kind?'

'Now that we don't know. Get onto our contact over there, Anthea. Ask them to do a full examination of the feather. I think it will prove to be the feather of a white eagle. I reckon our man has left his signature at the scene of another crime.'

'Signature crimes!' remarked Anthea. 'Oh yes, that's a business card we can do without. I'll follow it through.'

In an office situated at NATO Headquarters in Brussels a phone rang for over ten seconds before it was snatched from its cradle.

'Mouretti!' snapped the speaker. 'Just a moment.'

Grabbing a pencil from his desk, Mouretti swivelled a notepad towards him and began making notes.

'Whereabouts? When? How many dead? Feathers?' he enquired.

Mouretti listened and continued talking as he scribbled, 'The Hague! Yes, of course I'm attending the scene. Arrange a helicopter transfer for me please and whilst I'm away gather details of all the flight arrivals into the country in the last seven days. When you've done that compare it with the same data we took from the incidents at Istanbul and Paris. We're looking for the same name on at least two of the journeys. This is undoubtedly the work of the same team.'

Listening again, he shook his head and ordered, 'Then get more staff to help you. I want the results on my desk as soon as I get back. The helicopter! Arrange it now please. I'm on my way to the helipad… Thank you.'

Giuseppe Mouretti ended the call, closed his computer, and withdrew personal belongings from his desk. Approaching a wall safe, he entered a combination and pulled back the metal door.

'Sleep well, my beauty,' remarked Mouretti to his cockatoo in the cage. 'I will have an apple for you when I get back.'

Mouretti removed a shoulder holster and pistol from the safe and put it on beneath his suit jacket. Then he removed an ankle holster carrying a much smaller handgun. He fitted this to his ankle, took three boxes of ammunition, and closed the safe before heading for the helicopter pad.

The office door closed with a clunk as the security lock dropped into place.

The label on the door read, 'Special Investigations – Commander in Chief'.

In this building, Mouretti was a legend. The bit was between his teeth and he was chasing his prey down. He was in command but this one wasn't just historically linked to NATO personnel. For Mouretti, there was much more to it than that. Deep inside his heart and mind, it was personal.

His black suede shoes slid silently along the carpeted corridor as he adjusted his shoulder holster a notch. He reached the lift, entered, and pressed the button that would take him to the helipad on the roof of the building.

Ten minutes later, Giuseppe Mouretti secured his seatbelt when the AgutaWestland combat utility helicopter took off for The Hague.

The man from NATO was in pursuit but he wasn't planning to take prisoners.

*

# Chapter Seven
~

The American Embassy
Boltzmanngasein, Vienna, Austria
Two days later.

A black Volvo saloon car drew up close to the entrance of the American Embassy. The area was busy with people waiting to gain access to the building whilst others queued for taxis in a rank nearby.

Sporting a long ginger beard and wearing a distinctive red woollen bobble hat, bright red anorak, and red flared trousers, the driver tugged on the handbrake before flicking a homemade switch on the dashboard.

Seconds later, he stepped from the vehicle, locked the door with an electronic key, and zipped up his anorak. Casually, he strolled away towards an office block nearby.

A marine security guard, (and therefore member of the Marine Corps Security Group) hitched his holster into a more comfortable position, watched the driver walk away, and shook his head in astonishment.

'Did you see that, Joe?' quipped the guard nestling his hand on the butt of his handgun. 'Who on earth wears so many things that are red? He looks like a walking carrot, for god's sake.'

His colleague, stood beside him, shuffled from one foot to another and replied, 'He ain't gonna win no prizes in the fashion stakes, Jake. If he's a carrot then it's time he was uprooted, sliced, diced, and put in the pan.'

Jake began laughing as they watched the stranger walk away. He was tall, slim to medium build, and walked with purpose and commitment.

'Hey, man!' remarked Joe. 'Did you see that? He's parked in a restricted area.'

'No way,' replied Jake stepping out into the roadway. 'Excuse me, sir!'

There was no response from the Volvo driver.

'Excuse me!' shouted Jake. 'Oy! You!'

The man ignored the shouting. He was oblivious to the smartly dressed guard as he walked away in the opposite direction.

Joe unfastened the button on his holster, allowed his fingers to wrap around the trigger guard, and stepped into the road next to Jake.

His highly-polished boots crunched on the tarmac before he shouted, 'Hold it, man! Your car! You can't leave it there!'

Silence greeted the guards.

Jake stepped quickly towards the Volvo whilst Joe began to step out quickly towards its driver shouting, 'Stand still! Do you hear me? Stand still!'

Joe peered into the car, pressed his nose to the rear window, and squinted his eyes as he checked the contents.

'Jake, there's a mobile 'phone on the back seat.'

Turning a corner, the driver of the Volvo stopped, pressed his back into the wall of the building, withdrew a mobile phone from his pocket, and hit the digits. He pressed the green button on his mobile.

One hundred yards away, the mobile phone sitting on the back seat of the Volvo rang. The wireless signal activated an electronic current which raced down a thin red wire and ignited a detonator in the rear boot compartment of the Volvo. Simultaneously, a separate current sprinted along a blue wire that led to a plastic box held by a magnet beneath the engine block of the vehicle.

One hundred and ninety-five kilos of high explosives suddenly exploded and destroyed the Volvo saloon.

The engine block flew one quarter of a mile into the sky and landed six hundred yards away on the roof of a municipal building.

Glass in premises nearby fragmented into thousands of individual pieces. Firstly, it imploded and then exploded outwards on mass. Finally, it crashed to the ground below. Instantaneously, the boot lid fragmented into a dozen pieces when the bomb ripped asunder the sheet metal.

The shock wave from the explosion blew the two marine security guards from their feet and slammed their bodies into the embassy façade. Both men died in the next 24 hours because of the explosion.

Ground beneath the Volvo was gouged to a depth of two and a half feet. There was a crater in the tarmac where the bomb left its mark.

Thirteen people died because of the explosion. They included three members of the embassy staff and the ambassador himself.

As complete pandemonium engulfed the area, Darius, sporting a ginger beard and wearing a red bobble hat, bright red anorak, and red flared trousers, walked into Liechtenstein Park where he made his way towards the palace gardens. He mounted a pedal cycle which had been left near the staff entrance at the rear.

Cycling away, Darius whistled happily as he made his way out of the lush green park and gardens.

A short time later he arrived at Friedensbrücke: a line on the Vienna U-Bahn. It was the equivalent of London's underground train system. He entered the gents' toilets where, in the second cubicle, he removed a waterproof package from the cistern. He took off his bobble hat, anorak and trousers, untied the package, and dressed in a dark blouson and denim jeans. In the rear pocket of the jeans, he found a train ticket.

Leaving the toilets, he deposited the package – now containing his previous clothing – in a litter bin, and caught a train which took him across the River Danube towards Slovakia and the airport at Bratislava.

Enquiries commenced immediately and all points of travel were temporarily closed to try to contain the perpetrators within the Austrian capital. It was to no avail. Darius Yasin was gone from the scene of the bombing of the American Embassy in Vienna by the time the investigation had gathered any worthwhile momentum.

Giuseppe Mouretti stood amongst the devastation and scanned the embassy area. He took in the desolate faces of those around him, people who knew their friends were dead, staff who had lost their colleagues forever.

Tired, Mouretti looked across at his helicopter parked on the lawn of the Embassy garden.

Turning to a local investigator, he offered, 'The man who did this was responsible for the Brussels attack and the others.'

'But the suspect here has a ginger beard,' came the reply.

'Yes, and a red bobble hat, a bright red anorak, and red flared trouser,' confirmed Mouretti.

'That means he is probably cold and isn't very brainy,' replied his Austrian colleague. 'He stands out and will be easy to find.'

'Deliberately so,' replied Mouretti. 'His beard looks false and the red... the red is the colour of our faces. He's making fools of us and he knows it. He's doing that quite deliberately. Don't you see that? My friend, the feather, don't forget the feather!'

'What about the feather?'

'The feather is the key to who the man is and where he comes from,' replied Mouretti. 'But it's not just him. He moves from crime to crime too quickly. He has a team somewhere. I just feel it in my bones. I've been doing this for too many years, more than I care to remember.'

Mouretti stepped away, held the white feather in his hands, and studied the wreckage of a Volvo motor car.

Investigators later recovered CCTV footage from the approach to Friedensbrücke train station. Images revealed a tall man dressed in a red bobble hat, red top, and red jeans. His ginger beard seemed to be at odds with his dark eyebrows and the few strands of dark hair that had escaped imprisonment by his bobble hat. When his height was compared with street furniture, it was assessed that the suspect measured between six feet three and six feet six inches tall and was of medium build. His swarthy complexion remained apparent despite his beard.

Continued enquiries revealed no further trace of the described suspect. A package containing the suspect's clothing was found in a litter bin two days later during a police search. Forensic examination failed to adduce any positive leads.

Later that day, back in Brussels, Mouretti opened a secure chamber in his office and engaged the Ticker Intelligence system. The ignition lights changed from red to amber and then to green before they began flashing. Ten seconds elapsed before the light shone a constant green.

Happy that the system was secure and ready, Mouretti placed his fingertips on the keyboard, engaged a further level of encryption, and began to type a report.

Two hundred and thirty miles away, as the crow flies, Antonia Harston-Browne sat in the Special Crime

Unit office complex in Thames House, London. There was a flash on a computer screen. It was a notification.

Toni interrogated the Ticker system and realised, for the first time, that a senior NATO investigator had an interest in matters concerning the terrorist gang they were hunting.

'A deskbound detective,' mumbled Toni. 'Just a deskbound playing his part for NATO. That, we can do without.'

Her fingers rattled across the keyboard when she transferred the NATO file into their investigative intelligence file.

'That's the problem,' she said. 'It's all intelligence and opinion. There's hardly any real evidence to identify him. Of all the terrorists in the world to chase, we end up chasing a comedian and a master of disguise. How is that the police over there blast his photograph all over the media but they are no nearer to identifying him now than they were when it first started? Even NATO seem to think his beard is false. I wonder if he wears high heels too?'

'What was that? I thought I heard you say NATO,' murmured Boyd snoozing in his chair.

'Nothing,' replied Toni. 'Go back to sleep. It's not that important.'

'NATO?' queried Boyd. 'I didn't know they had any investigators.'

'Need to know, Boyd,' replied Toni. 'It looks as if we don't need to know about this one.'

'Do they have full access to our Ticker system?' enquired Boyd.

'No, partial only,' replied Toni. 'They can input and have first layer readability but can only skim the system.'

'What does this guy look like?' enquired Boyd.

'Stand by,' remarked Toni rattling the keyboard.

An image appeared on the screen and she declared, 'Giuseppe Mouretti, Commander in Chief, Special

Investigations, NATO Headquarters, Brussels. What a handsome man!'

'Careful,' replied Boyd chuckling. 'Don't let Phillip hear you say that.'

'Eye candy,' laughed Toni. 'Just eye candy.'

'Special Investigations?' queried Boyd. 'I wonder what is so special that he hasn't declared himself to other investigators. He doesn't appear to have flagged an interest.'

'I'm sure he has a legitimate interest,' proposed Toni. 'He's just not cleared to the same level as us. It is our system remember.'

'Good!' replied Boyd taking a long hard look at Mouretti's image. 'Not my type, Toni. He's male for a start.'

Toni nudged Boyd in the ribs and said, 'Go back to sleep. I'll wake you if necessary.'

Boyd snuggled into his seat and fell asleep again.

Mouretti checked the wall clock in his office. It was the one that gave him the precise time in Tel Aviv. He made the call and waited for a reply.

'Shalom, Benjamin! How are you?' asked Mouretti.

'Shalom! I am well,' replied a voice. 'And you?'

'You will be aware of a terrorist running around Europe leaving eagle feathers everywhere?' probed Mouretti.

'I am just a low-level diplomat, Giuseppe. How would I know of such things?'

'Benjamin, I think we both know better than that,' suggested Mouretti. 'It occurs to me that the man we are looking for is of Arab persuasion. It is only a question of time before your people are attacked.'

'Such things happen, replied Benjamin. 'It is to be expected.'

'Perhaps it is something we can work together on?' proposed Mouretti.

'Perhaps,' came the reply. 'I will need to consider the matter carefully.'

'Then do so, my friend,' advised Mouretti. 'Partners in these matters are hard to find and there is always something in the shop window that a man like you might want one day.'

The line went quiet for a moment before the diplomat replied, 'That is true. But the telephone, Mouretti… The telephone?'

'You once told me of a museum that you visited some years back.'

'Yes, I know where you mean,' replied the diplomat.

'I was thinking of visiting the exhibition there soon,' revealed Mouretti.

'You will be alone, my friend. You have nothing to sell and I'm not in the market at the moment. Perhaps another day?'

'Benjamin,' replied Mouretti. 'Have you ever heard of the Ticker Intelligence System?'

Benjamin paused before replying, 'It is what British Intelligence use. Why?'

'Not just the British,' suggested Mouretti. 'Their allies across Europe, the Commonwealth and elsewhere also have access to it.'

'And NATO?' enquired Benjamin.

'Perhaps!' replied Mouretti.

'The British are our friends,' ventured Benjamin.

'But they do not give you access to Ticker,' stated Mouretti.

'Your shop window appears to have brightened up,' suggested Benjamin. 'You have Ticker?'

'Yes.'

What do you want to know?' enquired Benjamin.

'I want to be ahead of the game,' revealed Mouretti. 'Your people have far better inroads into the Arab community than we could ever hope for. One of them killed my father. I want his name.'

'And if I don't know it?' queried Benjamin.

'This individual who brings his reign of terror upon Europe is of Arab extraction. That's the only thing we really know. One day he will put Israel in his sights. Mossad and Shin bet will then wake up and begin looking for the man that the west is so desperate to get their hands on. I want that man before he visits Israel and before he inflicts any damage to the Jewish State. Do you understand me?'

'I shall be at the museum at noon on Friday.'

The line went dead leaving Mouretti holding his phone and looking down the mouthpiece.

Smiling, he replaced the handset and removed a flight timetable from a drawer in his desk.

\*

## Chapter Eight

~

Tel Aviv
Israel
Three days later.

Deep inside an underground bunker in a village close to Tel Aviv, they were fighting a battle. The struggle had been raging for forty-eight hours now and there was still no sign of victory.

The only signs of warfare were several antennae sprouting from the ground and signifying the presence of a top-secret building far below the surface of the earth.

Row upon row of computer operators sat at their machines rattling the keyboards trying to fend off a cyber-attack on the Israeli infrastructure. One area defended the power grid whilst another tried to keep the financial quarter safe. Meanwhile, the biggest row of desks fought the cyber war by trying to uphold the military and public services.

They were tired, thirsty, hungry, and needed rest.

Once, this secret unit had thought they were impregnable and that their technology was at the forefront of the global cyber war. It was said that the Russians, Iranians, and Chinese would do anything to get their hands on the cyber arsenal protected within this building. The Israelis were unbeatable in the art of cyber warfare – until today.

'Situation report?' shouted from a desk at the top of the room.

'They're into the financial structure and we can't stop them,' reported a supervisor. 'The banks! Close the banks down now.

'How?'

'Rip out the power supply and then they can't feed into the computer systems.'

A left hand worked a switch whilst the right hand engaged a keyboard. Nearby, another member of the unit lifted a telephone and began contacting the financial sector.

'Closing! I am closing the financial rig down,' yelled an operator.

'Safe here,' stated another voice. 'The power grid is unassailable.

'Not safe here,' declared an operator. 'If they move resources and deploy more power to the bottom circuits we'll lose the entire public service infrastructure.'

'What about the military net?' from the command desk.

'Same as the public services net. It's going down. We're losing control.'

'Standby,' said a voice at the command desk.

A hand lifted a red telephone and waited. There was no number to dial or switchboard to bypass. It was a direct line to the President of Israel.

'Sir, they are about to breach the military and public service rigs. We are closing down the financial sector by turning off the power and...'

The commander held the phone, listened, and replied, 'That's not possible, sir. The two are on different power supplies. Yes, the electricity grid is also on its own system. It is the only one holding up now. No, we have no idea where the attack is coming from or who is behind it. We've never experienced anything like this before.'

Taking a deep breath, the commander listened, and then said, 'Sir, I ask for permission to deploy Crimson Gold. It's all we have left.'

Seconds later, the phone crashed to its cradle and the voice ordered, 'All desks, break off defence. Deploy Crimson Gold. I say again, deploy Crimson Gold.'

133

In a well-rehearsed ritual, one hundred and twenty operators ignored one computer system and turned to another.

A set of computer screens in one area flashed white and then red. Eventually, they turned to a crimson colour before resting on gold.

'Deploy!' ordered a supervisor.

'It's never been tested let alone used in anger,' replied an aide.

'It's our last resort,' suggested another. 'If we don't try this there will be nothing left in the morning. Deploy!'

In a micro second, the most advanced computer worm known to mankind entered the electronic world for the first time. Deviously, it calculated the route and origins of the cyber-attack before delivering a deadly virus to the assailant's platform.

The worm penetrated the lines, broke through firewalls and encrypted defences before attacking servers. Then, in a grand finale, Crimson Gold, tore through the attack protocol and began to infest back up and second layer defences. In a unique cyber-attack, the worm destroyed more servers, firewalls, motherboards, mouse controls, and drivers. Finally, the worm ignited its own power source, harnessed from the attack system, and mounted a ferocious assault on the enemy's servers. The secret of Crimson Gold was its ability to use the attacker's power source to deliver the final knockout punch.

Two hours later, it was all over.

Israel's military and public service computer systems had suffered and would be offline for the near future. The financial system had been saved but some banks and finance houses reported limited use of technology would be the order of the day for the next week.

The country's electrical power grid, however, remained untouched. It was invincible.

The unit rejoiced. The battle had been hard fought, not without loss, but victorious.

Twelve hours later, on the outskirts of Tel Aviv, Darius parked an old van in a layby. He removed a flask of hot coffee from a bag and poured himself a drink.

Relaxed, and confident, he looked at the sky above and thought, 'I am early.'

Sipping his coffee, Darius waited a short time before the night clouds rolled into place.

Reaching inside the dashboard, Darius removed a black balaclava mask and a loaded handgun. He donned his balaclava, manoeuvred the eyeholes into position, covered his beard, and stuffed the handgun into a belt near the small of his back.

Stepping out, he began his approach to the substation.

The unmanned substation was part of an electrical generation, transmission, and distribution system, that transformed voltage from high to low, or reverse. Essentially, as far as Darius was concerned, the substation was controlled by remote computers in what was known as the SCADA function (Supervisory Control and Data Acquisition). The entire complex was controlled elsewhere in Tel Aviv where operators ran the system by issuing computerised orders that increased or decreased voltage, or set changes of demand and supply, which connected to sensors and actuators inside the substation complex.

As Darius had grown from teenager to adult, he had learnt so much and was no longer an uneducated individual from an isolated mountain range. He grew up in a time and place where schools and electricity were not a natural part of the infrastructure of his homeland.

Yet today, he studied the substation from outside its iron fence and knew it was one of the most common types of industrial control systems in use. He knew

135

enough about SCADA systems to know they were very vulnerable to cyberwarfare and cyberterrorism attacks.

However, with no computerised device at his fingertips, Darius planned something different.

Using a small torch, he took his bag and approached the solid iron fence which provided a unique barrier between himself and the highly dangerous electricity. He threw his bag onto the other side, climbed over, and placed two home-made bombs at the base legs of the first transformer he found. All he could hear was his heart pounding like a big bass drum and the bizarre constant hum of electricity feeding around the substation.

'Or is that computer buzz?' he thought. He did not know.

All he really knew was that it was a dangerous place and he needed to be out of the complex as soon as possible.

Being careful not to venture further into the hazardous and potentially lethal complex, Darius set down two more home-made bombs at the base of another transformer.

Carefully, he retraced his steps, climbed back over the fence and returned to the van.

Sweating from the mental stress of being so close to danger, Darius wiped perspiration from his brow and took a deep breath.

Scanning the area in his vicinity, he realised he was alone and completely free.

'I will never forgive, I will never forget,' he shouted. 'Death to the allies of the western world.'

Darius flicked a switch on his console and activated a remote-controlled detonation.

Laughing, he watched the legs of the first transformer buckle inwards before slowly collapsing. The transformer hit the ground bringing down four secondary power lines above it. The electrical current rushed along the lines, were denied entry to the collapsed transformer, and exploded into a frenzy of sparks and ferocity that arced uncontrollably across the complex.

Darius flicked a second switch on his control panel.

The second transformer followed suit. A domino effect followed in which a chain reaction, caused by the explosion of the transformer, caused numerous transformers nearby to malfunction in an unprecedented manner.

As one transformer buckled to the ground, the next distorted, failed to remain erect when the power lines surrendered, and then bowed to oppression when it clattered to the earth.

One by one, the transformers exploded in a feast of pyrotechnics that collapsed and brought down the grid.

A terrific fellowship of escaped electricity suddenly energized and escaped from the complex. An arc of ferocious light rushed from the substation like a laser beam destroying and threatening everything in its path. Colossal arcs of electricity reached into the sky, threatened, subsided, and burst forth again when the transformers buckled and collided with each other in their dying moments. Wiring at the junction boxes near the top of the wooden poles abruptly began sparking, arcing, and shooting out flame in every direction possible.

An arc of electricity pulverized the front of Darius's van and narrowly missed the substation terrorist.

Then the grass nearby caught fire and the flames from the compound extended their reach and began consuming everything nearby. Their savagery ate up the oxygen and lashed out at Darius.

Scared stiff, completely terrified, Darius turned, ran, and fled the scene leaving everything behind – his control panel, sunglasses, thermos flask, and torch.

Turning, glancing behind, he saw the van burst into flame. The substation had rent its anger on the perpetrator by lashing out a tongue of revenge which had almost taken Darius.

Reaching a wooden fence about a quarter of a mile from the substation, Darius stopped, took breath, and promptly heaved the contents of his stomach into the ditch. He was shaking.

Gradually, he recovered, abandoned his balaclava, tightened his gloves, and made his escape on foot.

'Never again,' he thought. 'Far too dangerous. Never again!'

On reaching an industrial estate, Darius entered a phone box, made a call, and reported, 'Pick me up at the back up location. The job is done but the van is melted. Yes, the underpass… Now!'

Slamming the phone down, Darius made another call and volunteered, 'Mukhtar, it's done, totally destroyed. You are clear to go.'

Strolling away from the telephone, Darius heaved a sigh of relief, took a deep breath, and made for the pick-up point.

Glancing behind, he saw fire raging from the substation and flames stretching into the sky.

Darius felt alone and vulnerable. He broke into a trot and headed for the underpass.

In the aftermath of the attack, Tel Aviv was without full power for the next sixteen days.

Mukhtar, the Chosen One, ended the telephone and turned to his officers standing nearby.

'It is done. All is ready,' he said. 'We go in one hours' time. Brief the troops.'

That night, elements of Hezbollah - a Lebanese Shia radical movement sponsored by Iran – crept close to the Israeli border.

Mukhtar led his fighters through the sparse vegetation until they could see their target. Wearing night sights, the warriors crept closer, used an old rustic wall for cover, and then let rip at the border guards securing the crossing.

Three sentries fell immediately, mown down by the deadly chatter of Hezbollah machine guns, killed by their hate-filled anti-Semitic enemy in the name of establishing an independent Shia State in Lebanon.

Forward, they ventured, firing wildly every inch of the way towards the dark, powerless village. Only a candle burnt from the guardroom.

'Get closer,' ordered Mukhtar.

Using the darkness of the night, Mukhtar and his men stole nearer the guardroom, opened fire, killed, and moved on.

The black of the sky aided and abetted the invaders as they penetrated the lands of Israel and destroyed all who stood before them.

Gunfire resounded across the border signalling the only opportunity for villagers to escape before their houses came under attack. As Mukhtar and his killers went on the rampage, dozens of villagers fled their homes, chased by darkened shadows firing from the hip – destroying, killing those who dared to stand against them.

Simultaneously, elsewhere, three platoons of Hezbollah soldiers mounted a series of night-time rocket attacks into the heart of Tel Aviv.

Buildings and vehicles were hit by would-be Shia State artillery as Hezbollah pressed home their advantage.

Confused by the dark, with no electrical lighting, few standby generators, and a dangerous mix of noise and shadows, the people of Tel Aviv ran for their lives.

Masonry fell, woodwork twisted and contorted in its final throes, buildings crumbled to the ground, glass broke, and people ran screaming from their homes to get away from the hell that rained down upon them.

Over three hundred and fifty Jews, residents of the capital city, lay dead in the morning sunlight.

Inspired, gloriously happy, Mukhtar and his fellow Hezbollah warriors celebrated like never before.

Israeli investigators began their trawl, asking questions, and securing evidence wherever they could. It wasn't just another incursion; another chapter in a violent disturbing occupation. It was a comprehensive, well thought out attack by Hezbollah and it had been aided by a pre-planned operation to plunge the capital into darkness.

Israel wanted the names of those behind such an unprecedented assault, and they didn't care how much it cost or what steps needed to be taken to get them.

An old van was found burnt out in a layby near the substation. Examination by forensic experts revealed remnants of various articles that were found in the wreck. Enquiries in the area, amongst the local population, found witnesses who stated that the driver was a man in his mid-twenties. His hair was jet black and he sported a beard and moustache. Others argued that he was a much older man who was unshaven. The reality dawned that no one could really identify the enigmatic character to whom the destruction of the power grid was attributed.

No fingerprints or forensic evidence of a significant nature were found at the scene of the substation attack.

In the aftermath of the bombings, investigators discovered several white feathers discarded at various places in a field close to the substation. They were found to be the feathers from a pure white eagle.

Investigators, detectives, politicians, journalists, and even amateur sleuths, compared notes and concluded that several horrific, violent crimes in Europe, and this one in Israel, were connected. They realised that on each occasion under review the perpetrator, or perpetrators, had left the tail feather of a bird at the scene of each crime. It was the killer's calling card. His signature at the end of each adventurous murder. They also surmised that the number of possible motives involved suggested that the offender might be a terrorist for hire since he had attacked multiple targets of varying ideologies.

The only commonality found was that the offender was male and of questionable description and identity. He was tall, over six feet, had a beard and moustache, sometimes wore sunglasses, was of swarthy complexion, and his image had been captured on various CCTV systems. Yet no one in the law enforcement agencies knew him. It appeared that he was a man with no name and no previous criminal history.

The culprit was an enigma: an international figure of mystery and anonymity.

When asked, expert ornithologists reported that the feather left at the scene of this series of atrocities were attributable to the tail feather of a white eagle found only in parts of Europe and central Asia. Particularly, it was suggested, the recovered feathers of a pure white eagle might only be found in the Quandil Mountains.

Collectively, journalists, commentators, media representatives, police, and intelligence agencies across the globe, highlighted the search for a terrorist unit led by a man dubbed White Eagle.

Overnight, White Eagle ceased being a European phenomenon and became synonymous with global catastrophe.

When a train crashed headlong into another, in India, it was said that White Eagle must have been involved.

When an earthquake rocked Sri Lanka, locals wondered if White Eagle was somehow implicated.

When a volcano erupted in Hawaii, locals joked that it must have something to do with White Eagle, because no-one expected it and no-one saw it coming.

Whether such sayings were right, wrong, or indifferent, became irrelevant.

The legend of White Eagle was born.

Mouretti answered his telephone, listened, and replied, 'Shalom, Benjamin. How are you?'

'As well as a man with no answers can be,' replied Benjamin. 'In all my days of international diplomacy, I have never known such a blanket of negative information. They say he's done everything but when you investigate these matters, he hasn't done half the things they think he has.'

'It is the way of the world,' replied Mouretti. 'A legend only grows when people become afraid and cannot find a rational answer. You know that. How can I help you today?'

'The museum,' suggested Benjamin. 'I believe there is a section covering ornithology.'

'That is correct,' replied Mouretti.

'I'll be there at twelve noon on Tuesday,' replied Benjamin.

Sitting back in his seat, Mouretti deliberately paused, waited a second or two, and added, 'Just checking my diary… Yes, I can make it to the museum. Whereabouts?'

'In the area where they keep the eagles,' replied Benjamin. 'But then I think you knew that before I asked.'

'Perhaps,' ventured Mouretti. 'Tuesday, it is.'

The line went dead as Mouretti gently replaced the telephone in its cradle and wondered how he would handle the self-proclaimed diplomat from Shin Bet, the Israeli Intelligence Agency.

*

# Chapter Nine
~

The Special Crime Unit
London
One week later.

'So, there you have it,' declared Maude Black, the Home Secretary. 'This so-called White Eagle terrorist group are making us look like a bunch of idiots. There's a cartoon in a French newspaper today that compares the police with the Keystone Cops. Now please, tell me how I am supposed to deal with that in the national and international media?'

'You can't deal with it,' answered Sir Henry Fielding: The Foreign Secretary. 'Well, not effectively. You'll just have to make smoke signals as usual.'

'Your advice is beyond response,' replied Maude.

Turning to Antonia Harston-Browne, Sir Henry continued, 'I'd go further and remind everyone that the media are tearing our Intelligence services to pieces. British Intelligence is the lead organisation in Europe. For heaven's sake, we seem incapable of getting anything right. You have failed to produce any leads for ourselves or our counterparts in Europe despite a major financial investment in your unit.'

'The drones you promised have not yet arrived, sir,' suggested Sandy. 'Do you have a date yet?'

'Drones!' barked the Commissioner of the Metropolitan Police. 'Drones aren't the answer!'

Neil coughed and resumed with, 'Drones! Superintendent Peel, you have a million pound plus cyber package called the Ticker Intelligence system. The scheme, as you know, is protected by an extremely expensive anti-hacking system. You've been attached to Special Forces in the hope that such an experience would benefit the unit; re-educated in target penetration, cyber warfare, and anti-extremism; sent to Turkey to wave the flag for us and sort it all out, and we are no further forward than we were when this all started. As Police Commissioner, this really does worry me. What the hell are you people doing about this? You've got the best money can buy and we're going backwards! The only time this unit is mentioned is in the same sentence as the word complaint. Oh yes, complaint! From gung-ho armed operations at building societies to failed trips abroad to investigate crime. I've heard it all.'

'Settle down, sir,' advised Commander Edwin Maxwell. 'I head the unit not the Superintendent. Take it out on me, not her.'

'Where would you like me to start?' growled the Commissioner.

'Gentlemen!' ordered the Home Secretary. 'Shouting at each other like kids in the school yard won't get us anywhere. Now sit down and compose yourselves. I refuse to preside over such a rabble.'

The middle-aged and experienced, Maude tapped on the surface of the walnut desk, brought the meeting to order, and suggested, 'Now then, can we be constructive?'

Boyd shuffled his seat forward to the table, and commented, 'That does seem to be the way forward, I agree.'

'The way forward?' growled the Commissioner. 'How do you see us going forward, Boyd?'

'If all else fails, we rest, start again, and open a bottle of Bushmills for companionship,' replied Boyd with a smile.

'Dear god,' winced the Commissioner. 'I apologise, Madam Home Secretary but you can perhaps now understand why no progress is being made. Give me time and I will ensure the right people are in the right job, I assure you.'

'Unlike yourself, Commissioner,' replied Maude. 'I have been in post for quite a while now. I have every confidence in the unit. Indeed, I remind you that the Foreign Secretary – on the orders of the Prime Minister – insisted that we sent a senior officer to Turkey as a political gesture and in the hope that we might assist the enquiry. None of us expected the investigation to breach borders and encompass virtually the whole of the continent of Europe.'

'We are primarily a domestic unit,' added Commander Maxwell. 'There is Europol and Interpol, of course, but they have no powers of arrest and merely facilitate enquiries and police functionality rather than engage in on the ground investigations like ourselves.'

'Yes, they've always puzzled me,' remarked Boyd. 'Handbags at dawn?'

'Enough!' replied the Commissioner sardonically.

'With your permission, Home Secretary,' declared Commander Maxwell. 'You raised the conference in order that the way ahead might be discussed and I am pleased you were able to join us. Perhaps we might hear from Superintendent Peel as to her findings in Turkey.'

'Yes, please proceed,' replied the Home Secretary.

Commander Maxwell gestured his colleague and she stepped forward.

Settled in the conference room, Sandy cut an imposing figure in her dark blue business suit as she moved to the front of the gathering.

Commander Maxwell gestured to Sandy, engaged his audience, and said, 'I've asked Superintendent Peel to update us on the search for the people responsible for the attacks in Istanbul, Paris, The Hague, Vienna, and Tel Aviv. Here in the UK, it may not seem overly important to us now but we have been asked to investigate these matters in tandem with our European colleagues. Nationally, and internationally, our reputation is on the line but I must tell you that, so far, we've nothing to crow about. Listen up, I'll let the Superintendent explain.'

Speaking from the podium, Sandy began with, 'I'll sum up where we are with one word. Nowhere!'

There were murmurs of surprise and disapproval as Sandy's voice seemed to reverberate around the room.

'Yes! Nowhere,' repeated Sandra. 'To be fair, that really means that our suspect is still not yet identified. If you look around the walls, you'll see photographs of how these crimes came to light, what happened, and what the connection between them is. We're looking for a tall man who probably has size eleven plates of meat since we recovered the imprint of a size eleven Adidas training shoe at the Istanbul scene. Enquiries with shoe manufacturers suggest the subject may be anywhere between six feet and six feet nine inches tall.'

'At least that's something,' suggested Maude, the Home Secretary. 'A starting point, no less.'

'Images on the office wall reveal the crime scenes at Istanbul, Paris, The Hague, Vienna, and Tel Aviv,' reported Sandy. 'You can also see various images of a similarly described suspect which have been captured by various CCTV systems since this all began. No one knows him. I concentrated my efforts in Turkey because that was where I was sent. Interestingly, I will suggest to you that the culprit or culprits originate from Turkey.'

'A man between six feet and six feet nine inches,' pondered Commander Maxwell. 'That's most of the men in this room, although we haven't that many over six three.'

'Investigators did the usual at these crime scenes,' revealed Sandy. 'We checked local CCTV, fingerprints, footprints, DNA traces, house to house enquiries, and an intelligence trawl through French and Turkish criminal intelligence records. It took us nowhere. No-one saw a face in Istanbul. There were four raiders and not one person can be identified. We're pretty sure we've traced the van used to a lock up on an industrial estate a couple of miles away but there's nothing concrete anywhere.'

'Any forensics?' enquired Martin Duffy.

'None!' replied Sandy. 'The van and the contents were destroyed using a phosphorous bomb and an incendiary device. There's the connection to the airport incident – phosphorous – it suggests a military supplier or someone who has access to military stores. Enquiries have failed, so far, to identify any military unit that is missing a few phosphorous devices.'

'That might tend to suggest that a military regime supports the perpetrators,' suggested Anthea. 'Are we talking State sponsored terrorism?'

'Possibly,' replied Sandy.

'Or the PKK,' remarked Toni from the front row. 'What have you learnt about that organisation, Sandy?' she asked.

'That's really your department,' suggested Sandy.

Smiling, Toni ventured, 'After a few weeks in Turkey, you probably know more about the organisation than myself. That said, I think my Director-General might have something to say about that.'

'Not at all,' replied Sir Phillip Nesbitt. 'I'm glad a Detective Superintendent in the Metropolitan Police has taken the opportunity to research such an organisation. Tell me, Superintendent, 'Do you see a connection between Turkey and the man your unit has been following here in the UK – the one we call The Collector – with the Kurdistan Workers' Party, or Partiya Karkerên Kurdistanê, as they say in their native tongue? What do you think, Sandy?'

'It's also likely that the building society's robbers are with the same organisation,' suggested Boyd interrupting. 'Thinking forward progression, Madam Home Secretary, if we assessed the evidence and suspicion that we have here – only in the UK – then I would plump for the PKK. You see, we have no leads on

State sponsored terrorism, the Russians, Hezbollah, or anyone like that. The Collector, and the gang from the building society raid, are the only leads we have on anything remotely connected with Turkey, and we have absolutely nothing on the Tel Aviv attack. Yes, I know it isn't in Europe but we do have a relationship with Israeli law enforcement and, sad to say, there's nothing to go on at the moment. I'm sorry, but we're not even in the game as far as I can see. Plus, I must say, it seems the people that everyone wants are not active in this country.'

The Home Secretary nodded, and said, 'Thank you, Chief Inspector Boyd. Tell me, though. Have you had the opportunity to review the evidence available? Paris, for example, Chief Inspector, the killer rode a motor bike to the scene. Where was it stolen from?'

'As far as we know,' replied Boyd. 'The motor bike was bought for cash some weeks earlier by a woman. The number plates were changed and there's no sightings of the vehicle until the day of the murders. It's the same elsewhere. There are no hire vehicles involved so there is no driving licence or credit card involved in the transaction. There's no clues there for police to investigate. CCTV is non-existent because the sales are private and not recorded anywhere. A vehicle can be bought at an auction by a legitimate buyer and sold in an adjacent car park to someone looking for a specific vehicle. Car dealers meet customers every day of the week. They can hardly be expected to remember all their contacts.'

'A woman, you say,' remarked Maude. 'Does that surprise you?'

'Not really,' replied Boyd. 'And I'm not convinced by witnesses who can't describe their customers other than by recalling their gender.'

'And the weapons and ammunition?' enquired the Home Secretary.

'Similar,' revealed Boyd. 'There are no fingerprints, no DNA, and no traces although it is obvious that some of the weapons and ammo used are military grade. What does shout at me is that there is a Placer working away in the background. I'm talking about an accomplice so the way I read it is this – Our man gets a job to do and therefore begins planning with an accomplice that I'll call the Placer. The Placer doesn't carry out the job but does provide logistical support in the way of vehicles, firearms, ammunition, train tickets, and probably false passports and credit cards. I reckon there's a Placer operating. Find the Placer and we'll find our man.'

'Which brings us back to state-sponsored terrorism,' concluded the Home Secretary.

'Possibly,' admitted Boyd. 'I'm not convinced. I'm pretty sure our man has at least one accomplice. There may be more.'

'Thank you,' smiled Maude. 'Now then, Superintendent, how do you feel about Mister Boyd's remarks?'

'True,' admitted Sandy. 'I can't argue with any of that.'

Sir Phillip added, 'It is a fact, Home Secretary, that about half a million individuals of Turkish origin live in the UK. Ninety percent of them live in London. I understand well over half are Turkish Cypriots with about one hundred thousand from Turkey itself. We don't know, of course, how many of them support the PKK.'

'Tell me more about the PKK,' instructed the Home Secretary.

Sir Phillip smiled, bowed out, and gestured the Superintendent.

Sandy took a sip of water and replied, 'The PKK is a militant left-wing organisation based in Turkey and Iraqi Kurdistan. Since 1984 the PKK has waged an armed struggle against the Turkish state for cultural and political rights and self-determination for the Kurds in Turkey. The group was founded in 1978. Their ideology was originally a mix of revolutionary socialism and Kurdish nationalism, seeking the foundation of an independent, Marxist–Leninist state in the region, which was to be known as Kurdistan.'

'Sounds like the Russians might be interested in a Marxist-Leninist theatre,' suggested Anthea. 'That might lead us to the conclusion that State sponsored terrorism lies at the heart of this.'

'Well, things change and their leader was captured and imprisoned in 1999,' declared Sandy. 'Since then, the party has been influenced by the philosophy of communalism.'

'Communism?' queried Martin.

'Communalism.' confirmed Sandy. 'It sounds like communism but isn't.'

'What does it mean?' enquired Terry.

'It's the principle of political organisation based on federated communes,' intervened Commander Maxwell. 'It's driven by an allegiance to one's own ethnic group rather than to the wider society.'

'Och! You mean all for one and the one is me?' suggested Janice.

'Yes, something like that,' replied the Commander.

'In that case, where do I sign?' chuckled Janice. 'Och man, it sounds like home sweet home.'

'You might not want to sign up just yet,' laughed Sandy. 'In 2007, former members of the PKK helped form an umbrella organisation of Turkish, Iranian, Iraqi, and Syrian Kurds. They put their proposals to the Turkish government but it didn't work out. In 2016, in a joint declaration with nine other organisations, the PKK announced that they want a democracy based for people who are against imperialism, capitalism, chauvinism, fascism, and racism.'

'Utopia?' remarked Janice with a sly smile.

'If only,' replied Sandy. 'Realistically, in your dreams. Hence, the PKK is listed as a terrorist organisation by several states and organisations, including the North Atlantic Treaty Organisation (NATO), the United States of America, and the European Union.'

'That's right,' intervened Commander Maxwell. 'But some countries, such as Switzerland, China, India, Russia, and Egypt have not designated the PKK as a terrorist organisation. So, whilst respecting their opinion, you can also understand how the term State sponsored terrorism is alive and kicking because these are the countries who support the Kurds.'

'Yes,' added Toni. 'But it also might be the case that those countries have a better understanding of their grievances and look upon the PKK in a way different to us.'

'That's always a possibility,' admitted the Commander.

'It also explains why the war in the Middle East is so complex,' remarked Sandy. 'The Syrian army are fighting Islamic State and rebels who are battling against the Syrian State. The Kurds are fighting Turkey but both Turkey and the Kurds are fighting Islamic State. Meanwhile, some of the Kurdish armies are fighting amongst themselves because they all have their own ideas on what a new Kurdistan might look like, how big a geographical State might be, and who might lead it. I haven't even mentioned the tribal rivalries yet. Hey, I could go on but this helps explain some of the problems of the Middle East.'

'Did you get to the Quandil Mountains?' enquired Boyd. 'Or was that out of the question?'

'It's a war zone, Boyd,' reported Sandy. 'The mountains offer ideal terrain for guerrilla fighters and are accessible only through a network of narrow, near impenetrable passes. There's an odd road here and there – and I mean odd – because the highways are like what we might call a country lane. They loosely connect a series of almost medieval villages that are imprisoned in a time warp. There are no telephone lines, no electricity, no gas, no infrastructure other than what I've mentioned, and no life as we know it. Most of the water they use comes from wells, springs, or the mountain streams that dominate the area. The mountains serve as a launching ground for the PKK and their allied Iranian Kurds. The growing Turkish-Iranian alliance will do its best to make life as unpleasant as possible for the movement's militants in their mobile bases on the peaks. The Kurdish regional government will go on developing further south whilst looking nervously at its uninvited Kurdish compatriots in the mountains. I couldn't get anywhere near the Quandil Mountains, Boyd. It's a non-starter and I didn't want to go there because there might be no way back. There seems to be no end in sight. The beautiful, blighted border zone of Qandil will be ringing to the sound of gunfire, the shouts of insurgents and the periodic thunder of Turkish aircraft and Iranian cannons, largely out of earshot of a largely indifferent world, for a long time to come. Mind you, I did find out that these mountains are the command centre for the PKK. Approximately five thousand PKK members, and other armed guerrilla factions, control an area of roughly fifty square kilometres. It's been bombarded by the Turkish Air Force and shelled by the Iranian artillery for several years.'

'Motive,' announced Boyd. 'Oh, sorry. I was just thinking to myself.'

'The PKK uses heroin production and trafficking to support its acts of terror,' continued Sandy. 'They have been engaged in drug trafficking and money laundering activities and are well established. They are excellent smugglers and obviously use the revenue for purchasing firearms, munitions and other equipment.'

Toni intervened adding, 'Interpol, and the national police agencies of the EU member states, note that the narcotics route that runs through Turkey to the Balkans and western Europe benefits the PKK militants and their intermediaries. It also uses Romania and Moldavia. Drugs are sent to Europe by sea from the Libyan El Abde Mina Harbour, which is controlled by Syria. The PKK makes between three hundred and four hundred million dollars every year from drug smuggling. Germany reckons that eighty percent of narcotics seized in Europe have been linked to the PKK or other Turkish groups. The groups have used the proceeds to purchase arms. Our service suggests the PKK is responsible for forty percent of the heroin sold in the European Union.'

Martin whistled before saying, 'Incredible!'

'Thank you, ladies and gentlemen,' said the Home Secretary. 'That's most informative but it will not help either the Commissioner of the Metropolitan Police or myself in the media debate that is focused on the ability of our police and intelligence services. Do any of you have any firm ideas on the future?'

'Yes,' remarked Boyd. 'I do.'

'Such as?' enquired Maude.

'Some years ago, just after the banking crisis of 2008, governments cut public services in this country like never before. This included the NHS, the Prison Service and the Police Service. It's just not...'

'Chief Inspector!' barked the Commissioner in a cautionary voice.

'Let him finish,' responded the Home Secretary. 'He's entitled to his opinions.'

'I'm also answering your question,' suggested Boyd. 'It's about time some thought was given to increasing police numbers if we are to provide an adequate response to terrorism in the United Kingdom. The best deterrent in the future lies not only in technology and social interaction with those causing the problem but with boots on the streets getting to know the public and patrolling areas of concern.'

The Home Secretary nodded and replied, 'Recruitment is scheduled to rise, Chief Inspector and I tend to agree with you. Do you have a policing response in the short term?'

'Yes,' replied Boyd. 'But you might not like my answers.'

'It may be time to shut up,' suggested the Commissioner.

Commander Maxwell threw the Commissioner a disapproving look, glanced at Boyd, and asked, 'What's on your mind, William? Come on, don't keep it to yourself. I want to hear what you have to say.'

'All the money, fancy gizmos, surveillance clones, phone taps, electronic interceptions, and fortune tellers in the world haven't worked, Commander,' explained Boyd. 'They haven't worked because we've failed to profile the offender properly and we're using the wrong tactics against him.'

The Commissioner shook his head in disappointment whilst the Foreign Secretary pursed his lips and Maude looked on with interest.

'What do you suggest?' enquired the Commander.

'Yes,' added Sir Phillip. 'I'd like to hear what road you would go down.'

Boyd studied his audience and replied, 'We put all our sources to work – every last one of them – I don't care if they've only ever given us a shoplifter when we were young detectives in a CID office years' ago. I'm not bothered if they slipped the name of an armed robber last week. Make it happen. Turn the dustbin upside down and see what comes out. He's making a fool of us and I, for one, have had enough. We lead. We do not follow. Technology only works if someone is using an electronic device or is mentioned in an electronic transmission of some kind. I think this guy uses semaphore.'

'Or an eagle,' quipped Janice.

'Maybe a pigeon,' suggested Anthea.

'Do you get my drift?' enquired Boyd as he sought to carry the gathering with him. 'He talks to someone. Someone talks to him. Someone somewhere knows this guy. There's a link. The man has travelled across Europe to attack specific targets.'

Boyd delved in his desk, recovered half a dozen shot glasses and a bottle of Bushmills, and began filling the glasses.

The Home Secretary's eyes shot up. Startled, she watched Boyd thread his way thought the group as he poured drinks.

'If we find the link, we're on the road to success,' Boyd explained. 'In Istanbul, he attacked the Turkish State and we all thought it might be a shot at either the Turkish government or NATO. In Paris, he killed three NATO generals and we were sure we were looking for an anti-NATO man, maybe a Russian. In The Hague, it was a cyber warfare man of ours so some thought our suspect might be connected to organised crime or the Mafia, something like that. In Vienna, it was the American Embassy, so Interpol and the Yanks were looking for anyone who hates the Stars and Stripes; and in Tel Aviv, he attacked the State of Israel and paved the way for Hezbollah to launch multiple attacks on the city. On its own, you might think the Israeli attack came from someone who hated Jews. Add all those attacks together and look at them as if they were one entity and I suggest that the man we are looking for is a terrorist for hire. Don't you see? The law enforcement agencies can become so very easily entrenched in looking for a terrorist from Islamic State that we haven't thought outside the box. I know there's a needle in the haystack. We need to find the needle. Is that understood?'

Boyd handed the Commissioner, the Home Secretary, the Commander, and the Director-General, a glass of Bushmills each.

Raising the glass to his colleagues, Boyd took a sip and said, 'And we won't do it thinking about Ireland and this little tipple.'

'We'll need to give some serious money away,' frowned Anthea.

'And buy a lot of beer,' remarked Terry.

'Or Champagne?' chuckled Sir Phillip.

'Wine and maybe a few promises,' added Janice.

'Cake!' suggested the Home Secretary.

Boyd looked at the Home Secretary and queried, 'Cake?'

'Why not? What price is freedom?' enquired the Home Secretary.

'Priceless!' replied Boyd.

'Then dig deep and make sure that what you pay for is what you get,' suggested the Home Secretary. Smiling, Maude raised her glass to Boyd and the group and continued, 'Good luck!'

'It looks like it's time for me to wind up our friends in Legoland,' suggested Toni. 'MI6 have eyes and ears everywhere. Who knows, if we don't tell them what we're looking for we might all end up in the dark. Sir Phillip?'

'Yes,' replied the Director-General. 'Leave that with me and I'll make a call to my counterpart.'

'Thank you,' indicated the Commander with a nod.

'So, what are we waiting for,' announced Boyd. 'Let's make it happen. We have a long-term interest in the Collector. If White Eagle comes to the UK, he'll need help. We've found the Collector. Now we need to find the Placer.'

Maude Black smiled, took a sip, and announced, 'I'll drink to that. After the week, I've had with the media then I'll go with anything that might lead to success. Boyd, you're off the wall again. You want to abandon the proven methods of electronic intelligence gathering and go back to a rather old-fashioned concept of policing. But, the way I see it is simple. What have we got to lose at this stage? Yes, I'll drink to that. Commissioner, it's your call.'

'Fine, nodded the Commissioner. 'For now, that is. I'll go with it but I'll reserve judgement.'

The Home Secretary surprised everyone when she downed the contents of her glass, held it towards Boyd for a refill, and said, 'Well, what are you waiting for, Boyd?'

'Terry,' quipped Boyd. 'Contact Patient Lamb. We've not heard from him for a while. It's time to rattle his cage. We've made things too easy for him.'

'Good!' interjected Commander Maxwell looking at a disillusioned Commissioner. 'Consider this, our man just ups the ante every time. He's gone from airports to organisations to capital cities to who knows where? I mean, where will he strike next?'

Boyd began filling glasses again and, as he strolled from one to another, revealed, 'It occurred to me as you were all discussing the Quandil Mountains. This isn't a group we are looking for. It's an individual who enlists the support of a group when he needs to.'

'How do you work that out?' queried the Commissioner now happily sipping his drink whilst watching every movement of the Home Secretary.

Sir Phillip leaned forward and said, 'Boyd, he's a terrorist for hire that enlists a group when he needs to. Is that what you are saying?'

'Not quite, but close,' replied Boyd. 'They are all signature crimes as far as I can see. Our man leaves the feather of a white eagle at the scene of every crime. The feather comes from an eagle found only in the Quandil Mountains. The mountains have been bombed, blasted, and bombarded for over a decade. Here, in those mountains, lies the motive to the crime. Revenge! Someone from that area wants revenge.'

'That's every Kurd who has been dispossessed since time immemorial,' proposed the Commissioner. 'Only a few million suspects there then.'

'No,' responded Boyd moving to the wall and pointing to an image of an eagle's feather. 'With respect, sir, you don't understand the psychology in play.'

'I do,' intervened Ricky. 'It's a big part of my criminology degree. Psychology is the study of behaviour and the human mind. It embraces all aspects of conscious and unconscious experience as well as thought. It's an academic discipline, and a social science, which seeks to understand individuals and groups by studying and researching their actions.'

'That's what I mean,' explained Boyd. 'There's something going on in the killer's mind. The man we are looking for is between six feet three and six feet nine, wears a size eleven shoe, is a master of disguise, and comes from the Quandil Mountains. I'll lay odds that he once lived there and suffered some great catastrophe in his earlier life.'

'Something going on in his mind? Such as?' enquired Anthea.

'I don't know,' replied Boyd. 'But I'll hazard a guess. Did he lose a wife, a brother, or children, during a bombing raid when he was a younger man?'

'Maybe he lost his entire family,' suggested Ricky. 'Whatever it was, it turned him into a serial killer as well as an international terrorist. If you can understand the difference between the two?'

'Oh, I do,' replied Boyd. 'I certainly do. We're looking for a terrorist who also has a personal score to settle. He's a signature serial killer and you know what that means?'

'I've heard the term before,' revealed Maude. 'But in my time as Home Secretary, I have to tell you that I have no experience of the phenomenon.'

'No, me neither,' said Toni. 'What does it mean, Boyd?'

'I've heard the term before,' revealed Sir Phillip. "The day will come when he wants the world to know who he is. Fame! He wants to be a terrorist, yes, but he also wants to be remembered as a serial killer. Isn't that right, Boyd?'

There was a silence in the room before Boyd continued, 'Yes, it is and I know what you are all thinking. It just doesn't fit the normal profile of a terrorist but it goes a long way to explaining why he hasn't been caught yet. Dedicated terrorists often look death in the face and are prepared to die for their cause. This man leaves his signature everywhere because he doesn't want to be caught. His ego is bigger than his actions. He's like a camel drinking from a watering hole in the desert. The man can't get enough of it. He has to keep drinking from the well of fame until he's had his fill, and then he still wants more.'

'Fascinating and frightening too,' remarked the Home Secretary.

'At the moment,' proposed Boyd, 'Our man wants everyone to know about him. He's much cleverer than your normal terrorist. One day, he will want to be a globally recognised figure. This man is a megalomaniac in hiding but one day he will want to be world famous and that's our problem.'

'I think you're exaggerating, Boyd,' argued the Commissioner. 'You're putting him on a pedestal and making him into something he's not.'

'I disagree, sir,' contended Boyd. 'He'll continue doing what he's doing until he gets involved with the big one – a blockbuster of an attack somewhere. Hopefully, not here, but one that receives worldwide acknowledgement.'

'Where, precisely, are the Quandil Mountains, Boyd?' enquired the Commissioner.

'Here,' indicated Boyd pointing to a map on the wall. 'Right here, sir.'

\*

# Chapter Ten

~

The Quandil Mountains
Iraqi-Kurdistan
The following day

Driving a dark coloured Land Rover towards the Qandil Mountains - a mountainous area of Iraqi Kurdistan situated near the Iraq–Iran border - Darius shaded his eyes from the sun before pulling down the visor. He removed his sunglasses from their hideaway and put them on as he continued to head south towards the Zagros mountain range. Homeward bound, Darius made for a settlement in the Quandil Mountains.

Eventually, the tarmac highway gave way to a narrow single lane that, in turn, petered out into a rough track. The route became difficult to negotiate where the terrain was uneven. Darius found himself bouncing up and down in the driver's seat. Gradually, he began climbing from the base of the mountains in order to ascend one of the narrow access points into the mountain range.

In the end, the road became rutted and rocky. It was impossible to drive the vehicle further without risking a half shaft or some other essential part of the Land Rover.

Swinging the 4 x 4 from the track, Darius drove it beneath a stand of trees. He got out of the vehicle and studied the route he had just driven. Using binoculars, he scanned the lane and assured himself that he had not been followed.

'I am clean,' he said to himself. 'I've been clean since I left these mountains long ago. Always clean!' Then he laughed and muttered, 'One day they will be all over me and then the whole world will know it. But until then...' He looked over his shoulder once more and whispered, 'I'll stay one step ahead in the game that we play.'

Looking north, Darius made out the faint uneven horizon where the towns and cities of Turkey and its borders clawed skyward. Turning south, he marvelled at the high peaks of the mountain range that lay before him. Some of the peaks reached over 4,000 metres high and were snow-capped throughout the year. The mountain range stretched 1,200 miles from South-East Turkey to the Straits of Hormuz. They were formidable yet it was to his original home in the Quandil Mountains that he now journeyed.

Darius walked into the stand of trees where he found a horse.

'What a lovely horse they have left me,' he said.

Standing back, Darius admired the beautiful white stallion. It had been groomed to perfection and fitted with a luxurious leather saddle. He stroked the animal's neck and nuzzled close to it.

The horse responded firstly by swinging away but when Darius gently persisted by stroking its back, the horse settled and seemed to warm to its newfound admirer. Slowly, gradually, Darius bonded with his equine friend.

Grooming the horse's back led Darius's fingers to some saddlebags. He opened the bags and found a leather canteen full of fresh water, bread, sugar, and apricots.

Taking a sugar lump, Darius placed it in the palm of his hand and spoke soothingly to the horse as it ate the sugar.

Gently, he stroked the horse's mane and whispered, 'My friends have cared for you and made you quite magnificent. Oh, what should I call you? You are such a supreme being.'

The horse remained still as Darius continued to nuzzle the animal. The two were swopping scents, appreciating each other, and becoming more relaxed.

'Today,' remarked Darius. 'I shall call you Xerxes.'

Darius found more sugar lumps and treated his horse to the sweet delights.

'Did you know that long ago there was once another man called Darius?' he declared. 'He was the King of the Persian Empire and his son, Xerxes, became King of Kings – King of all the lands and people of the Persian Empire and more. He rode to glory and to victory on a white horse. You are named after him – the King of Kings.'

The horse whinnied and shook its head playfully.

'Come, my friend,' proposed Darius laughing softly. 'Father and son – Darius and Xerxes – are one again. Let you and I ride home together. It is to glory we ride.'

Removing his haversack from the rear of the vehicle, Darius slung it over his shoulder and locked the Land Rover. He secured it with a key, which he placed inside the pocket of his combat trousers, and approached Xerxes once more.

Mounting the horse, Darius rode off on the thin narrow path that steadily climbed towards the snow-capped Quandil Mountains.

Bit by bit, the track gradually became less discernible until it resembled a narrow uneven bridleway.

Every now and again, Darius stopped, drank water from his canteen, and then rode on. His journey lasted over three hours before the pass narrowed still further.

He knew they were there. He was expecting them.

As he drew closer, Darius let go of the reins and raised his arms above his head. He spread his fingers out so that they might see that he was unarmed.

Armed guards were stationed on the edges of the mountain pass that was wide enough only for a man on a horse. The two guards occupied the high ground and could see Darius long before he could see them. Bearded, wearing a black bandanna, and riding a white horse, his arrival was anticipated. The area was so sparsely populated that they seldom welcomed visitors. Only smugglers and drug couriers used this path and the procedure was to approach with your arms in the air until you were cleared.

Both guards cradled long barrelled sniper rifles but they also wore holstered side arms.

One of the guards turned his back on Darius and waved his rifle at those in the village below. Then he turned, held his rifle above his head, gripped the stock with one hand and the barrel with the other, and thus gave Darius the signal he was expecting.

Lowering his arms, Darius picked up the reins and continued his ascent. He was nearly there.

The guards returned to their duty – watching the approaches to the village.

Darius rode on, made the top of the pass, and then descended gradually into the village.

His impending arrival spread like wildfire in the village as Xerxes carried his noble master back to the lands of his birth.

On the descent into village, Darius noticed how dense the thicket had become. It was ideal for hiding in whenever a drone or aircraft flew over. As he rode through the waist-high dense bush, Darius saw the village open out before him. He made out the tobacco fields, rows of potatoes under cultivation, and scores of apricot trees sagging with their fruit.

Smiling to himself, Darius realised that nothing seemed to have changed. The village was still locked in a medieval time warp that denied the existence of any kind of modern infrastructure.

Eventually, the path levelled out and Darius entered the village.

People gathered on the route into the centre to see him. No-one smiled or cheered. They did not know him and had never met him. What they understood from their upbringing was that the guards at the mountain pass had allowed the man on a white horse to enter their lives. He must be important, they thought. Perhaps he is a new trader, one who has arrived to barter with the elders over the price of tobacco or the produce they grew? Maybe he was a drug dealer wanting to do business? They did not know but they knew they were safe in the village located in the deep belly button topography of the Qandil Mountains.

'See, Xerxes,' remarked Darius as he rode on high. 'We are Kings, you and I. Kings from another time and another place, and they do not know us.'

There was a sudden screeching from above and a bird took off from a rocky outcrop and flew above the horse and rider.

Stretching out his arm, Darius shouted, 'White Eagle! Come to me, White Eagle. Today, we are one. I said I would return one day and it is today. Fly to me, my friend.'

The eagle circled the pair, swooped low, and landed on Darius's outstretched arm.

'The eagles of the Quandil Mountains!' remarked Darius. 'Oh, how you have watched over our people. My soul lies deep within the spirit of an eagle.'

The crowd huddled together. Some of the people were afraid, others intrigued and mesmerised by the man they had never seen before.

Sporadically, the villagers began clapping when Darius shouted, 'It is I. This is my home. I have returned to the land of my fathers.'

Gradually, they warmed to him as he repeated, 'This is the land of my father, my grandfather, and my great-grandfather. This is Kurdistan. It is my home. It is the land of my fathers.'

Darius rode through the community, pointed at a school that had been rebuilt, and shouted, 'My school! You have rebuilt the school. It was my school.'

The villagers drew nearer to him, wondered who he might be, and why he had returned to their mountains.

Darius rode past a drugs laboratory that had been modified and reconstructed in the side of a mountain where a natural overhang protected its roof, and a stream where once he had played and built dams with Ilya and Suz.

Pulling his horse up, Darius smoothed the neck of the eagle, and said, 'Go! Hunt, White Eagle! Eat! You are our guardian, our Emperor of the skies.'

The eagle took off and began circling in the skies above.

Darius dismounted in the centre where the flag of Kurdistan flew from a solitary flagpole. He studied the flag, smiled, and then approached a group of elders.

Bowing before the village leader, Darius announced, 'Malik, Lord of the Kings, servant of our deity, I exalt you in the name of Allah. I am your servant returned to the land of my fathers to attend our people.'

Malik stepped forward, held out his arms, embraced his hero, and said, 'Welcome home! We had a message that you were coming and have been expecting you for days now. A good journey?'

'Yes, yes indeed,' replied Darius. 'No problems.'

'Join us,' instructed Malik. 'It is time to eat the fruits of your labours and drink to the future.'

'Thank you,' replied Darius. 'And thank you for the horse. He is such a beautiful stallion. I have never seen such a creature before.'

'White horses are special to those of us who seek lands in the old Persian Empire,' explained Malik. 'The white horse is associated with the sun chariot, with warrior-heroes, and with fertility.'

Chuckling, Darius responded, 'It is written that there were once horses with great powers. One had wings and some had horns which gave such creatures' phenomenal power.'

'Pegasus and unicorns,' laughed Malik. 'It is just history, my friend, just the mythology of an ancient world. Come, join us in our meal. We have much to talk about.'

Time moved on and a slight breeze ruffled the leaves on the apricot trees. Gradually, the leaves blew into the centre of the village.

Malik, Darius, and the elders, ate their fill and drank their wine before Malik announced, 'We have one last job for you.'

'One last job?' queried Darius. 'I have fulfilled a vow I made as a child and made our organisation millions of pounds in the process.'

'Yes, I understand but….'

Interrupting Malik, Darius continued 'Singlehandedly, I have expanded our network of couriers and suppliers across the continent of Europe. What more do you want of me?'

'Just one more,' pleaded Malik. 'Just one more? I can place you there. It is all arranged.'

Despondent, Darius lowered his head and gradually turned it to the skies above.

White Eagle flew closer and perched on a rock about a quarter of a mile away.

'Please,' pleaded Malik. 'You say I am the servant of Allah. You tell us that you have returned home to help our people. So, kindly listen to what I have to say. My friend, Allah has spoken to me. He tells me that revenge can be even sweeter when the truth is known.'

'What truth?' asked Darius.

'Once we had millions of pounds in bank accounts in Britain and various European countries,' revealed Malik. 'Our collectors moved amongst our supporters in such countries and deposited donations to our cause in their banks. When we needed the money, we transferred the funds into our master accounts. Now the cash no longer flows and we grow weaker by the day.'

'I know nothing of this,' replied Darius. 'Tell me more.'

'The accounts are frozen,' indicated Malik. 'We have been betrayed by our enemies and our bank accounts have been immobilised. The cash cannot be transferred from the banks. Those donations are withheld and I cannot get at them.'

'And the effect on us?' queried Darius.

'They are bleeding us dry, my friend. It's like turning off the water that nourishes our people. They are cutting off a vital supply of revenue that is necessary for the continuation of our cause.'

'I did not know,' replied Darius.

'How were you to know?' suggested Malik. 'You were not here. You have spent most of your life travelling and recruiting. You have given us your time and money to fight the good fight, and you have fought our battles too.'

'I fought for revenge but I also fought for the highest bidder whoever they were,' explained Darius. 'That's all I did.'

'And in the process scared half the world into fearing you,' declared Malik.

Silent, Darius considered the eyes of the village elder.

'I know,' suggested Malik. 'I know that you like the moment of the kill. I see it in your eyes. It is more than just revenge. Allah has gifted you with the power to kill.'

'There is no such gift in the Quran,' suggested Darius.

'No, but then it is Allah's gift to you.'

'I do not walk with Allah,' revealed Darius. 'And neither do you. Not in the way that devout Muslims live. You and I, and the other elders, we drink wine and enjoy the fruits of our labour. Yet you do not pray in the way others do and I see no Quran to read or recite from. Malik, in my life, I have kept safe only because I have done things my way. I walk alone. I have no religion. You know that, Malik.'

Nodding, twisting his face as if he had been hurt, Malik replied, 'I know that Allah has watched over you.'

Darius smiled and suggested, 'I think Allah has watched over the Placer, Malik, and that is you.'

'It is what the other elders call me,' chuckled Malik. 'A strategist might be a better description. You know that I place the Placers. We teach them until they become skilled in planning action to be taken and how to do it. We are cut off from the world here but then you and I have the wherewithal to travel anywhere on the globe. From this mountain base, I can formulate our tactics and advise others. I can make plans, teach people, and project the future of our organisation.'

'I am indebted to your team for helping me to accomplish so much, Malik,' revealed Darius. 'Things would have been much harder on my own.'

'We try to make it easier for people like you to kill and walk away without risk of capture,' explained Malik. 'Are you telling me now that you are a kafir – a non-believer?'

Darius did not answer.

'Do you no longer believe in the Prophet, Muhammad?' enquired Malik. 'Are you telling the elders that you have abandoned your Muslim origins?'

'I was born a Muslim,' admitted Darius. 'Yet my life has changed so much that I no longer follow the five pillars of the Islamic faith. I have no place for the confession of the faith, and no time for prayer. I have given millions to the organisation in the name of almsgiving but I have never fasted, not even in the month of Ramadan.'

'Hajj?' enquired Malik. 'Not even a pilgrimage to Mecca?'

'No,' confirmed Darius. 'Such things are not in my life now. I have abandoned the five pillars of Islam. A man who kills like me has no God, Malik. In the journey I have taken, it has often paid me to be a Jew or a Christian. These are falsehoods that I have created to smooth my passage through Europe.'

'And leave no trace behind?' suggested Malik.

'Not so that you'd notice,' replied Darius.

'Allah will forgive you and embrace you into the faith when he receives you,' pronounced Malik. 'He understands why a wolf might need to wear a sheep's fleece. Can I promise you seventy-two virgins in the paradise that will one day await you?'

'Such virgins are not mentioned in the Quran, Malik, that much I do remember. The virgins are a false promise made by those of the Muslim faith who should know better. It is a promise made to attract those easily fed by such false pretences.'

'A pity,' chuckled Malik. 'But I live in hope.'

'Allah is no more than a good politician and an adventurous businessman,' suggested Darius.

'Okay, perhaps it is best we know but then it will not spoil our business,' suggested Malik

'Which is?' enquired Darius.

'We have been sold down the river by the politicians of the west,' continued Malik. 'They promise us a homeland but squeeze us ever closer to Islamic State and anyone they can label us with as their enemy. Our friends, the Greeks, have even found it harder to help us because they are now a poor country reliant on European Union bailouts. In times gone by, their military helped to train us but not anymore.'

'Malik!' yelled a voice. 'Malik, it is time. Two minutes!'

A bell rang loud and clear and could be heard throughout the village.

The guards at the pass hid their weapons and clung to the ground using the uneven terrain to hide. People scurried to nearby caves hewn from the mountainside. Everything went quiet as Malik ushered Darius beneath a rocky ledge that jutted out above the drugs laboratory.

'What is it?' asked Darius. 'I can't see anyone.'

'The drones,' replied Malik. 'They send a drone on the same day of every week. It flies overhead and we hide so that they cannot see how the village has changed over the years.'

'But the school?' queried Darius.

'They will see the school and a couple of dwellings where a handful of our people live but they will not see the drugs laboratory or the caves where most of our people are situated.'

'The caves!' remarked Darius.

'Yes, the caves,' repeated Malik. 'When they destroyed the village years ago, you were the only one left. You used the raw heroin and strychnine to good effect. You used it well and made a fortune from it, Darius. It is you that financed the new laboratory and the equipment we used to gouge out the rock so that we might live in caves and beneath the ground.'

'Yes, I did. That was a long time ago,' suggested Darius.

Quietly, a drone flew over the area, circled, and then disappeared to the south.

'Still, after all these years, they send people to bomb us,' enquired Darius.

'Not quite,' replied Malik. 'It is a surveillance drone. They fly over the mountains and take pictures. They do it on the same day of every week. When they compare the pictures, they look for changes and buildings that are new. They no longer have an interest in this valley because they do not fly jets overhead to bomb us anymore. They think we are nothing, just

172

irrelevant farmers living a frugal lifestyle in the land that time forgot.'

A bell rang again only this time it sounded six times and then fell silent.

'The all clear,' observed Malik. 'It has gone.'

There were cheers when the drone flew over. People applauded and the wine flowed once more.

'No more for me,' ordered Darius. 'Water only, please.'

Malik poured his man water and then said, 'Your mission is to visit England. There is no bounty from Hezbollah or any of our other friends like in the past. The mission is one of revenge and, if all goes well, blackmail. We want you to blackmail the British Government.'

'You make it sound so easy,' suggested Darius.

'It is,' replied Malik. 'The plans are made. People are in place. We are ready.'

'Why do such people – the Placers – not carry out these attacks?' asked Darius.

'Because often they are older than one might believe,' revealed Malik. 'Unfit and lacking in the courage needed to actually carry out the kill. They are not trained in warfare, my friend. We do not give them guns to shoot or explosives to detonate. They are taught the ways of the unseen. In the world in which they live, they move quietly in the shadows, always watching, always looking for an opportunity, seldom failing in the work that they do. It is their way, my friend. Better to know how to make a false identity and a fraudulent passport than to not take part at all. We only need to get it right once. The enemy must get it right every time and we know, as you do, they often fail.'

Darius nodded in agreement.

'Everything has been perfect so far, has it not?' enquired Malik.

Darius looked towards the eagle. It was still perched on the rock.

'I said I was finished,' remarked Darius.

'You may not come back from this one,' suggested Malik. 'Britain is an island. You'll be flying in and flying out. The only other way is by boat. It's not like Europe where you can drive or catch a train for twelve hours and never get stopped.'

'Yes, I know what you mean,' replied Darius.

'But then you may also secure our cause for generations to come,' continued Malik. 'They will write your name in books and sing songs about you. Many will die. You could make it happen for us this time. Your name will be enshrined in our history. Mothers and fathers will speak of you and tell their children your story. Such children will pass on your story for generations to come. I know you, my friend. It is deep within your soul.'

'What is?' asked Darius.

'A desire not seen before by me,' explained Malik. 'You have a need to revenge but also to inspire others to follow you. Something burns deep within your soul. You are a special kind that one seldom finds.'

'It's that bad?' enquired Darius.

'Yes! I dream of white feathers lying on the streets of London. I dream of you and a revenge fulfilled,' pronounced Malik.

Darius stepped away, turned, and replied, 'If White Eagle flies to me when I call then I will stay here with my people. If the eagle circles in the sky and flies north, then I will do as you ask.'

Snapping his fingers, Darius turned to the eagle and whistled.

There was no response other than a flutter of the wing and a turn of the eagle's head.

'And if there is no response?' queried Malik.

'He will respond,' replied Darius.

Nothing! The eagle did not move a muscle.

'Will the eagle ever fly?' asked Malik. 'Or as he determined then you will never live out your life in Kurdistan?'

The eagle stepped forward, launched itself into the sky, and flew northwards towards the Turkish border.

Moments later, Darius looked into Malik's eyes and asked, 'What do you want me to do?'

'Drink your water,' advised Malik. 'Your mission is to destroy those who turn the tap on and off.'

'I don't understand,' said Darius.

'Here are the co-ordinates,' replied Malik handing over a piece of paper.

'To the north,' replied Darius as he read the handwritten note.

Malik nodded.

'When does it begin?'

'Now, come with me,' instructed Malik. 'There is much you need to know.'

Together, the two men entered a cave hewn from the rock of the mountain where a television set was broadcasting a news channel.

'A television,' remarked Darius.

'How else do you expect us to keep up with the news?' queried Malik with a smile. 'It runs from a generator and receives a satellite signal. It's very useful for keeping contact with things going on in Europe and elsewhere.'

'I'll bet it is,' chuckled Darius. 'Come on, what is it that you want to show me?'

With a homemade brush, a man patiently swept away the leaves from beneath the flagpole. Ageing now, only a thin cruel wisp of hair crept over his head and made no pretence at shading his body from either the sun or the snow that would arrive in winter. His body was frail, under nourished, and in need of a new set of clothes that might render him some pride in his appearance.

Gripping the brush tightly with his arthritic hands, he gradually moved closer to the mouth of the cave where Malik and Darius held their talks. The guards ignored him. He was just an old man who swept all day, carried wood for the fires, and water from the stream. No one was interested in him. There were those in the village who had forgotten his name, could not recall how long he had been there, and didn't care anyway. He was just a piece of furniture that everyone looked down upon and banished from their mind.

Sweeping, brushing, ignoring those around him, the individual watched, listened, and remembered.

'This visitor has no name,' thought the old man. 'Not once did Malik call him by his name. A new man! A new drugs courier from Turkey wanting to deal. I must learn his name.'

Later that night, the man settled in his outhouse and thought of the day's events that had unfolded before him.

'Who was this man,' he wondered? 'They say he once lived here and has returned. Yet, I heard them say he was going away again. One day a man returns with an eagle but the next he marches back to who knows where? I do not understand and the narrowness of my ageing mind does not allow me to work things out. I know what I must do.'

When the night skies were dominant, the man checked his watch and approached a corner of his room. He stripped away the carpet, removed a small satellite dish and tripod, and checked his watch again.

At the right time, as arranged, the man connected the dish to a mobile phone and sent his encrypted words to an unseen satellite in the sky. The satellite captured the text and relayed it to a building in Cheltenham where it was decoded and forwarded to MI6.

In an office in MI6, in London, they knew of the man. His codename was Persian Leopard and he was an agent of Britain's Secret Intelligence Service. The old man was charged with reporting the comings and goings of those involved in life in the Quandil Mountains whether it be heroin production and distribution, or training terrorists who had sworn allegiance to the Kurdistan Worker's Party.

Two minutes later the satellite had moved out of the reception area and the signal was lost.

The old man took a match from the folds of his clothes, struck it, and lit himself a cigarette before burying his equipment in the corner of his house. He did not know when he would need it again. It would depend purely on what he learnt of his enemy in the days or weeks ahead.

As he began to relax, he removed an old photograph from his battered wallet. Frayed at the edges, the black and white image had seen better days. The old man kissed the image of his wife and daughter and returned the photograph to the folds of his wallet.

Relaxing, the man lay back and thought of what might happen tomorrow. Then he reminded himself why he was committed to sweeping, carrying water, and bringing wood. His wife and daughter were killed by a bomb that exploded in a shopping mall in Istanbul ten years earlier.

Persian Leopard – driven by revenge - stubbed out his cigarette, yawned, drew a blanket across his shoulders, and slept.

*

## Chapter Eleven

~

Tower Hamlets
London
The Next Day

Adem Sidik hauled himself out of bed, pulled on his dark blue denim jeans and trainers, and made himself a black expresso coffee, which he downed in one swoop. Stretching, he threw open the bedroom windows, took a deep breath, and decided he should have stopped in bed where it was warm.

Not used to the cold, Adem selected a roll neck sweater, a leather jacket, and a scarf from the wardrobe. He then bent down and removed a black briefcase and a maroon canvas holdall from the bottom of the wardrobe. Turning, he threw the holdall on the floor, placed the briefcase on the bed, and then dropped down onto his knees. He rummaged beneath the bed with his left hand.

Finding the pistol, Adem pulled it from its hiding place, checked it was loaded, and shoved it into his jeans belt at the small of his back.

Decoding the briefcase fastenings, Adem smoothed his fingers across the banknotes inside, closed it, and coded the lock with a new set of numbers. He then placed the briefcase inside the holdall and slung it across his shoulder. Finally, he removed several passports and credit cards from the wardrobe and flicked through them. Each one carried the forename Adem or Adam but each also boasted a different surname. Examining his credit cards confirmed that he held numerous false passports and cards. He removed a money belt from beneath a pillow on the bed, filled it with the passports and credit cards, and then added an air flight ticket from his wallet. Adem then secured the money belt around his waist, pulled his roll neck sweater down, and tidied himself in the mirror.

Checking his watch, Adem turned the door handle then stood and scanned the room. Leaving nothing behind, he vacated his room and wandered downstairs into the hotel lobby where he checked at reception for messages.

The young man behind the counter, smiled, shook his head, and engaged the next person waiting.

Moments later, Adem stepped onto the footpath outside. Casually, he looked around and checked the street as he suppressed a yawn and pretended he was not yet switched on for the day's proceedings. Yet there was nothing further from the truth when he closed the door behind him. The Collector hailed a taxi and set off for Tower Hamlets.

Fifty yards away, a rider adjusted his crash helmet, kick-started a motor bike, and followed the vehicle towards the south of the capital.

As the taxi drew up at traffic lights, Adem sneaked a view to his rear, satisfied himself that he was not being followed, and patted the money belt fastened to his body.

The motor cyclist hung back, blended into the busy London traffic, and allowed his quarry plenty of room. Negotiating the traffic lights safely, the motor cyclist resumed his surveillance.

Enjoying an uneventful journey, Adem looked for the tall buildings that signified his closeness to Canary Wharf. He didn't know the capital that well, but he knew it well enough to know that he was headed in the right direction and they would soon be there.

When the taxi reached the crossroads at Poplar, Adem reached forward, tapped the window, and instructed the driver to pull in at the post office on their nearside.

The driver nodded his understanding, negotiated the traffic lights, and cruised to a standstill outside a sub post office near the East India Dock Road.

An aircraft roared overhead on its inbound route to London's City Airport when Adem leaned forward, paid the taxi driver, and stepped from the taxi.

The taxi moved off and Adem watched the traffic pass by. There was a couple of buses, numerous cars, a van, a motor bike, and a few cyclists with their heads down racing towards the Isle of Dogs. No one stopped to look at him; nobody seemed interested in his presence on the street.

Adem turned, stared into the post office's plate glass window, and waited. Seeking reassurance, he eased his torso slightly and felt the pistol firm against the small of his back. Then he slid his hand to his stomach and felt the documents in his money belt. Vulnerable and alone, Adem glanced to left and right, and tightened his grip on the holdall.

Nervous now, Adem felt a bead of sweat trickle down his neck and slip down to his shoulder blade. It's not that he feared the police or the British authorities. It was the quarter of a million pounds in the briefcase that worried him.

'You made it then?' sounded a voice.

Swivelling around, Adem saw his friend, Baris, and replied, 'I'm a few minutes late, sorry.'

'No problem,' replied Baris. 'You have the cash?'

'Yes,' replied Adem.

'And protection?'

'Of course,' revealed Adem. 'I'm carrying. Where is Hakan?'

'I'm here,' announced Hakan approaching from behind Baris. 'I haven't forgotten anything and we know what to do if they try to rip us off. We are ready, yes?'

Adem looked at his friends carefully, smiled, and said, 'Yes, we are ready. I'm not expecting problems. My friend will not let me down. Come on, let's go.'

The three Turks set off down the street, reached a junction, and turned left before crossing the road towards a housing estate.

All three men wore training shoes, denim jeans, sweaters, and dark coloured leather jackets of varying lengths. They walked purposefully, penetrated the estate, and approached the Bull and Unicorn public house.

A motor cyclist switched his engine off, ditched his crash helmet on the rider's seat, and followed cautiously from a safe distance.

'They are inside,' stated Adem.

'Good!' replied Hakan feeling the butt of his handgun. 'Let's do it.'

'No! Wait!' suggested Baris. 'I will go in first and return shortly. Give me ten minutes to see if it is too dangerous. Okay?'

Adem and Hakan glanced at each other but Baris continued with, 'It is what we agreed.'

'Okay,' the men nodded.

'Be quick,' suggested Adem. 'This bag is rubbing my shoulders and making me sore.'

'Wuss!' quipped Baris. 'Wait here.'

The tallest of the three, Baris, made his way towards the front door.

Following Adem had changed into a bit of a challenge for Mehmet, their pursuer. Reading the situation, he decided they were making for the Bull and Unicorn public house. Running now, Mehmet gained ground, sneaked into a telephone kiosk, and dialled a number.

The number rang out as Mehmet kept his eyes on the three Turks, the entrance to the Bull and Unicorn public house, and a row of Harley Davidson motor bikes parked outside the premises.

In the office of the Special Crime unit, a red phone rang and was immediately answered by Terry Anwhari.

Seconds later, two more incoming calls to the same number were relayed by an automatic switching system to neighbouring phones on the same desk.

'The phones are red hot this morning, Anthea,' remarked Boyd.

'Well, you said you wanted them to turn over every snout, grass, informant and source that they'd ever used and that's the result. Even the East End gangs and the Wild West Enders are in on this one. Someone mentioned money and this is the result. We've spooked every crook and crony in London. They're crawling all over the place for us.'

'We needed to start somewhere,' suggested Boyd.

Commander Maxwell, dropped two paracetamols into his mouth, took a slug of water, and replied, 'The East End, oh yes Remind me never to go to my old haunts again. I've a throat like sandpaper and a brass band playing somewhere inside my skull.'

'Too much to drink, sir?' enquired Boyd mischievously.

'Of course, not,' snapped the Commander before he chuckled and added, 'Well, never again. That's all I can say, Boyd. Never again!'

'Guvnor!' yelled Terry covering the mouthpiece with his hand. 'There's a big supply of heroin just hit the town and it's up for sale to the highest bidder.'

'How much?' queried Boyd.

'Ten kilos!'

'Fact or rumour?' enquired Boyd.

'Rumour so far but there's a meet in a pub in the East End going down today,' explained Terry. 'That's all the man knows.'

'You're joking,' suggested Boyd. 'In a pub?'

'Well, they have to do it somewhere, I suppose,' suggested the Sergeant.

'Line two, Terry,' snapped Bannerman. 'Someone asking for you personally.'

Terry thanked the first caller, replaced the phone, and diverted his attention to the second call.

'Who is it?' asked Boyd.

'Patient Lamb!' replied Terry covering the mouthpiece.

'At last,' nodded Boyd.

'Pick up,' suggested Terry.

Signalling a thumbs-up, Boyd snatched a nearby phone, punched a button, and listened in for a while.

'Okay,' nodded Boyd to Terry. 'Get as much as you can, Terry. Tell him to stay in that phone box until we get there.'

Stepping towards a map on the wall, Boyd said, 'Gather around, chaps. The first call was from an old informant responding to our trawl last night. It's all a bit hazy and nothing is precise. The second call was from Patient Lamb and he's delivered what may be a big heroin deal in Tower Hamlets. It's just about to go down.'

'Whereabouts?' enquired the Commander.

'The Bull and Unicorn just off the East India Road,' revealed Boyd.

Terry Anwhari nodded, exchanged confirmatory glances with Boyd, and began scribbling notes.

Shaking his head, Boyd turned to the Commander and said, 'Yes or no?'

'Cover it, Boyd,' ordered Commander Maxwell.

'Convince me why I should drop one case for the other,' argued Boyd. 'Yes, I know it's one of our sources but it's drugs not terrorism. I can pass it to Drugs and Organised Crime along the corridor and forget it.'

'No!' ordered the Commander. 'Firstly, ten kilos of heroin on the streets of London have a street value of between six hundred thousand and a million pounds. Major crime alert! It's what this unit does. Secondly, I didn't get a touch in the East End last night but someone has. We've got to go with it, William.'

'Where were you last night, sir?' asked Boyd.

'Tower Hamlets,' replied the Commander.

Turning to Terry, Boyd asked, 'Whereabouts is the meet again?'

'The Bull and Unicorn, Tower Hamlets,' revealed Terry covering the mouthpiece.

'Okay, let's do it,' ordered Boyd. 'Everything! Find out everything you can from Patient Lamb before you put that phone down.'

'Done!' snapped Terry as he returned to his phone call.

'Interesting, William,' remarked Commander Maxwell. 'How did our source in the Turkish field get involved in the drugs world?'

'I think we're about to find out, sir,' replied Boyd.

'Get a move on, Chief Inspector,' smiled the Commander. 'Draw firearms. Standard operational briefing applies. I'll organise a search warrant for you.'

Fifteen minutes later, the team were travelling at high speed to Tower Hamlets.

A display of blue lights flashed from the squad car roofs as the convoy advanced and Boyd radioed, 'Central Control, this is Red One Alpha responding to the Bull and Unicorn, Tower Hamlets on an intelligence led operation. Estimated time of arrival five minutes. Request Armed Response and Territorial Support to travel and await further instructions.'

'Central Control, all received. Advise caution in that case.'

'Red Alpha One received,' replied Boyd. 'Advising caution.'

'I have that,' came the reply.

'You're going too fast. Slow down, Boyd,' delivered Anthea.

'That makes a change,' replied Boyd. 'But then you usually drive. Hang on tight, Anthea.'

Boyd manoeuvred through another set of red traffic lights as Central Control passed on his message and organised an armed response from the uniform section to position themselves in the area on standby.

The area they drove towards included much of the redeveloped Docklands region of London, including West India Docks and Canary Wharf. Many of the tallest buildings in London occupy the centre of the Isle of Dogs in a borough, which has a population of more than a quarter of a million people. The area has one of the highest ethnic minority populations in the country with an established British Bangladesh community. Yet much of the area has retained its traditional East End with its Brick Lane restaurants, street market, and varied shops of all sizes.

As they turned into a street leading to the Bull and Unicorn, Boyd killed the flashing lights and stopped when a uniformed police sergeant standing in the centre of the highway waved him in.

'Are you lot the Special Crime Unit?' asked the sergeant.

'That's us,' replied Boyd. 'And you are?'

'Sergeant Ryan! This is my patch. We got your message. I'm with Armed Response and Territorial Support. I have four vehicles situated about half a mile from the pub. They are all static. Two men in each with standard police armoury.' In addition, I have three minibuses on route. Each one is carrying a sergeant and ten officers. This had better be good because the borough commander mobilised everyone as a result of your radio call.'

'It is much appreciated, Sergeant, thanks,' replied Boyd. 'Let's hope the guns aren't needed but it's a drugs buy apparently. A big one! You never know.'

'Our armed officers are in position,' revealed Ryan. 'This is Ripley territory and the Bull and Unicorn is their local.'

'Who are the Ripley's?' asked Boyd.

'Self-styled local hoodlums involved in drug supply in these parts,' revealed Ryan. 'I took the liberty of preparing a hand-written plan of the interior of the building. Here!'

Boyd took the piece of paper and replied, 'Excellent, thanks. You're obviously the man for the job. You know the pub. What do you suggest?'

'An entry at speed by Territorial Support led by a shield party. There are three main areas to concentrate on. The main bar, the snug at the back, and the cellar area. Old man Ripley is usually in the snug playing cards. If there's any drugs in the place they will be in the cellar or the snug under his control. I'd recommend one team to each area.'

Nodding his understanding, Boyd remarked, 'I agree. You're on the ball, Mister Ryan. Thank you.'

'If they get the chance,' suggested Ryan. 'They'll kick off big style. They can be quite violent. By the way, is that your man in the phone box over there?'

Ryan pointed to Mehmet covertly pretending to make a call from the kiosk.

'Why do you ask?' enquired Boyd.

'Because he's been in there since before we arrived, that's all,' winked the Sergeant.

'Leave it with me,' replied Boyd. 'We'll sort it.'

Ryan persuaded a sly smile and stepped away.

'Terry,' radioed Boyd.

'I see him,' replied Terry.

'All Red Alpha units, wait one,' radioed Boyd stepping out of the squad car.

Together, he and Terry made for the phone box and a very worried Patient Lamb.

'Mehmet,' began Terry. 'What do you know?'

'I can't hang about here, that's what I know,' declared Mehmet. 'I'm done for if they see me.'

'How did you get here?'

'On my cousin's motor bike,' explained Mehmet. 'He doesn't know I borrowed it and I need to get back before he realises its gone.'

'Okay, you got my message?' asked Terry.

'Yes, I've been on Adam for a while. Word in the mosque is not good.'

'How come?' asked Terry.

'No-one is talking aloud but I heard a whisper that the Collector had fallen short of his target and was in trouble.'

'Is that so?' suggested Terry.

'That's what they say but some of us don't believe that,' revealed Mehmet.

'Why?'

'People tell me he's been collecting for months. He should have hundreds of thousands by now. The man has been all over England. I think he's about to rip everyone off.'

'How is he going to do that?' enquired Terry.

'By using money he's collected to buy drugs,' explained Mehmet. 'He's been to somewhere called Glasgow, in Scotland, a place called Newcastle and all over the Midlands. And places, I've never heard of and never visited.'

'Where exactly?' probed Terry

'Sheffield, Huddersfield, Doncaster, Birmingham, Wolverhampton, Bradford, places like that,' replied Mehmet. 'I wrote them all down for you. That way I remembered the names. Oh, yeah, and somewhere called

Hull! I don't know where that is but I heard he went there.'

'Who is he buying the drugs from?' asked Boyd.

'The biggest biker gang in East London: the Ripley bothers,' indicated Mehmet. 'Joe Ripley is the boss. He runs the pub. Big guy, be careful. They've been dabbling in drugs for years now.'

'Have they indeed?' stated Boyd. 'Interesting, and that's their bikes parked outside the pub?'

'Yeah, all brand new sparkling Harley Davidsons. They were bought with drug money and violence,' suggested Mehmet.

'Anything else?' asked Terry.

'There's two men from the mosque with him inside the pub. Adam is carrying a big holdall and it looks heavy. I'd say they were all tooled up just in case,' announced Mehmet. 'One more thing, Adam's girlfriend is Ripley's daughter. Black haired girl, biker like her dad, and a stunner. She's the connection.'

'You mean she set the buy up?' asked Terry.

'I think so,' replied Mehmet. 'I don't know for sure. I'm just guessing because I can't think of any other way Adam would get connected to these druggies.'

'Why here?' asked Boyd. 'Of all the places in London, why here?'

'It's mainly Bangladeshi,' clarified Mehmet. 'No Turkish population to speak of. Lots of English obviously but not a mosque to be seen for miles. Adam has no Turks to spoil his little plan. Just the Canary Wharf and those huge skyscraper things. But the houses and small businesses are Bangladeshi. Fancy a curry?'

'Maybe later,' quipped Boyd.

Three minibuses arrived at the scene, discharged three sergeants and thirty officers, and waited for instructions from Ryan and Boyd.

Speaking to the sergeants, Boyd outlined the intelligence and then declared, 'I want unarmed Territorial Support to go in first, at speed, and secure every room as seen on this plan from

Sergeant Ryan. I'm sorry it's not drawn to scale but this is a fast mover of an operation. Shield parties to lead and protect backed up by Territorial Support officers to secure and hold every room. Armed officers will be right behind you in case they are needed. Speed is the key to success here. Are you happy with that?'

'It's what we train for,' replied Ryan. 'We'll split into three teams. Leave it to us. We'll cascade the briefing down to the troops and be ready to go in five minutes.'

'Excellent, good luck,' remarked Boyd.

The rear door of a minibus opened and reinforced plastic riot shields were handed out to the officers. Gloves and protective gear was donned as the officers were given their tasks.

Bannerman arrived with a warrant, got out of his squad car, took a megaphone from the boot, and made his way towards Boyd and the front of the convoy.

Standing six feet seven inches tall, Bannerman dominated the area as he approached.

'Who owns these?' asked Bannerman.

'Whoever is in the pub,' replied Boyd.

'I see,' nodded Bannerman. 'By the way, I brought this.' Revealing the megaphone, he said, 'Just to talk to people.'

'Okay, let's do it,' replied Boyd engaging his throat mic and radioing, 'Red Alpha One to Central Control. Move Armed Response to scene and instruct them to prepare. We're going in soon.'

'I have that,' came the reply.

'Cover up,' ordered Boyd.

Within minutes, the unit had donned bulletproof clothing and the Armed Response officers had moved their vehicles much closer to the pub.

'Red Alpha One,' radioed Boyd. 'There are two entrances, front and rear. Terry, take your line to the rear. We'll take the front.'

'I have that,' came the reply.

Sergeant Ryan acknowledged Boyd and said, 'We are all ready to deploy. Rapid entry and no hanging about, okay?'

'Excellent,' replied Boyd.

Ryan engaged his throat mic and radioed, 'I have control. Phase Two, execute.'

Four car boots were opened and protective clothing put on. A shotgun was selected, then a backup gun for an ankle holster. There was a quiet 'click' when the boots came down and a driver's door was opened. An ignition fired and the cars moved closer.

The adrenalin rushed down the veins when a hand tightened around a pistol butt, a finger slid along a trigger guard, and a female torso moved to accommodate uncomfortable body armour.

'Safety catches off,' instructed Boyd.

Two unmarked squad cars cruised towards the back door of the pub at the same time as three minibuses took closer order on the building.

Anthea moved towards the front door. Janice smoothed the barrel of her shotgun. Martin's fingers tingled. Terry Anwhari began to wonder if Patient Lamb could be trusted.

'Guvnor!' remarked Terry Anwhari. 'I sure hope we're not being set up.'

'Put it this way,' replied Boyd. 'We're about to find out. Come on!'

Bannerman walked casually towards the pub, kicked the first Harley Davidson over, and then watched it fall against the next one, and the next one. The domino effect resulted in a pile of very expensive motor bikes lying on their sides on the Bull and Unicorn car park.

Turning to Boyd, Bannerman declared, 'We're ready now! No-one is leaving!'

Boyd grimaced, and then radioed, 'Red Alpha One, I have control... Stand by all units. Stand by... Stand by...'

The front door of the pub opened and a tall man dressed in oily denims with a long scruffy beard appeared on the front step.

'The bikes!' he screamed. 'What happened to the bloody bikes?'

'Strike! Strike! Strike!' radioed Boyd.

On the first call of Strike, the party at the rear burst through the door. On the second call of Strike, the front party complimented their colleagues and dominated the building. By the time Boyd had called the third Strike, Bannerman had placed his hand on the biker's chest and pushed him back into the pub. Simultaneously, three shield teams, their uniformed support, and armed back-up, made their way into the building at a ferocious speed, dominating the ground, and taking the initiative.

'Police! Armed police,' they yelled. 'Freeze!'

A gang of bikers sat in one corner of the room next to the snug. By the time they realised what was happening, they were looking down both barrels of Janice's shotgun.

'Twitch,' she said. 'Go on, twitch. It will be the last twitch you ever make. Make it a good one, why don't you?'

A biker made to stand up and suddenly felt the barrel of a shotgun thrust into his stomach.

'Down, boy,' ordered Janice quietly. 'Nice and easy. Now put your hands on the table in front of you.'

No one moved.

'Now!' yelled Janice at the top of her voice. 'Do I make myself clear?'

At the front door, Bannerman found an angry biker complaining about damaged motor bikes parked outside the pub.

'Wind!' remarked Bannerman. 'Must have been the wind. Now sit yourself down and rest a while.'

'Like hell, I will,' replied the biker.

Again, Bannerman placed his hand on the biker's chest. This time he hurled the man backwards into the wall and said, 'Sit! It means sit! Understand!'

With the wind knocked out of him, the biker dropped his head onto his chest and waited.

A dark-haired girl dressed in a black leather waistcoat, tight fitting sweater and jeans, and sporting a whip, stepped backwards into the snug.

Seconds later, a team of officers rushed into the snug bearing shields and dominating the ground.

'Freeze!' they shouted. 'No-one move.'

A group of men sat at a table in the snug. They had no time to react when armed officers appeared with the shield party and again ordered, 'Freeze! Remain exactly where you are.'

Lifting the megaphone, Bannerman announced, 'We are the police. We are armed. This is a raid. We have a search warrant. Remain exactly where you are. Do not move and put your hands on the table in front of you.'

From the other end of the room, a huge man wearing a denim waistcoat and a pair of jeans stood up and shouted, 'You gotta be joking, Mister. You gonna shoot me for standing up?'

'No, he won't,' remarked Anthea pointing her handgun an inch from the man's temple. 'But I will.' The pistol barrel brushed the man's ear as she held it close and menaced him with, 'You'd best sit down and do as you're told. I get nervous at times.'

The man dropped onto the nearest seat.

'Where's the licensee?' asked Boyd.

Someone nodded towards the snug and Boyd stepped towards the door saying, 'Search the place!'

Boyd burst through the lounge door to find three men in biker gear sat a table with three men of Asian appearance. They were surrounded by officers carrying shields whilst armed officers covered their every move.

The table was littered with beer bottles and a half-filled ashtray.

'Which one of you is the licensee?' demanded Boyd un-holstering his gun.

No one replied.

Unperturbed, Boyd continued with, 'No matter! I have a warrant to search these premises for drugs.'

One of the bikers shuffled his feet and was quickly met with an icy glare from Boyd who barked, 'We are all armed. Don't push your luck today, gents. Hands on the table now!'

Boyd motioned with his arms and the barrel of his gun bobbed up and down a little as he moved closer to the men.

'Table!' barked Boyd. 'Now! Spread those fingers!'

Pure speed had won the day allowing Boyd and his team to dominate proceedings.

'Where's the drugs?' enquired Boyd.

Greeted with silence, Boyd turned to Terry and Martin and ordered, 'Do a quick search of the room. I'm feeling lucky.'

'Let me see the warrant,' growled an older man.

'And you are?' asked Boyd.

'Joe Riley! You know who I am,' came the reply.

'I do now,' revealed Boyd. 'We've reason to believe there are illegal drugs on the premises. We will be here as long as it takes to find those drugs. Unless, of course, you want to help us.'

'Drugs? Nothing to do with us,' growled Riley. 'People have been accusing us for years but it's just our enemies. People get jealous when you run a good business, you know.'

'You have enemies? You should make friends more,' suggested Boyd.

Scanning the faces of the Asian contingent, Boyd recognised Adem and proposed, 'You three seem to be out of your jurisdiction, gentlemen. Tell me you're here to either buy a Harley Davidson or a sack full of drugs?'

Adem's eyes dropped to the floor. His colleagues looked away.

'Thought so,' observed Boyd.

In the adjoining bar a ginger-haired biker screamed, 'I'm out of here!'

Within seconds, pandemonium broke out when half a dozen well built, broad-shouldered, bikers suddenly exploded in anger.

Ginger made a bolt for the door, shoved a uniform officer out of the way, and then kicked out at Bannerman. It was as if someone had lit the blue touch paper on a firework. Within seconds, more individuals made a bolt for the door.

Another uniformed officer fell to the ground and was trampled in the process. An unarmed greasy biker who was overweight, grubby, and just wanting to get out of the pub, made a bolt for the exit.

Anthea stepped back. Balancing herself perfectly, she kicked Ginger in the groin, heard him scream in pain, and then stepped backwards again to fend off the next challenge.

An empty beer bottle sailed through the air and smashed against the wall behind Anthea. She ducked the first one but didn't see the second bottle smash into her forehead when she bobbed back up to engage the would-be escapees.

She collapsed to the floor.

The ginger-haired, self-styled, leader of the pack regained his feet and dived into Janice pushing her towards the front door. Wrestling her all the way, he used his weight to overpower the Scottish detective who eventually rolled free and rammed the buttstock of her shotgun into his face.

A shower of blood gushed from Ginger's nose like an overeager waterfall and covered Janice's face and upper body.

Meanwhile, at the front door, a wild kick displaced Bannerman's megaphone. When it rolled uncontrollably across the floor, someone deliberately stood on it and rendered it unusable.

Angry now, Bannerman locked horns with the two nearest bikers and smashed their heads together.

In the snug, and to the surprise of Boyd, a door to a lady's toilet opened and a female in her late twenties appeared. With long flowing jet-black hair and a stunning figure, she stepped forward. Her skin-tight jumper under a leather denim waistcoat were complimented only by her even tighter jeans.

Boyd glanced towards the door, saw the woman, and felt the end of her whip when she cracked it from twenty yards away.

'Arghh!' he screamed.

Boyd recoiled, clutched his shoulder, and threw himself under a table as she moved forward thrashing the air in front of her with a succession of 'cracks'.

Rolling clear, Boyd was up on his feet again pointing his gun at those around the table.

Moments later, the shield party smothered Miss Whiplash, disarmed her, and forced her back into the wall.

In the main bar, another officer keeled over from the weight of two men trying to force their way passed him.

Sergeant Ryan withdrew his Taser – a conducted electric weapon – and discharged an electric shot into his nearest enemy. The biker's body stiffened in resistance, buckled, and pirouetted in a bizarre fashion, before falling to the ground out of the game.

Anthea murmured, shook her head, and began to come around.

A terrific explosion occurred when Janice pulled both triggers and two shotgun cartridges blasted into the pub ceiling.

'Enough!' she yelled.

Janice broke her shotgun, reloaded, and fired again.

A ton of plaster and light fittings crashed to the floor at the same time as reinforcements burst in through the front door.

'At scene. Shots fired!' bellowed a voice into a radio. 'Shots fired! Engaging!'

In the snug, Adem's hand went to the small of his back.

Boyd spun quickly to the table and shouted, 'Freeze! Don't get any ideas. I'm likely to pull this trigger any second now.'

The sound of sirens squealing from outside greeted Boyd's ears when he backed into the main bar, and shouted, 'Enough! That's it! Enough!'

As fresh officers bounded into the pub, sheer weight of numbers overwhelmed the biker gang and restored order.

Blood!

Blood oozed from Anthea's forehead.

Boyd bled from a gash on his shoulder, which had been caused by the whip slashing both his jacket and shirt.

More blood!

Terry and Martin both looked at each other, and then looked at a deep red pool forming on the floor in front of them. The whip had cut them both.

'Ambulances on their way,' snapped Bannerman from the door. 'Need a hand?'

'Please,' remarked Boyd.

Sergeant Ryan appeared at the door and said, 'Will I do?'

'You certainly will,' replied Boyd. 'Can you cover this lot until we get organised?'

'Of course,' snapped Ryan. 'Hands! Keep them exactly on the table!'

Ryan nodded at his colleagues and released a couple of officers who immediately turned their attention to the main bar.

'Is Anthea okay?' enquired Boyd as he relaxed his posture.

'Just groggy, that's all,' revealed Bannerman.

'Okay,' nodded Boyd. 'We need to talk to our friends here, but I'm not quite sure that friends is the right word to use.'

Retreating from the gathering, Bannerman quipped, 'Friends, Boyd? We could have a whip-round for the damage. Janice has blasted the roof to kingdom come.'

'Whip round! Later, Mister Bannerman. Much later!'

The door closed on the small group as Boyd strolled around the table with Ryan in support. Easing his shoulder slightly, Boyd then grasped the woman and sat her down on a seat at the table.

'Now then,' remarked Boyd coiling the woman's whip. 'What were you doing in the ladies?'

She shuffled uncomfortably.

'Terry, Martin!' quipped Boyd.

The woman did not reply but as Terry took closer order to the table, Martin forced his way past and kicked down the toilet door.

197

Joe Riley tried to stand up but Terry weighed down on his shoulder and offered, 'Listen to what my guvnor has to say, Mister Riley. It will do you good.'

'Yes, Mister Riley,' suggested Boyd. 'Hardly a wonderful welcome to your illustrious premises but we will find what we came for. I take it you all know each other?'

A silent response caused Boyd to continue with, 'Of course you do. You are all so happy sitting here in the back room, the adjoining lounge, the snug – what do you call it?'

Joe glanced at Boyd and held his stare.

'It doesn't really matter what you call it, Mister Riley. I take it these two are your sons and the young woman with the whip is your daughter?'

Joe nodded in agreement. The woman spat on the floor.

'Charming,' remarked Boyd.

Engaging his throat mic, Boyd radioed, 'Janice, come through please.'

Martin reappeared lugging a briefcase and disclosed, 'I found this half way out of the window. Another couple of inches and it would have been in the back yard.'

Turning to the woman, Martin asked, 'What was the matter, couldn't you get it through the gap?'

The woman turned away as Janice entered the room.

Shouldering her shotgun, Janice approached the party and nodded at Boyd.

'Open it,' ordered Boyd. 'Let's see what all the fuss is about.'

Heaving the briefcase onto the table, Martin flipped the lid to reveal a stash of neatly stacked banknotes.

'Wow!' remarked Martin. 'How much is there, guvnor?'

'We'll have it examined for fingerprints and DNA first, I think,' replied Boyd. 'Then we'll count it.'

'Okay, I'll bag it and tag it for evidence,' revealed Martin.

'We've got the money,' declared Boyd as he feasted his eyes on the find. 'Now where are the drugs?'

Silence was met by Boyd who ordered, 'Search them!'

Terry walked around the table, paused where Adem sat, and said, 'Stand up, young man.'

Reluctantly, Adem placed his hands on the table and pushed himself up to reveal a maroon canvas holdall.

Ignoring the holdall for a moment, Terry began padding Adem down and soon felt a couple of bulges around his waist. Releasing Adem's sweater, the detective sergeant removed a loaded gun from Adem's belt, and a money belt wrapped around his stomach.

Terry broke the gun as he said, 'What have we got here then?'

There was no reply as Sergeant Ryan took possession of the weapon and shoved it into an evidence bag.

As Ryan covered the gathering, Terry and Martin padded down the others. Moments later, two flick knives, a locking knife, and another pistol – taken from Joe Riley – lay on the table.

'Your gun?' probed Boyd when he looked into Joe's eyes.

Joe nodded but declined a proper answer.

'And typical biker gear?' remarked Boyd as his hand hovered the knives. 'Offensive weapons and loaded firearms,' he continued. 'The drugs? Are they in the bag? Shall we take a look?'

Terry hauled the canvas bag onto the table beside the briefcase.

Boyd nodded and Terry unfastened the bag to reveal blocks of a white-grey substance individually packed inside cling film material. The bag was lined from top to bottom.

'Heroin!' declared Boyd. 'What a surprise,' remarked Boyd. 'One briefcase full of money and one holdall packed with drugs. What happens next?'

'I've done nothing wrong,' argued Adem. 'And I've nothing to say.'

'This one, I don't trust,' remarked Boyd to the amusement of Terry and Martin standing nearby.

'What's this?' probed Terry pointing to the money belt on the table.

'Nothing!' replied Adem. 'Just a private money belt, that's all.'

'What's your name?' asked Boyd as he watched Terry open the money belt.

'No reply! I have no name.'

'But plenty of passports, credit cards, and some travel tickets,' suggested Terry as he separated his findings from the money belt.

'Where to?' enquired Boyd.

'A train ticket for Heathrow and an air ticket for Panama,' replied Terry.

'Panama!' exclaimed Hakan. 'You never said…'

'Didn't he?' remarked Boyd. 'A one-way flight ticket to Panama, gents, and he didn't tell you. Tut-tut!'

Hakan's eyes bore into Adem.

Okay!' replied Boyd. 'We can do this here or at the nick. I don't care.'

'Are you deaf? I've nothing to say,' repeated Adem.

Boyd turned to Adem and revealed, 'Actually, we know who you are. To most of your friends you're Adam but your real name is Adem, isn't it?'

Adem looked Boyd in the eye but did not respond.

'You are Adem Sidik and we've been following you.'

Adem's mouth dropped slightly and he took a step back.

'You've been seen collecting money from various locations for the PKK – the Kurdistan Worker's Party – but then you know what the PKK is, Adem, and so do I,' revealed Boyd.

'You'll need to prove it,' snapped Adem.

'Oh, I don't need to say anything else, Adem. Other than two things! We have you on video and, if you need to be reminded, do you remember this lady?' Boyd indicated Janice and continued, 'A restaurant wasn't it, Janice?'

The Scot nodded, walked straight up to Adem, pushed a glass from the bar into his chest, and said, 'Och aye! Adem remembers me, don't you, Adem? You remember the drunken Scottish woman in the restaurant. I mean we all know what you've been doing. There's no way out for you, bonny lad!'

'You are a Collector,' stated Boyd. 'And we know exactly what that means as far as your friends back home are concerned. You collect money from your friends and contacts and send it back to Turkey to fund terrorism.'

Speechless, Adem immediately recognised Janice. He rocked slightly on his heels and fought for a reply that wasn't there.

Adem's lips trembled when he managed to ask, 'What does this mean?'

'It means you are in trouble,' advised Boyd.

Boyd's eyes scanned the contents of the holdall once more and said, 'Big trouble! Now you're all in big trouble! This is what your little meeting is all about, isn't it?'

They remained silent until Boyd revealed, 'We'll take your fingerprints and compare it with prints on the bag, the briefcase, and the packets of heroin. Whose do you think we'll find?'

Walking between the suspects, Boyd probed with his questions asking, 'Which one of you, or all of you? Does it really matter, I ask myself? You're all technically in possession of the heroin and the money that has funded the buy anyway. Not to mention loaded guns and knives.'

The group exchanged glances but no one spoke.

'Five, ten, fifteen, twenty!' mentioned Boyd. 'Am I practising my five times table or trying to work out how long you'll get for guns, knives, drugs – and oh, yes – money laundering somewhere along the line.'

Again, there was a shuffle of feet. Only Joe Riley managed to keep a solid face. It was like granite and showed no emotion.

'From here on in it's all about how deep you are all personally involved and how much stir you will get because of it,' revealed Boyd. 'Anyone had a long sentence before?'

One or two glances were exchanged but no-one wanted to talk to Boyd. His was the only voice audible.

'I thought not,' remarked Boyd. 'I'd say it's not very pleasant living in prison. No motor bikes in there. Nothing to get excited about. No beer either, and a few other things I can think of.'

'I want a solicitor,' demanded Joe Riley.

'Of course you do,' replied Boyd. 'And you shall have one. There's no need for anything else to be said, is there?'

Joe Riley's mind worked overtime before he asked, 'I want a deal. I don't want a solicitor anymore. A solicitor won't get me the type of deal I need. Can we do a deal?'

Pausing mid step, Boyd said, 'Did someone say something?'

'I did,' replied Joe. 'These two are my sons and Miss Whiplash over there is my daughter, Roxy.'

'Cool!' replied Boyd. 'Real cool. You've found a voice at last.'

'Will you do a deal?' enquired Joe.

The table erupted in a show of anger when the two sons leaned across and shouted, 'No, Dad! Say nothing!'

'I'm listening,' disclosed Boyd as he signalled the two brothers to quieten down. 'What have you got that I might be interested in, Joe?'

'Shut up, boys,' remarked Joe. 'I'll take this one on my own if I must. It's like this Roxy is my daughter.'

Turning to the raven-haired beauty with the whip, Boyd asked, 'You mean, Miss Whiplash, I presume.'

'Yeah,' replied Joe. 'She's Adam's girlfriend.'

Boyd's eyebrows shot up when he heard the news.

Considering Joe's remark for a moment, Boyd replied, 'You call him Adam but his real name is Adem. Agreed?'

'That's right.'

'Is she really his girlfriend? Now that explains why three Turks sit down at a table with three bikers and a woman cracking a whip.'

Nodding in agreement, Joe continued, 'About a month ago, Adam asked me to put together a heroin deal. He told me he had a million pounds.'

'And did you?' enquired Boyd pointing at the heroin in the maroon bag

'Yes, it wasn't a problem.'

'Presumably, this is the heroin,' remarked Boyd.

'Yes!'

'With your fingerprints on the packaging and your DNA all over the place?' suggested Boyd.

'Maybe, maybe not,' admitted Joe. 'But I'm not trusting those three to tell the truth. I'll turn Queen's evidence on them.'

'Queen's evidence!' exclaimed Boyd. 'It's a long time since I heard that one but if you know what it means then I reckon you've probably got a criminal record. Am I right, Joe?'

'I've done stir for drugs, assault, robbery, and stuff like that.'

'It sounds like the next sentence might be a long one for a man of your age,' hinted Boyd.

'Yeah! I worked that one out all by myself. Are you in the mood for dealing, Mister Boyd?' enquired Joe. 'Queen's evidence in return for a very short sentence?'

'How much cash is in the briefcase?' probed Boyd.

'A quarter of a million,' replied Joe. 'It's been counted.'

Boyd strolled around the table looking at the display of guns, knives, drugs and money before he explained, 'I might be able to help you there, Joe. It's not actually my decision. Only the Attorney General can grant you full immunity from prosecution if he's happy with things. He might not be. At this stage, I don't know. But I can tell you that ordinarily you'd be charged with the offences the same as everyone else. Then you'll need to plead guilty and get your brief to argue for a reduction in sentence. That's the law. It's not opinion or false promises. It's the law.'

'I know the score,' replied Joe. 'It's the supergrass thing. Right?'

'Something like that,' admitted Boyd. 'But you've a long way to go yet, Joe. It's a nice display on the table. Every article is a criminal charge and the more we put together the more time you'll serve. Let's face it, you're all bang to rights. There's no walking away from this one.'

Drumming his fingers on the table, Joe leaned back, and then looked at his sons and daughter before admitting, 'I put a million quid's worth of gear up for Adam, or Adem as he calls himself. That's the street value of the heroin you can see once it's cut and made into wraps. One million! Where do you think he got the money from, Mister Boyd?'

'I can guess but I'd rather you told me,' intimated Boyd.

Hakan leaned forward and threatened Joe with, 'My people will hunt you down and kill you wherever you are, you fool. Our organisation is far bigger than you would ever imagine.'

'Which organisation would that be?' probed Boyd.

'You know which organisation,' seethed Hakan.

'And you're a member of it by the sound of that reply,' voiced Boyd.

Roxy Riley swung her hair across her shoulders and shouted, 'It's not like that. Adem doesn't kill people.'

'No, he only funds the purchase of the bullets and bombs,' implied Boyd.

'Be quiet, Roxy,' ordered Joe. 'We can all walk away from this one if we're lucky. You guys too, if you listen up. Isn't that right, Mister Boyd?'

'I'm listening,' replied Boyd. 'But I'm not promising. I'm sure you wanted to count the money when you sold the drugs. I'm in the same boat. No deal until I know what's for sale.'

'You know as well as I do where the money came from,' explained Joe. 'The difference is I can prove it. Adam collected a million pounds for that organisation you're on about.'

'The PKK!' confirmed Boyd.

'You collected a million pounds for the PKK?' demanded Boyd.

'Yes!' snapped Adem. 'I kept a quarter back to buy the drugs. That way I would have quadrupled the amount I syphoned off.'

'You never had any intention of sending that money back to Turkey though, did you?' responded Boyd. 'As long as you sent something back they'd be happy because they would never actually know how much you had collected, would they?'

'No, they never knew how much I collected,' replied Adem. 'I've no-one looking over me.'

205

'You were flying to Panama on your own according to this air ticket,' proposed Boyd. 'You decided to rip the organisation off and then recruited your mates here to help you. Am I right? Of course, I'm right. You'd worked it all out. Three quarters for Turkey and a quarter for you, isn't that right?'

Adem nodded and murmured, 'I don't want to go back to Turkey.'

'Traitor!' snapped Hakan.

'You greedy fool,' endorsed Baris.

'Greedy? Traitor?' snapped Adem. 'You didn't say that when we talked about how much we could make. You were in it with me.'

'So where is the other back account, Adem? You weren't travelling to Panama without a bean in your pocket. You were offloading the drugs somewhere on route, weren't you?'

Adem nodded but looked away.

'Right!' replied Boyd. 'Terry, do the honours please and arrest these people. We've got enough to hang them all out to dry.'

'What about our deal?' begged Joe.

'To use your own words, Joe, you know the score. Come clean right across the board. You'll be interviewed later and asked to make a statement about your criminal activity. Who knows? You might just impress the Attorney General enough to give you the nod.'

Terry Anwhari moved in, cautioned the gathering, and made the arrests.

'Wait!' ventured Adem. 'We can't win. You have us cold but you are only listening to Joe. Why don't you listen to me?'

'I'd like to,' admitted Boyd. 'Right now, I see you on a terrorism charge and a few more to count. How are you going to get out of that?'

'I'll make a deal with you. If he can do it so can I,' suggested Adem.

'I'm tempted to say form a queue,' replied Boyd. 'This had better be good. For starters, Adem, I'd need to know where your bank accounts are. We both know you weren't going to Panama without a bean in your pocket. You were going to offload the drugs on route, weren't you?'

'I'll tell you everything if you'll make a deal with me.'

'That might not be enough, Adem,' revealed Boyd. 'It will take us time to find your bank account – the one we don't know about – but we will find it. As for the drugs, we have them anyway so I'm not going to lose sleep over where you thought you might offload them. You'll have to do better than that. The Attorney General pushes a hard bargain. What do you know that will make my day?'

Adem eyed Boyd for a moment.

''Nothing,' suggested Boyd. 'You've nothing to trade, have you, Adem?'

'The man is coming,' revealed Adem.

Boyd's brain switched into overdrive when he replied, 'Who? Who is coming, Adem? Where from and why?'

'Say nothing,' advised Hakan. 'You're dead meat.'

'Allah is listening,' suggested Baris. 'Are you crazy, Adem. You will sign your own death warrant.'

'So, you all know?' enquired Boyd.

Scanning the faces of Hakan and Baris, Adem turned to Boyd and said, 'No! They don't know, but I do.'

'What the hell are you talking about?' snapped Joe.

'Shush!' whispered Boyd. 'Adem wants to tell us something, don't you, Adem?'

'Death awaits the man who speaks against us,' bellowed Hakan.

'Shut up!' shouted Terry.

Adem faltered, looked uncertain, and tried to back away.

'Who is coming and why?' persevered Boyd.

'I don't know his name,' revealed Adem. 'But he's coming to destroy the water. That's all I know.'

'Who placed him here?' probed Boyd.

'What do you mean?' asked Adem.

'You're the Collector, Adem. You collect people's donations to the cause. Someone placed you here so that you could collect. They set you up with money, passports, and credit cards. If I decided to believe you then I would suggest that someone has the job of placing the man who is coming to destroy the water. Someone has a task and that means they help with somewhere to stay, money, credit cards, vehicles, whatever. Who is the Placer?'

'Later!' replied Adem glancing at this friends. 'Later when I have thought about it.'

'We need to talk,' revealed Boyd. 'At the nick. Take them, Terry. All of them.'

As the prisoners were escorted into waiting vans outside, Janice sidled up to Boyd and said, 'Good arrest! Dodgy operation when we got here though, and Anthea is helping Bannerman with the loose ends. A ton of money and easily a million pounds' worth of heroin recovered. Street value that is, and a few weapons off the streets. It must be good. But tell me, guvnor, will any of them get charged with anything?'

'Probably,' stated Boyd. 'I expect they'll all get charged but how long they will serve in prison is another story. We'll know what charges to put to them later this week, I expect. Right now, we need to get them back and talk to them at length. They're bang to rights and they know it. You see, Janice, the old man – Joe – worked out they haven't a leg to stand on. They felt safe here. Safe because it was their patch and the job has been watertight for weeks, then along comes Patient Lamb and upsets the apple cart for them. Joe offered a deal because he can see the writing on the wall. It took Adem longer but he followed suit.'

'You're not answering my question, guvnor,' persisted Janice. 'Will they walk?'

'Maybe, maybe not,' replied Boyd. 'Sometimes things are done for what they call the Greater Good, Janice. Joe will sing like a bird because he doesn't want to die of old age inside a rotten prison. Adem is different. He's holding something back because he's afraid. I want him to tell us about the PKK importing drugs through the European route and we'll check it out with Toni. What we really need to know is who is the Placer and who the hell is coming to destroy our water.'

'And how,' offered Janice.

'Absolutely, fancy half an hour on the firing range before we finish for the day?' suggested Boyd.

'Sounds good,' replied Janice. 'It will get some of that adrenaline out of my body. I'll take sniper's alley. You take the Gloch 17.'

'Okay,' replied Boyd. 'I've yet to try out the new sniper range. It's only fifty yards long they tell me.'

'Technology, guvnor,' advised Janice. 'Aim, pull the trigger, and the electronics record your score.'

'Sounds good,' replied Boyd.

'Oh, I meant to tell you,' remarked Janice. There was a call from Millwall nick. Something about a stolen motor bike found near the Bull and Unicorn. They've arrested one guy and he's asked for you.'

Boyd stopped in his tracks and declared, 'Just what I need. You go on and have a good snipe, Janice. I'll need to make that call and get someone out of trouble.'

## Chapter Twelve

~

The Pass
The Quandil Mountains
Next day

Scorching!

The old man had been up since dawn and had quietly made his way out of the village without anyone noticing. A shadow of a man, people took no interest in him anyway. Pitiful, that's how he heard them describe him.

Now the sun scorched the ground on which he stood causing him to pull a hat tight over his head to protect himself from the rays.

Rubbing his arthritic hands, he smiled to himself as he made his way through the apricot trees to climb the pass. Pausing for a moment, he distinguished the guards standing with their rifles looking north. From their rear, they could not see him. They faced the other way because they were guarding the approach to the pass from their enemies to the north.

On high ground, the guards shouldered their rifles, smoked their cigarettes, and occasionally used their binoculars to scan the path below and the skies above.

It was a boring job being a guard but also a responsible one.

The old man walked through the rows of apricots trees and crept into the thicket where the shrubbery partially hid him from view. He climbed towards the summit, parallel to the mountain path, and then dropped to his knees. He crawled to a point where two rocks jutted from the ground. They were both partially covered by vegetation but here, his fingers clawed the earth.

Retrieving a camera from the soil, the old man wiped sweat from his brow, and waited. He had chosen his hiding place well. It was close enough to the path for him to find the spot in the dark and far enough away from the path not to be easily seen during the day. Anyone leaving the village below had to use this route. The old man lifted his head slightly, heard not a sound, saw not a movement of any kind, and reconciled his patience.

The sun rose higher in the sky but by then Darius had made his promises and said his goodbyes. Only the eagle accompanied him on his journey.

Riding Xerxes out of the village, Darius dismounted by the stream which he had tried to breach as a youngster so many years earlier.

He walked along the bank for a while, found the location, and then gathered wild flowers from the vegetation nearby.

Approaching the site where his family was buried, he removed his bandanna, stroked his beard, and knelt on the ground. Placing the wildflowers beside a rock, Darius recounted the days when the Turkish Air Force had flown overhead and bombed their village. It was the day that changed his life. Things had never been the same since.

Forcing back a tear, Darius wiped the corner of his eye with the bandanna, and arranged the flowers into a position that pleased him.

'For you all,' he whispered. 'I love you.'

Xerxes neighed and bobbed his head up and down but Darius merely held up his hand to settle the horse and quieten him down. He had a way with animals that constantly amazed him.

'Devotion is a sweet tasting stream constantly flowing from the mountains into our valley below,' remarked Darius at the graveside. 'Vengeance is death to those who sour our water. I shall return, my loved ones. I shall return when I have annihilated those who spoil our stream. You are forever in my heart.'

Retreating, Darius remounted and took the path that meandered north towards the mountain pass. His mind thought back to the dam across the stream, a drugs laboratory hewn into the mountainside, a school, and the way ahead.

Clouded with memories from long ago, Darius turned his back on the graveside and stretched out his arm.

'In the Christian Bible,' he recited, 'There is a book called Isaiah. In it, it says... but those who hope in the Lord will renew their strength. They will soar on wings like eagles; they will run and not grow weary, they will walk and not be faint...'

A white eagle flew from the crags above and landed gently on his outstretched arm before hopping onto the man's shoulder.

'I am no Christian,' voiced Darius. 'But we will renew our strength and soar on wings like the eagles that we are.'

Gradually, Darius rode north towards the guards.

There was an inaudible click when Darius came into focus and the old man took a photograph.

Unaware his image had been captured by Persian Leopard, Darius persuaded Xerxes onwards and upwards.

When the sun had reached its zenith, the old man hid his camera in a threadbare shoulder bag, and moved deeper into the thicket where the shrubbery reached above his head. When he felt safe, he checked his watch. It was too late. The satellite he relied on had passed over. It would be twenty-four hours before he could send the image of the man with a white eagle to his paymasters in MI6.

The time difference between the Quandil Mountains and England was slightly over two hours. Tomorrow, at twelve noon, he would return and send his image via the satellite dish. Cheltenham would receive his message at about nine thirty in the morning.

Resting, the old man smoked a cigarette. Deep inside, he knew time was of the essence, and he was behind in the race.

In England, the Placer was shopping in a department store in the Trafford Shopping Centre, off Barton Dock Road, in Manchester.

Strolling through the aisles, the Placer came to a display and studied the promotions on offer.

Selecting a perfume bottle, the Placer felt the weight, marvelled at the thin diameter, and held it up to the light for a closer inspection. The article measured approximately an inch long.

'They are only on promotion,' revealed the shop assistant. 'They're not usually for sale but the manager decided to cut the price and see how they went.'

The Placer smiled, unscrewed the top from the tiny bottle, and took a sniff.

'Yeah that's what they are for really,' explained the shop assistant. 'They're even smaller than the miniature range but they give you a chance to take in the odour and see if you prefer one from the other.'

'All of them,' replied the Placer. 'I'll take all of them.'

'Why not try one of the larger containers? They come in various shapes and sizes, and at different prices too.'

'No, these are just what I want, thank you. They will fit nicely into my luggage when I travel. All of them please.'

Grinning, the shop assistant reached across, gathered the perfume, and gift wrapped the goods for sale.

'Cheque or card?' asked the assistant.

'Cash,' replied the Placer.

Leaving the centre, the Placer drove directly to a lock-up garage.

Taking a spanner from a tool kit, the Placer removed a set of number plates from the car boot and fixed them to another car parked in the garage. The Placer then carried a holdall from the first car and put it into the boot of the one fitted with new number plates. The car was then driven out of the garage. The other car was then driven into the garage which the Placer locked.

An engine fired and the car was driven to a multi-story car park. A ticket was bought for cash at the automated entry system and the vehicle was left, locked and secured on the third floor of the car park.

There was a slight breeze in the air when the Placer walked from the car park and pulled the anorak hood tighter across their face.

Later that day, Darius arrived in Istanbul where he checked into a hotel near the airport and relaxed in his room. He drank black coffee before standing in front of the mirror and shaving. Removing his moustache and beard, he cleaned the sink, and took a long shower before dyeing his hair a deep black.

Annoyed with himself for spilling the dye, he washed again and scrubbed his hands for a second time.

Dressing in a fine linen suit, Darius boarded an aeroplane to Athens where he took a flight to Manchester.

When he arrived at Manchester airport, Darius produced a passport and strolled through the arrivals lounge with only his hand luggage. Pausing, he stopped at a newsagent and bought an English newspaper – The Times - and a selection of ordnance survey maps. Then he checked his appearance in a mirror. Gone were the trappings of the Quandil Mountains. Clean shaven, fresh, and smartly dressed, Darius took on the appearance of a jet setting traveller. Perhaps a businessman, an executive of some kind, or a man of importance. Either way, the man who rode through the pass on a white horse was no more.

Negotiating the Manchester streets in a taxi, Darius booked into an expensive hotel and unpacked. He visited the restaurant, ate an all-day breakfast, and then retired to his room.

Unzipping a netbook bag, he removed a vehicle ignition key and a compact laptop. He opened the lid, logged on, and waited for the search engine to dominate the page. It didn't take him long to click into maps, define the route he intended to take, and check the News for any holdups.

Finishing his coffee, Darius left the hotel and walked to a nearby multi-story car park where, as planned, he located a motor car that had been placed there for his use. Using the ignition key retrieved from the netbook cover, Darius opened the car boot, donned a pair of leather gloves, and checked the contents. Satisfied, he secured the boot and set off northwards in the car.

The surface of the water resembled a dull mirror that gleamed back at Peter Foster. It was only upset when he cast his rod and watched the line ripple across the surface before lazily dropping to the deep.

'Carp!' he muttered. 'I'll get that twenty pounder if it kills me.'

'You think so?' quipped Bill, his colleague.

'I've a couple of quid says I'll get it today,' replied Peter.

'In that case, you're on,' chuckled Bill. 'You know what they say. A fool and his money are soon parted.'

'You wish,' snapped Peter. 'Here, have a sandwich.'

The two men sat by the reservoir fishing, eating sandwiches, drinking tea from flasks, and mulling over life in general.

Occasionally, one would stand up, stretch, and then cast his line across the water once more. Not the best of fishing days, but a great day to relax.

The fish didn't bite.

Yawning, Peter shrunk down into the vegetation at the side of the bank, pulled a hat over his eyes, and said, 'Wake me if you catch something, Bill.'

'Will do,' remarked the older of the two men.

Bill propped his rod onto a Y shaped fishing rod holder, sat back deep into the grassy bank, and declared, 'Maybe the fish can see us if we're too close to the water.'

'Old wives' tale,' replied Peter. 'Good idea though!'

There was barely a ripple across the water when Peter eventually dropped off and began quietly snoring.

Bill studied the surface of the reservoir, scanned the edges of the water looking for more fisherman, and realised how tranquil the area was.

Joining the Bury Old Road, Darius took the turning for Heaton Park and pulled up next to a small square building which housed the pumps for the nearby reservoir.

He got out of the vehicle and scrutinized the building. On the front wall, he looked at a carved relief which depicted the bringing of water from Haweswater, in the Lake District, to Manchester. Beneath the carving, Darius examined five plaques telling the history of the Haweswater supply and how water had been routed through a long system of aqueducts and tunnels from Cumbria to the northern edge of the city of Manchester.

The water travelled both above and below the ground.

Whilst the pump house was constructed from Yorkshire sandstone, the plaques were made from Westmorland greenstone, which had been brought from Broughton Moor, in Cumbria.

Darius studied every detail on the slate plaques and realised the water in the reservoir had travelled eighty-two miles by pipeline to Heaton Park. According to the five plaques, Manchester Water Corporation owned the reservoir. He read and understood that there were six tunnels of 2.6 metre diameter. Of the eighty-two miles, thirty-one miles of the aqueduct, in Cumbria, were big enough to drive down.

Shaking his head, Darius marvelled at the reality that five hundred and seventy million litres of water flowed from Cumbria to Manchester every day. The system had taken over twenty years to build and went into operation in the mid-fifties.

Turning, Darius opened the boot of his car, removed a bait box, and approached a gate by the side of the building. Accessing the reservoir, he made his way down to the water's edge and stood looking out across the expanse of water.

It was deserted. No boats, no people, nothing! Just an empty area used as a basin to capture water from the Lake District.

Darius knelt and removed a glass phial from his bait box. As he poured the content into the reservoir, he was about to add a second when a voice behind disturbed him with, 'What the hell are you doing?'

Surprised by the intrusion, Darius stood up and blustered, 'I'm taking water samples.'

'No, you're not,' barked Bill. 'You're putting something into the bloody water! What's going on?'

Standing to face his interloper, Darius harangued the man with, 'I told you. I'm taking samples for the scientists. Mind your own business!'

'Scientists? Which scientists would they be?' enquired Bill.

'I'm a scientist for Manchester Water Corporation,' replied Darius.

'Really! That's a lie,' snapped Bill. 'The corporation closed down years ago. Peter! Come here. This guy is...'

Before the words escaped his mouth, Darius closed with Bill. His hand stretched out like a claw, snatched his throat, and squeezed.

Bill's tongue suddenly protruded from his mouth as he fought for breath. Lifting Bill from the ground, Darius used his superior height and strength to slowly throttle him.

'What the...!' ventured Peter running up the bank towards the two men. 'Hey!'

Darius felt Bill's body go lifeless as his vice-like hand clutched the man's throat, throttling him, strangling him, denying him any oxygen.

Alive now, his mind on fire, Darius reached inside his jacket, withdrew a pistol, and shot Peter Foster twice in the forehead.

Both bullets pierced Peter's skull and he immediately fell back towards the water's edge. His life ended before his spine hit the ground.

A trickle of blood ran down Peter's head, across the bridge of his nose, and onto his face before gradually forming a pool on the ground.

Calmly replacing the pistol in its shoulder holster, Darius placed both hands on Bill's throat and finished strangling him to death.

Bill's feet kicked out, shook, and went into spasm when the last tingling throes of his life flowed through his body.

Gently, almost reverently, Darius knelt and brought Bill's body to the ground with him. He squeezed the man's throat one last time and then let go.

Nearby traffic noise alerted Darius to others in the area. With no time to lose, he abandoned his plans and checked the path from the pump house. It was still clear.

Anxious now, Darius looked to his left and right, stood up, and quickly scanned the area from which the two men had appeared. Finding fishing gear, rods, keep nets, and various belongings on the bank of the reservoir, he pushed it all into the water and watched it disappear beneath the surface. Then he returned to Bill's body, dragged it to the side of the bank, and deliberately left it close to the water. Moments later, Peter's body joined him.

Standing back, Darius looked at the two bodies side by side resting close to the water's edge. He heard a gentle splash when the keep net refused to sink and bobbed back up again to float on the surface of the water.

Gathering his bait box, Darius placed an eagle's feather upright in soft soil near a pool of blood where Peter's body had lain. Adding more feathers to the ensemble, Darius carefully placed them on the ground and made the shape of the Sun.

'Game On!' he thought before casually strolling to the roadside. 'But I did not expect this. I cannot return to the hotel. I need to be far away from Manchester.'

Unlocking his car, Darius jumped into the driver's seat, fired the engine, and headed north.

Overhead, a cloudbank dulled the sky above the Quandil Mountains but the old man knew enough about his calling to know that somewhere in the planet's atmosphere - known specifically as the thermospere - a satellite was orbiting about sixty miles above the Earth's surface. It was within range of his equipment.

Hurriedly, he unpacked his shoulder bag and set up his Special Forces issue satellite transmitter and dish. The dish measured nine inches in diameter and was connected to a lithium-ion battery that was two thousand times more capable than a normal battery. Arthritic fingers did little to help him connect the dish to a cylindrical transmitter – the size of a hand torch - that, in turn, was connected to his camera and mobile phone.

Once the image and had been transmitted from his camera to a mobile phone, the old man added a text message and then uploaded his product via the transmitter to the dish.

Persian Leopard tapped in the transmission codes and watched the digital read out.

Moments later, the uplink to the satellite above was established.

There was an almost inaudible buzzing sound for a moment when Persian Leopard realised the photograph of Darius was finally on its way to the taskmaster in the sky. On arrival at the satellite, the photograph would be sent by a downlink to a screen in Cheltenham where a desk officer would read the old man's accompanying script, understand its importance, and retransmit the content to the Secret Intelligence Service in London.

The old man closed the satellite dish, packed away his equipment, and placed it in his bag with the camera.

'You!' shouted a guard. 'What are you doing here?'

The old man was speechless. He stood up and took a pace backwards. Dominated by fear, his hands automatically reached for the bag.

Immediately, the guard levelled his rifle and took aim at the old man yelling, 'Stand still! Drop the bag! Drop the bag!'

Allowing his bag to fall to the ground, the old man stepped further back, looked around for a way out, and waited for the guard to respond.

'Back! Stand back!' shouted the guard as he bent low and retrieved the bag.

'What is this?' shouted the guard. 'What are you up to?'

'Nothing,' mumbled the old man. 'It's just nothing.'

The transmitter, mobile phone, camera, and wiring fell out of the bag when the guard shook it upside down and watched the contents fall out.

Finally, the satellite dish rolled out of the bag and clattered on top of the camera.

Stunned, the guard looked again at the old man, prodded him with his rifle, and shouted, 'Spy! You are a spy!'

Turning, the old man set off through the shrubbery striding out as fast he could. He broke into a stiff run when he tried to combat his aching joints. Ignoring the guard yelling behind him, the old man ran towards the village.

'Stop or I'll shoot!' shrieked the guard. 'Stop!'

The guard fired into the air.

Guards on the narrow mountain pass heard the shooting. Aware of the commotion, they turned, began pointing and shouting, and watched the old man struggle in his getaway.

'Stop!' shouted the guard.

The old man found a new lease of life, made the path, and sprinted for the village.

A succession of gunshots followed, struck the old man in his legs, and brought him crashing to the ground face down.

The guard raced to the old man, stood above him, and rolled him over onto his back.

In terrible pain, blood seeped from the old man's lower limbs and soiled the ground beneath him.

'Get up,' order the guard.

The old man shook his head and blurted, 'Never!'

'Why?' yelled the guard. 'Why did you spy on us?'

'Revenge!' spat the old man.

'What do you mean revenge?'

The old man forced a laugh and bit into a cyanide pill lodged in his teeth at the back of his mouth.

Cyanide exploded from the capsule, trickled down the old man's throat, and burnt his stomach.

Cutting off the oxygen supply to his body, the old man died a quick but agonising death.

Malik arrived at the scene on horseback.

Dismounting, Malik looked at the guard and demanded, 'Why did you kill him, you idiot?'

'I didn't kill him,' replied the guard. 'Look! He's taken a pill of some kind.'

Kneeling, Malik seized the old man's chin and turned it to one side slightly. The skin was still warm but a creamy white liquid dribbled from the corner of the old man's mouth.

Malik dabbed his finger in the finger in the substance, tasted it, and announced, 'Cyanide! He took a cyanide pill.'

'Look,' pointed the guard. 'He was spying on us. Look at the contents of his bag.'

Others from the village joined Malik when he and the guard gathered around the body of the deceased.

Malik studied the old man's possessions and allowed his fingers to settle over the satellite transmitter, dish, and camera.

'Yes,' stated the guard. 'He is a spy, Yes?'

'Yes,' nodded Malik reluctantly. 'Why else would he have all this equipment?'

The guard let out a distinct cry of relief and pleaded, 'I tried to stop him running away, Malik. I didn't intend to kill him.'

Grabbing the old man's mobile phone, Malik tapped the digits and examined the phone's recent history.

'He has sent messages,' stated Malik. 'And photographs but I do not recognise these numbers. They might be coded numbers of some kind but, whatever they are, they are the numbers he uses to contact people outside the village. I do not like this.'

'I am sorry, Malik,' beseeched the guard steeping back, obviously afraid of the village leader. 'I did not mean to kill him. I aimed to bring him down. That's all.'

Malik placed his hand on the guard's shoulder and asked, 'It's okay, my friend. Calm down. We are not going to punish you because you killed him. You found him spying. The rest is history. He was always going to do that if he was caught. He is lucky. If I had caught him I would have throttled him, torn him limb from limb, and then fed him to the eagles.'

Nodding, genuinely relieved, the guard relaxed.

'Thank you, Malik. May Allah bless you every minute of the day, Malik. Thank you!'

'What do they call him?' probed Malik. 'What's the old man's name? Tell me!'

The guard shook his head and replied, 'I don't know. Someone in the village must know him.'

Looking around the assembled crowd, Malik insisted, 'His name! Does anyone know his name?'

A woman raised her hand and offered, 'He lives in an old shack near the stream. I think his name is Serkan or Sergei. Not sure, maybe something like that.'

'You know him?' enquired Malik.

'Only because he sweeps up and keeps the fires going in winter,' replied the woman. 'You must have seen him wandering around gathering wood and stock piling it beside the laboratory wall.'

Concerned, Malik said, 'The laboratory! What was he doing there?'

'He told me he was putting the wood against the wall so that it would be kept dry by the heat from the building. I said hello to him most days because I thought he was your father or maybe your uncle.'

Malik's look of scorn shredded the woman of all dignity when, aggressively, he probed, 'So, you know his name?'

'Sorry,' she offered. 'I can take you to his home. I will show you where he lives but I do not have his name.'

'Yes,' stipulated Malik. 'You do that. Take us there. Guard, you will search the place. Search everywhere he was ever seen. Get me a name. A name, you understand. Someone must know him.'

'I will,' replied the guard. 'I will get you a name because I caught an American spy.'

'American?' queried Malik, slightly confused.

'The satellite dish is American, yes?' suggested the guard. 'Or is it British? Look,' pointed the guard. 'The writing on the dish is American. Or maybe it is English? There is a difference, yes?'

'It's neither,' replied Malik studying the writing on the outside of the satellite dish. 'It's Russian. This is the type of thing they issue the Russian Spetsnaz with.'

Confused, the guard offered, 'Russian? Are you sure?'

'Oh, I'm sure,' confirmed Malik. 'You can be certain of that. Our problem is that we have had a spy in our midst for some time, maybe a long time. I don't know. More importantly, we don't know who he was working for. Certainly not the Russians, that's for sure. He's working for whoever these numbers in his phone belong to. Maybe they are co-ordinates or... of course, they are satellite co-ordinates, aren't they? A satellite! Of course!'

The guard looked down at the body and said, 'A spy, though. A spy!'

'Yes,' agreed Malik looking at the sky above. 'For all we know this man might have been spying on us for months. It makes me wonder if the heroin trail from Afghanistan has been jeopardised.'

'No!' remarked the guard. 'How can that be? It is possible, yes? What about the couriers? They will no longer be safe.'

'The route and the couriers may be blown,' intimated Malik.

'No, I hope not,' ventured the guard,

Nodding his head, Malik offered, 'And now someone knows what Darius looks like and where he is from.'

'And that he has left this place,' added the guard.

'Search the village,' ordered Malik angrily. 'Turn it inside out. What else will we find? Do it. Now! All of you! Quickly!'

Gazing at the satellite dish and mobile phone, Malik pursed his lips and said, 'I thought we were safe here. I thought we were impenetrable yet someone managed to place a collector amongst us. Someone collected intelligence for our enemies and I was blind and stupid to the basics of defence. Darius, wherever you are know that they are onto you and I - my friend - I want revenge too.'

The guards moved towards the village as a Persian leopard stalked the high ground above and the body of an old man that no-one knew lay blistering in the sunshine of the Quandil Mountains.

In a restaurant in the west end of London, Toni's pager vibrated as she poured wine into Phillip's glass and then offered Boyd and Meg a top up.

'No, thanks,' replied Boyd. 'Lunch has been really lovely and we've enjoyed catching up with you both but we must be off soon.'

'Yes,' added Meg. 'I hope you can make it to Cumbria next weekend. It will be great if you can join us.'

'We're already looking forward to it,' replied Sir Phillip.

'Excuse me,' revealed Toni. 'This is important. I must make a call.'

Stepping outside, Toni rang a number from her mobile and took a message from her contact in the Secret Intelligence Service.

Returning to her guests, Toni sat down, took a gulp of wine, and announced, 'Two things! One – that was Legoland. An MI6 source in the Middle East has delivered a photograph of the man they call White Eagle into the hands of the SIS. They believe the photo was taken yesterday but we only received it today. An accompanying message states the individual is heading to the United Kingdom to destroy our water.'

A look of astonishment saturated Boyd's face before he ventured, 'Name?'

'None given,' replied Toni. 'Which usually means the source doesn't know the name.'

Boyd nodded as he considered the new intelligence.

'And secondly?' enquired Sir Phillip.

'Two bodies have been found on the banks of a reservoir in Manchester,' revealed Toni. 'One has been strangled, the other shot twice in the head at close range.'

'They can't relate to White Eagle,' suggested Boyd. 'It's merely a coincidence, surely?'

Sir Phillip's pager vibrated and he moved away to respond using his phone.

'Some white feathers have been found at the scene, Boyd,' explained Toni. 'Plus, the source information is over twenty-four hours late.'

'Why?' asked Boyd. 'Is the source unreliable?'

'No,' replied Toni. 'I wouldn't expect our friends in MI6 to tell me anything about the source but I'll guess it's a field agent at the sharp end of somewhere they'd rather not be.'

'Oh, I see,' replied Boyd.

'Put it this way,' suggested Toni. 'If my friends at Vauxhall tell me something like this I'm inclined to believe them.

They're on the same side as us and if they tell me the source is trusted and approved then I'll go with that. Let me put it this way, Boyd, we both know that Operation Angarum is now in its tenth year. It's taken that long to define the heroin smuggling routes from the poppy fields in Afghanistan to the United Kingdom and the rest of Europe. I rather suspect the source has been working on that although I can't be sure.

'Angarum?' queried Boyd.

'Do you ever read anything I send you?' probed Toni.

'Well, usually,' confessed Boyd. 'I must have missed it. Tell me again.'

Disappointed, Toni shook her head.

'Please,' ventured Boyd.

'During the time of the Persian Empire,' explained Toni reluctantly. 'Messengers would convey information – what we now call military intelligence – by horseback from one riding post to another. The first rider delivered his message to the second and the second passed it to the third, and so on. The message was carried from hand to hand along the whole line until it reached its destination. We're talking about carrying messages along a route in excess of one thousand miles by the quickest means possible. No-one rested their horse. They just handed the message over to the next messenger who was waiting with a fresh horse at the riding post for the next part of the journey. The Persians gave the riding post the name of Angarum. Read heroin for message and you might understand why we picked Angarum as the name of the operation. It's all about defining the couriers route from the Golden Crescent of heroin production to Europe.'

'Good!' acknowledged Boyd. 'How people have the balls to get involved and provide intelligence for us is beyond my comprehension. You must pay them a lot of money.'

'It's not just money that inspires people,' ventured Toni. 'Often revenge is cited as one of the main reasons people work for the intelligence services. But then I don't know enough about their source to comment further. Need to know and all that.'

'I understand,' replied Boyd.

'The balloon has just gone up,' suggested Sir Phillip returning to the company. 'That was Maude: The Home Secretary. I've strongly advised her that the reservoir in Manchester is closed and water tests taken. She agrees but government has gone into overdrive. Panic is the order of the day and the Prime Minister is on the verge of an apoplectic fit because the Press is aware of the two murders.'

'We can't hide that from the journalists,' declared Boyd. 'But there's no need to disturb the rest of the population yet. It's madness to even mention the water problem at this stage. Let's not go overboard on the strength of one source report. Tell the Home Secretary to get a grip.'

'Of course,' chuckled Sir Phillip. 'I'll pass on your regards too, shall I?'

Boyd's mobile rang and he answered it.

Nodding, and shaking his head at the same time, Boyd listened to his caller and then replied, 'I'm on my way, Commander.'

'Actually, Boyd,' considered Phillip. 'The media! I'll recommend a D notice to the media. I know we can't stop them printing about the discovery of the bodies, it's too late now, but we can issue a D notice to prevent further escalation and speculation by them. Yes, I'll ring Maude back.'

Sir Phillip made the call.

Meg topped up her glass and offered, 'Cheers everybody! You are all awesome. I'll look after the wine, shall I? Go get 'em, Billy.'

'I'll…' offered Boyd.

'Just go do it,' said Meg interrupting. 'We've been there before. I'll see you when you return and not before. Don't come back without a scalp.'

Returning to his phone call, Boyd said, 'Commander, I want Bannerman on the Ticker system. MI6 have a photo of the man we know as White Eagle. I want it but I want it for us only at this stage. I don't want to create panic. Blasting a photo all over the media might drive him underground. If White Eagle has arrived in this country I want him out in the open, running like a wild rabbit, not disappearing into the undergrowth.'

'Agreed!' declared Commander Maxwell. 'I'll make a call and make sure we get his photograph. How recent it is?'

Boyd glanced at Toni and replied, 'It was taken between twenty-four and forty-eight hours ago, as far I'm aware, sir.'

'Brilliant!' chuckled the Commander. 'It's a hot potato in our world then. Boyd, you'll need a scientist to examine the feathers at the murder scene and I'll arrange Sandy to begin a trawl on all air passengers arriving at Gatwick, Luton and Heathrow in the last 48 hours.'

'Great,' replied Boyd. 'But can you ask Sandy to start with Manchester and Liverpool airport passengers. This man is a quick mover. He doesn't hang about and if he planned to attack the reservoir then I'm pretty sure he arrived in this country and drove straight there from either Manchester or Liverpool. Check the inbound flights. There's the lead.'

'Leave it with me, Boyd,' stated the Commander. 'Get a move on. I'll ring the locals and let them know you're coming and what the score is.'

'Thanks, boss,' replied Boyd ending the call.

'I'm coming with you, Boyd,' suggested Toni. 'Phillip, I need a helicopter.'

'You know the procedure,' replied Sir Phillip. 'I'll get back to the office and activate coverage and security protocol. Meg, can I get you a taxi to your hotel?'

Hours later, Boyd stood at the entrance to the reservoir at Heaton Park with Toni and their colleagues from the Special Crime Unit. The entrance was roped off and protected by a uniform officer who refused entrance to everyone.

As their helicopter lifted and returned south, a suited gentleman approached and introduced himself as Detective Superintendent Bob Smith.

'Boyd?' enquired the detective with a smile.

Shaking hands, Boyd replied, 'That's me. Thanks for closing the road for the helicopter. It's appreciated. This is my team.'

Introductions complete, Boyd said, 'I expect Commander Maxwell has been on the blower. I'll make it clear. We're not here to take over. We'd like to examine the scene for similarities to a series of events we are investigating and…'

'There's no need to explain,' remarked Smith. 'Your boss filled me in. I'm in charge of the murder squad. Come with me but keep inside the roped area. Don't disturb the scene or I'll have you arrested and busted down to ground zero. You know the procedure. Two of you only, please. There's one way in and one way out and the boys are doing a fingertip search at the moment.'

The uniform officer stood to one side as Smith escorted Boyd and Toni through the roped area. A team of officers wearing white forensic suits were on either side of the ropes on their hands and knees searching for clues on the ground. At the end of the route, Boyd recognised Professor Wilkinson who stood by the water's edge with a test tube in one hand and a phone in the other.

'Professor Wilkinson,' said Boyd.

'Just about to call you, Boyd,' replied the Professor. 'Strychnine traces, I'm afraid.'

'Seriously?' probed Boyd. 'You mean the reservoir has been laced with poison?'

'Oh, I'm serious alright, Boyd,' delivered the Professor. 'But the water is as clear as crystal. No, you'd need a milk tanker full of strychnine to contaminate the reservoir and render it fatally poisonous. Look at this. It's this patch of ground here.'

Professor Wilkinson pointed to the earth in front of him and offered, 'Before I forget, the feathers are from an eagle. My problem is that I need to get the feathers back to the laboratory to examine them properly. I've never actually come across a white eagle before you see.'

'How can you tell they are from an eagle then?' asked Toni.

'The plumage,' explained the Professor.

Toni and Boyd exchanged glances before Boyd ventured, 'Sorry, Professor, but we've just gone into watertight evidence mode. Imagine you're in the witness box at the Old Bailey and the defence barrister requires you to prove the feather is a feather from a white eagle found only in a certain mountain range on the Turkish – Iran – Iraq border. The judge leans forward across the bench and says, 'Professor, explain.' I mean, what you are telling us so far worries me. I need you to define the knowledge, Professor. It's as simple as that.'

Professor Wilkinson laughed, looked scornfully at the pair, and then replied, 'Boyd, you never change, do you?'

'Nah!' grimaced Boyd.

'Okay,' agreed the Professor. 'Feathers are among the most complex integumentary appendages found in vertebrates and are formed in tiny follicles in the epidermis, or outer skin layer, that produce keratin proteins.'

'Whoa!' roared Boyd. 'What the hell does integumentary mean?'

'You should have gone to school, Boyd,' replied Professor Wilkinson. 'As we all know, the integumentary system is the organ system that protects the body from various kinds of damage, such as loss of water or abrasion from outside. The system comprises the skin and its appendages and includes hair, scales, feathers, hooves, and nails.'

'Of course, it is,' acknowledged Boyd. 'It just slipped my mind.'

'I'll continue giving evidence to the judge then, shall I?' suggested the Professor. 'The β-keratins in feathers are composed of protein strands hydrogen-bonded into β-pleated sheets, which are then further twisted and crosslinked into structures even tougher than the α-keratins of mammalian hair, horns and hoof. The exact signals that induce the growth of feathers on the skin are not known, but it has been found that the transcription factor cDermo-1 induces the growth of feathers on skin and scales on the leg. You see, Boyd, a feather consists of various components which include the Vane, Rachis, Barb, Afterfeather, and Hollow shaft. They are like fingerprints because they all enjoy different lengths, depths, curve lengths, arcs, designs, shapes, and colourations. If I compare these feathers with others from birds throughout the world I will clearly show to the judge and jury that the characteristics of these white feathers are such that they could only come from an eagle. Understood?'

'Thank you,' replied Toni.

'Yes, yes of course,' acknowledged Boyd. 'Absolutely.'

'Good, that's settled then,' announced the Professor.

'You mean a white eagle?' probed Boyd.

'Yes, yes, yes!' snapped the Professor. 'I shall be able to extract inner substances from these feathers to prove that they originate from a given area. I'll be looking for minute traces of things like seeds, leaf, and soil. Substances that point to the original location of animals' genealogy. Anything else?'

'The strychnine, Professor,' pleaded Boyd. 'Tell us about the strychnine. I'm sure Bob would like to know too.'

'Oh yes,' ventured Bob Smith. 'I'm all ears.'

'Not you too?' quipped the Professor.

'Well, I just wondered,' replied Smith.

Professor Wilkinson stroked his beard and replied, 'The way I see it is this – I arrived. I saw the feathers planted in the ground as if they were signpost. Someone stuck the feathers in the ground and made a round shape with them. They didn't fall from the sky and land upright in the soil like that.'

Nodding, Boyd said, 'Agreed! That's his signature! Go on, Professor.'

'Ahh! You know about signature killers, Boyd?' enquired the Professor.

'I'm not an expert,' admitted Boyd. 'But I have some knowledge of the associated criminal behaviour.'

'Good!' smiled Professor Wilkinson. 'Now bear with me for a while as I explain things to you.'

Boyd acquiesced.

'Because the feathers are white,' declared the Professor. 'Presumably from an eagle, I immediately thought back to Commander Maxwell's briefing when he called me out and asked me to cover the scene. I began to think about strychnine and went to the water's edge to have a look. I'd expect to see a cloudy surface – almost creamy like a half-diluted candy floss - but that's never going to happen. No, what I see on the ground, beside the bank, is a slightly discoloured patch of land that is a different shade to its surroundings. I tested it and a quick test tube analysis tells me that strychnine has been spilled here very recently. See, the test tube turned purple, Boyd.'

Professor Wilkinson held the test tube up for Boyd, Smith and Toni, to see before continuing, 'I'm no detective but I'd say our two victims disturbed someone putting strychnine into the reservoir. Whoever it was panicked and dropped the poison here on the ground. Hence the residue I found. The individual then reacted by viciously killing both men.'

Boyd looked across to two corpses lying inside black body bags. A uniformed officer and a couple of undertakers were about to zip the bags tight when Boyd bent down to examine both men.

Moments passed before Boyd nodded and said, 'Thanks.'

The undertaker zipped tight the body bags and arranged for their removal from the scene.

'Photographs taken, I presume?' enquired Boyd.

'All done,' replied Bob Smith. 'We've also got plaster casts from the footwear of the two victims as well as a footprint from nearby. I think the footprint belongs to the killer. I'll have copies done and forwarded to your office. No problem!'

Boyd nodded and asked, 'Cause of death, Professor?'

'One was shot at close range with a handgun. Two shots to the forehead. The other was strangled to death.'

'That suggests to me that the killer was male,' replied Boyd.

'And well over six feet tall by the size of his footprint,' suggested Smith. 'Take a look.'

Studying the footprints, Boyd agreed and said to Toni, 'I'm afraid the scene fits the bill. Unless I'm wrong and I'm jumping to conclusions, I'd say this is probably the work of the man we are looking for. What do you think?'

'I think you've missed something, Boyd,' submitted Toni. 'Look at the pattern of the feathers in the ground.'

'They have been photographed,' remarked Smith.

'It's a circular shape, Toni,' replied Boyd. 'What do you see? I see his signature in the feathers of a white eagle. Am I missing something?'

Toni stepped forward, looked down at the circle of feathers and pointed, 'I see the flag of Kurdistan, gentlemen. The image on the flag is that of the Sun on a green, white and red background.'

'It's just a shape in the soil, Toni,' suggested Boyd. 'I can't see anything.'

'I see the emblem of the sun disc with twenty-one rays pointing outwards from the centre. Look,' Toni indicated, 'The rays are represented by the twenty-one feathers pointing outwards. It's their flag. The Kurds use it as a symbol for the desire for independence. You're looking at a representation of the official flag of the autonomous Kurdistan Region in Iraq.'

Gobsmacked, Boyd studied the feather design, glanced at Toni, and then replied, 'So help us all. You're right. Bob, do you see what we see?'

'Yes,' said Bob Smith slowly. 'And before you ask, I'm not aware of a local Kurdish enclave.'

The trio spent time at the scene, spoke with the scenes of crime and forensic officers, and then returned via the roped area to the road.

'Is it our man?' asked Anthea as Boyd approached.

'We think so,' nodded Boyd.

'In that case, you'd better take a look at this,' proposed Anthea pointing to a plaque on the pump house wall.

Stepping forward, Boyd read the history of the reservoir and the origins of where the water came from.

Turning to the group, Boyd declared, 'Toni, you'd better get that helicopter back. Thanks for your help, Bob, it's always a pleasure to work with a professional. Next time you're in London give me a bell.' Boyd handed over a business card and said, 'We're always looking for the best.'

'Not me, Boyd. I'm planning my retirement,' chuckled Bob Smith.

'Maybe,' remarked Boyd. 'But then you know who is up and coming and worth keeping an eye on. Look, how about I leave you a couple of officers here to help with your enquiries. Our man arrived from abroad and stayed somewhere in the area. If nothing else, we need to turn the hotels and bed and breakfasts over.'

'Be my guest,' replied Bob. 'I need all the help we can get. We've never enough hands in a murder enquiry, you know that.'

'Great! Thanks again. I'll leave Anthea and Martin here. They can pick up some of the workload for you. Meanwhile, it's time we moved on.'

'Where to?' queried Bob Smith.

'Cumbria,' replied Boyd. 'And this, I don't like. We're too far behind. We need to work out our suspect's next move and be there waiting for him when he turns up.'

'I'd say that was pretty much impossible,' suggested Bob.

'It is when you're behind in the game, Bob.'

Nestling on the shoreline of the Solway Firth, in North West Cumbria, England, the port town of Silloth sat twenty-two miles west of Carlisle. Historically, the town is one of the finest examples of a Victorian seaside resort in the North of England.

Darius guided the Ford rental along the cobbled road which ran parallel to a large expansive green that separated the highway from the sea and dominated the town.

Glancing to his offside, Darius noticed that a group of kite flyers had gathered on the green and were toggling their flying lines to guide the kites high into the sky and towards the Solway.

Ignoring the kites, and the people, Darius swung a right at the crossroads near the harbour and drove down Lawn Terrace to a car park at the end of the road. Parking beside Silloth Lifeboat Station, Darius noticed he was in a pay and display car park. Not wanting to draw attention to himself, he fed the machine with a couple of coins and placed the ticket on the dashboard inside the Ford.

Excited now, Darius approached the sea. It was the Solway Firth but to Darius it was an ocean and he had never been so close to one in his life before. He'd flown across them, seen pictures of them, and even heard tales from people who had swam in them. But he'd never experienced the fresh smell of a seaside before.

What's more, the tide was coming in.

Stretching towards the hamlet of Skinburness, Darius ventured down the steps of the Promenade and enjoyed a long walk by the Solway Firth. He felt the wind lash at his face whilst the sunshine fought to caress his cheeks. Marvelling at the sea, and surroundings, he studied the waves rolling in. They were grey and unique. Something he'd never seen close up before. He shuddered when they rolled onto the beach, crackled on the pebbles, and then drew back into the ocean before coming again.

Eventually, he turned around and walked back to the boat station. Satisfied, and with another tick on life's bucket list completed, Darius fired the Ford and drove back into the town.

At the crossroads, he drove straight across and stopped in Eden Street. He glanced casually to his offside and saw a post office next to a chemist shop. They were both open.

Locking the car, Darius stepped smartly across the road and bought a selection of envelopes at the post office before returning to the Ford.

Driving off, Darius headed past the old police station and the rugby club. Both were closed and the police station was boarded up and out of action.

'Virtually derelict,' thought Darius as his vehicle rattled on the cobble stones.

At Skiddaw Street, he took a left and then a right before pulling in near a row of holiday caravans.

Locking the car, he made his way towards one of the caravans whereupon a voice shouted, 'How'st the going on, marra?'

Looking over his shoulder, Darius saw a uniformed man carrying a parcel towards him.

Immediately, Darius's hand reached inside his clothing and sought the handgun.

'No,' he thought. 'This uniform is not police. What is it?'

A courier's delivery van was parked nearby and Darius quickly surmised that the man was the courier. He released the handgun and offered a smile.

'Ist thou number six, marra?' enquired the man. 'I take it you are number six?'

Checking the number on the caravan door, Darius removed a key from his pocket and checked the number on the tab.

'Yes, that's the one. Number Six,' confirmed Darius. 'Is that for me?'

'Aye, lad, sign here,' replied the courier.

Darius accepted the parcel and squiggled a signature on the electronic pad offered by the courier as proof of receipt.

'What's the craic today then?' asked the courier jovially.

'Sorry,' replied Darius suddenly looking extremely worried. 'There's a crack in the parcel? Whereabouts please?'

'No there's nothing wrong with the parcel,' offered the courier. 'It means... Oh, never mind. I reckon you're not from around 'ere then, marra. On holiday, are we?'

'Holiday! Yes holiday, it is,' confirmed Darius.

'Good for you. Have a good day, marra,' said the courier as he retreated to his van.

Ignoring further interaction, Darius felt confused and unsure.

'I hope they don't all speak like that in England,' he thought. 'It's bad enough as it is people talking like that.'

Put off guard by the courier, he quickly unlocked the caravan and went in. Opening the parcel, he assured himself of the contents, and then pushed it under the bed. Removing a map from his bag, he spread it out across the table and read the figures on a piece of paper in his notes.

Darius read the figures 54°31'08"N 2°48'17"W and then checked the map. Carefully, he worked out the location of the co-ordinates before making himself a black coffee. Removing his lap top computer, he double checked the laptop result against his own findings on the map and studied the area closely. Darius took in the road system and the topography of the land and committed them to memory. Then he removed a note book from the inside of the netbook bag and reminded himself of Malik's briefing.

Cautious, Darius closed the curtains, lit an oil lamp provided, and removed the parcel from beneath the bed. Untying the string, he unwrapped the brown paper and opened the wooden box.

Smiling now, Darius removed the envelopes from his jacket and began his work.

## Chapter Thirteen
~

Two Days later
Lytham St Annes, Lancashire.
Morning

The sound of an envelope landing on a doormat made John Carpenter drop his newspaper and head for the doorway. Returning to the breakfast table with the post, he downed the last of his tea, bit into a piece of toast, and then studied the newly arrived package.

'Interesting,' he remarked to his wife. 'What have we here? Something the good lady has arranged, I expect.'

'Not from me, dear,' replied his wife, Carol.

In his mid-fifties and wearing a dressing gown, John ripped into the padded parcel. Pausing for a moment, he checked the address on the front of the envelope.

'John Carpenter, Director of North West Water Facilities,' he read. 'Yes, that's me but I wonder who gave them my private address?'

'What is it?' enquired Carol pouring tea.

When the envelope was torn, a thin bottle of liquid – the diameter of a pencil – was apparent.

Lifting the bottle, John held it to the light and read the label.

'Free perfume sample,' he reported. 'Someone at the office is having a laugh.'

'Kind of them, though,' remarked Carol, also wearing a dressing gown. 'Here, let me try it before I get dressed and go to work. It's one of those miniatures they use to introduce new products.'

John passed the bottle over with, 'Be my guest, I'll stick with my own aftershave, if you don't mind.'

Carol unscrewed the tiny top and held it beneath her nose.

'Not much of a smell,' she said before dabbing the liquid onto her fingers and then onto her neck. 'Maybe a hint of almonds but what a strange thing to use in a perfume.'

The phone in the hall rang causing John to vacate the kitchen once more.

''I'll get it,' he said as he wandered off. 'It'll probably be my secretary.'

Carol lifted the bottle again and said, 'Mmm... I wonder what she wants?'

Holding the perfume under her nose, Carol inhaled the perfume deeply.

Coughing slightly, she dropped the bottle and said, 'It's terrible. It's...'

On the telephone, John listened and replied, 'A government warning and security advice? Mmm... That's bad news, Madelaine. Can you make sure all senior managers are informed of the threat to our water supply and that all appropriate security measures are put into action. Inform the manager responsible for Heaton Park Reservoir to put a twenty-four-hour security presence in place. We'll look stupid if something like that happens again. Next, just a moment while I think... Yes, set up a video link and arrange a conference with those responsible for the water supply from Thirlmere, Haweswater, Lake Vyrnwy, and the River Dee in Wales. I want to speak to all relevant managers at 2pm this afternoon. These areas provide over half the region's water supply. I'll be in the office by then and I'll....'

Breaking into muscular convulsions, Carol's heartbeat increased at an incredible speed. Her neck bulged and her shoulders began shaking uncontrollably. She tried to steady herself on the side of the table but lost it and crashed to the ground bringing with her cutlery, crockery, and a dish of cereal.

On the floor, Carol involuntarily turned on her back when her legs began kicking out in a wild manner. It was as if the devil himself had taken her into his fold and was destroying her body piece by piece.

John heard her fall, slammed the telephone down, and ran to the kitchen.

'What's happened?' he yelled.

He saw Carol on the floor shuddering, jerking, her body going into spasm with all the violence the devil inside could muster.

Racing to her side, John pushed the bottle of perfume away and tried to restrain his wife.

'Settle down!' he pleaded. 'Easy now! What's wrong, Carol?'

Unable to speak, Carol continued to thrash her arms up and down as if she were marching like a soldier on a parade ground.

Wide eyed, and nodding her head determinedly, Carol kicked out at the bottle of perfume and tried to point at the bottle.

'Perfume?' queried John. 'Is it the perfume?'

'Mmm…' muttered Carol. 'Mmm…'

John picked up the bottle, held it to the light, and smelled the content.

'Oh, my god!' he screamed. 'No! No!'

Placing the bottle on the table, John ran back into the hall and dialled 999.

'Ambulance! Then police! My wife! She's been poisoned.'

By noon that day, Carol Carpenter was sat up in bed attached to an intravenous drip whilst her husband sat close by listening Doctor Elliott.

'The worst is over, Mr and Mrs Carpenter,' explained the doctor. 'It is the case that two sniffs from an alleged bottle of strychnine pretending to be a brand new perfume can hardly be described as a serious dose. Yet the strength of the undiluted poison is clear to see. On a one to one basis, the excess inhalation of even a small amount of strychnine can easily cause convulsions and, in some cases, lead to a heart attack and death. Fortunately, you are quite fit for your age and were able to endure the attack.'

'Thank God,' mumbled John squeezing Carol's hand.

'I'm alright now, John,' remarked Carol. 'Thank you, Doctor Elliott.'

'My pleasure,' smiled the doctor. 'Some years ago, athletes used to take a mild ingestion of strychnine in the belief that it aided their performance. You can see how close some of them were to fatality had they over subscribed to that belief.'

'Oh, yes,' replied John. 'We've been very lucky.'

'The police are here to see you, Mrs Carpenter. Do you think you are fit enough to speak to them?'

'Yes, show them in,' agreed Carol.

Escorted by the doctor, Anthea and Martin walked in, sat down next to the bedside, and began their questioning.

'Good day,' remarked Anthea. 'I'm DI Adams and this is DC Duffy. We're glad to see you are improving.'

Holding up two see-through exhibit bags, Anthea stated, 'We recovered a jiffy bag and an exceptionally small bottle of perfume from your kitchen. The perfume has been examined and, as you know, it is strychnine. Can you tell us what happened?'

The witness interviews moved on.

In Cumbria, Darius entered a telephone box, dialled a number, and asked, 'Is that the Home Office?'

Listening to the reply, Darius continued, 'This is your first warning. Your people will know me as White Eagle. Several people will open their mail today and a short time later they will suffer from the effects of poisoning. These postal attacks will continue until the British Government deposits twenty-five million pounds into the following bank account. I do this in the name of Kurdistan.'

Darius recited a bank account number and finished with, 'You have twelve hours to make the deposit.'

The call ended when Darius replaced the transmitter and left the kiosk.

Elsewhere, eleven other people had received suspicious packages through the mail. Each package was a brown jiffy bag – also known as a padded envelope – that contained a thin and small bottle of liquid that was smaller than a miniature. A printed note accompanied each parcel and invited the recipient to try the enclosed perfume for free. They had all been especially selected as brand testers for this new and exciting perfume that was about to hit the High Street in the near future.

Six of the recipients were male, and six were female.

Throughout the day, the twelve victims who had been targeted by the poisoner, gave in to the bizarre complexities of a strychnine poison attack, ended up in hospital, and caused a nationwide alert.

It didn't take long for Anthea and Martin to confirm that all twelve victims had a connection to the country's water supply system, and the parcels, according to the postmarks on the envelopes, had been posted in Cumbria and the South of Scotland.

In the Bullring Shopping Centre, Birmingham, the door of a telephone kiosk closed behind the caller. A selection of coins dropped into a phone and the caller waited for an answer.

The Placer made the call.

When the man at the Israeli Embassy answered, the Placer asked, 'Put me through to an Intelligence Officer please. I have some information for Shin Bet.'

'What? I beg your pardon,' replied the telephonist hurriedly pushing a series of buttons in an attempt to trace the telephone call.

'You heard me correctly,' declared the Placer. 'Not Mossad. I want a man from Shin Bet. I have information about the cyber-attack on Tel Aviv and the Hezbollah missile attacks that followed. Now please or the phone goes dead.'

The telephonist put the call through.

'Can I help you?' asked a voice in the Embassy.

'No, but I can help you,' insisted the Placer. 'I have information about the man who is responsible for terrorist attacks in Israel. If you are from Shin Bet, do you want to deal?'

'To deal?' questioned the voice. 'How can I deal with a person who offers no name and promises something that is offered every day of the week by numerous callers. Please, put the phone down and don't play games with me. We get far too many hoax calls as it is.'

'White Eagle,' declared the Placer. 'Not just an eagle. Do you know which mountain range the eagle flies from?'

There was a noticeable pause before the voice on the phone in the Embassy replied, 'From where does the eagle fly?'

'The Quandil Mountains!'

'Okay,' replied the Embassy man. 'I'm listening.'

The Placer replied, 'Good! I have some information for you but it comes at a price and with terms and conditions.'

'What price did you have in mind?'

'I'll get to the price shortly,' replied the Placer. 'The terms and conditions are that you, and your allies, will not launch an aerial attack on a location that I give you.'

'Why do you come to me? Why not speak to our allies as you call them?'

'Because they will come to you when they want the name of an Arab who is slowly destroying Europe by terrorising the population. I take it you are a Jew and wage a secret war against those of an Arab persuasion. Or do you think I am a fool?'

Confused now, but burning with interest, the Israeli official proposed, 'Call me Benjamin, and you are?'

'No-one important, I just place people.'

Benjamin could not believe his luck when he switched on a tape recorder and said, 'Tell me your story and then tell me what you want.'

Five minutes later, the Placer ended the call and set the phone on the cradle.

Benjamin pressed a button on the Embassy telephone device and asked, 'Did you get it? Did you trace the call?'

'Birmingham,' replied the telephonist. 'The Bullring Shopping Centre, Birmingham.'

A hundred miles away, the door of a phone box in the Bullring Shopping Centre swung lazily on its hinges when the Placer walked down Dudley Street.

Two minutes later, the Placer boarded a train at a New Street railway station.

In an Embassy in London, an Israeli diplomat called Benjamin rubbed his hands in glee.

'Luck!' he shouted aloud. 'Things don't get much better than this.'

Darius entered a phone box, dialled a number, and asked to speak the news desk.

'Just a moment,' replied the switchboard operator. 'Putting you through now.'

When a reporter on the news desk responded, Darius read from a pre-prepared script and said, 'This is the voice of the man the media has dubbed White Eagle. I am responsible for attacks in Istanbul, Paris, Vienna, Brussels, Tel Aviv, a reservoir near Manchester, and elsewhere. In order to verify that this is not a hoax, I suggest you ring the Home Office and ask them to confirm that they received a telephone call from White Eagle earlier today. In addition, ask them how many feathers were left in the soil at Heaton Park Reservoir. The answer is twenty-one. Got that?'

'Got that,' replied the reporter anxiously.

'Today I give you, the Home Office, the Prime Minister, and the people of the United Kingdom a warning,' continued Darius. 'Tell your people not to open their mail. Tomorrow, many will die when the postman arrives. I shall continue to attack the United Kingdom, its people, and its government if the following instructions are not complied with.'

'Wait one!' replied the reporter. 'Who are you again?'

'White Eagle,' replied Darius. 'Do not play games with me or try any stupid tricks like trying to trace this call. These attacks, and others, will continue until your government transfers twenty-five million pounds into the following bank account. The money will be transferred from that account into another account. Any attempt to track the money by electronic means will lead to a renewal in attacks.'

Darius announced the bank details before continuing, 'In addition, the following members of the Turkish community falsely held in prisons across Europe will be released immediately.'

As Darius related the details, the reporter activated a recorder and scribbled away at his notes before finally saying, 'Hey, slow down. Slow down, man.'

'I will not slow down,' revealed Darius. 'Your government has twenty fours to comply with my request otherwise these attacks will continue and things will worsen. Beware, you have been warned.'

Darius replaced the telephone, left the kiosk, and crossed the green towards the sea front and the embracing air of the Solway Firth.

'Shit!' yelled the reporter. 'Where's the boss? We've got a scoop! Some guy calling himself White Eagle is trying to blackmail the British government.'

'Not that White Eagle?' asked a colleague. 'Not the one that has been terrorising Europe?'

'That's the one. He's here. He's attacking us next and, what's more, he's trying to blackmail the government to the tune of twenty-five million smackeroos.'

*

## Chapter Fourteen
~

The Embankment
London
Next Day

'Are you sure about this meeting, Toni?' probed Boyd.

'Put it this way, Boyd,' replied Toni. 'White Eagle has gone to ground and we haven't a clue where. Cumbria, the South of Scotland? I don't think so. He could be anywhere and Sandy tells me her team has contacted every hotel, motel, bed and breakfast and accommodation spot in the county and not got a sniff of the man.'

'Sniff?' queried Boyd. 'Not the best word to use when talking about tracing a poisoner, Toni.'

'Well you know what I mean,' replied Toni. 'What I do know is that the government are close to apoplectic. Fury knows no boundaries at the moment. The cheek of the man. Phillip tells me our man telephoned the Home Office and a national newspaper. White Eagle is trying to blackmail the government into giving twenty-five million quid to his terrorist group in exchange for not attacking our country. What do I hear?'

'Go on, tell me,' stated Boyd. 'What do you hear?'

'We're in trouble for not catching him,' replied Toni.

'Yeah,' murmured Boyd. 'I overheard someone in the canteen saying that heads would roll soon.'

'Yours might be first,' suggested Toni.

'Don't I know it,' admitted Boyd.

'Be honest, Boyd, it didn't take Sandy long to work out that there wasn't anyone on our radar when she trawled the passenger lists for Manchester and Liverpool airports. Yes, I know she has a team going through the video footage at arrivals but that will take time. Come on, you know as well as I do, our suspect must be travelling on a false passport under a false identity. He can hide in a haystack and we'll never find him. What have we got to lose making this meeting?'

'But the Israelis?' questioned Boyd.

'They owe me a favour,' replied Toni. 'We're late. Let's get a move on, please.'

The pair left the office in Broadway, caught a taxi, and got out on the Embankment overlooking the River Thames.

Boyd paid the taxi driver, turned to walk down the pavement with Toni, and asked, 'So, who is this man we are about to entrust the nation's secrets with?'

Toni smiled and replied, 'My contact with the Israeli Security Agency.'

'Really?' probed Boyd. 'Mossad presumably?'

'No,' revealed Toni. 'Mossad is foreign intelligence; Aman is military intelligence, and Shin Bet covers internal security.'

'Like MI5,' replied Boyd. 'So how come you've got a meeting with a man from Shin Bet if the organisation only works inside Israel?'

'He owes me a few favours and he's on holiday, I believe. Or so he says. Before you ask, their motto is 'Defender that shall not be seen' or 'The unseen shield'. Remind you of anyone?'

'Unseen?' queried Boyd. 'That probably describes White Eagle admirably.'

'That's what I was thinking,' agreed Toni.

'What favours?' probed Boyd. 'You mentioned he owed you a few favours.'

'They want the same man for the Hezbollah rocket attacks on Tel Aviv and the power outage that brought the country to a standstill for a while. They might want to work together on this one. It's been done before. They've helped with the IRA and some of the Islamic bombings in central London. In return, we keep them posted about movements they might be interested in. They've nothing to lose and neither have we.'

The man from Shin Bet left the Israeli embassy in Kensington Palace Gardens in a car fitted with blacked out windows and diplomatic number plates. He took a ride to a location about half a mile from Thames House where he got out of the car to walk.

Boyd and Toni met him and strolled along the Embankment with the man from the embassy.

Toni opened the conversation with, 'Shalom!'

'Peace be with you,' replied the diplomat. 'You are well?'

'Very well,' replied Toni.

'I can't stay long. It will be frowned upon if I am seen with you.'

'But not necessarily a problem,' remarked Toni. 'It's just that you shouldn't be seen doing the work of Mossad.'

Smiling, the diplomat asked, 'Your friend?'

'Detective Chief Inspector Boyd,' replied Toni introducing her colleague. 'He's with our unit. It's....'

'I know about Boyd and your unit too,' replied the diplomat. 'Just as you know about ours. How can I help?'

Stepping towards the wall that separated them from the Thames, Toni peered out across the river and enquired, 'Have you seen the photograph I sent you?'

Standing beside her, the Israeli replied, 'Yes, is that the man we are all looking for?'

'If you mean the Hezbollah rocket attack and a blackout at Tel Aviv then yes. We believe so.'

Nodding, the man withdrew a piece of paper from a wallet, and passed it over saying, 'He has a passport in the name Joshua Shalom Cohen. He acquired it, we believe, via his contacts in Hezbollah. The man passes himself off as an 'Arab Jew'. It's a term used during the First World War by Jews of Middle Eastern origin living in western countries to support their case that they were not Turks and should not be treated as enemy aliens. The Jewish identity, some believe, is a matter of religion rather than ethnicity or nationality. Some consider the term to be offensive. Either way, the man can wear both hats when it suits him.'

'That's his real name?' enquired Boyd.

'No,' replied the diplomat. 'His real name is Darius Yasin.'

'Where from?'

'The Quandil Mountains.'

'How do you know this, Mister...?'

'I have no name for you,' replied the diplomat. 'And if I gave you one it would be meaningless.'

'How did you get to him?' asked Toni.

'Sometimes you recruit people to work for you. Sometimes they are already working for someone else. I suggest you try to find him before we do.'

The Shin Bet man nodded, tucked in his collar, and walked off.

'Yes, perhaps lunch sometime?' ventured Toni.

The man did not reply, didn't even turn to acknowledge Toni.

'Or a coffee even,' she ventured. 'Maybe feed the ducks in the Serpentine?'

The man turned, smiled, and replied, 'I was never here, my friend but you know how to get hold of me. Perhaps we will speak again if the climate is right. Who knows?'

'Indeed,' responded Toni. 'Perhaps we will.'

'You will find this man soon, but he will be dead when you find him,' suggested the diplomat. 'Good day to you both.'

'Yeah, shalom,' offered Boyd.

A vehicle bearing diplomatic plates drew up. The man entered the car and disappeared behind the black windows.

'What the hell,' said Boyd shaking his head. 'And he's on our side, you say?'

'He's on his own side, Boyd,' revealed Toni. 'If he gets the man before us, he'll be a hero in a certain office in Tel Aviv. If we find this Darius guy first, then he'll remind everyone back home that he guided us to him. People like him never lose. He's got a foot in both camps.'

'Sounds like Joshua has too, or shall we call our suspect Darius from now?'

'Yeah, Darius it is,' confirmed Boyd. 'We have his name at last and I'll judge that our Israeli friends have someone searching for Darius too. We need to find him first. It's our job and our patch, and your man has just told us what to expect if they find him before us.'

'It could be the gunfight at OK Corral all over again, Boyd,' suggested Toni.

'A gunfight possibly but I'd venture such a killing might be much subtler and less headline grabbing,' ventured Boyd.

'I agree,' replied Toni. 'Any shouting can be done in Tel Aviv. They'd probably prefer a quiet murder if there is such a thing.'

'A Mossad inspired murder on our patch would be a monumental loss for us,' stated Boyd. 'It would make your office look like fools and we'd be hung out to dry because we're supposed to be defenders of the realm.

The media would have a field day making the headlines up. We've got to find this man before the Israelis do.'

'Any ideas?'

'We'll start with a major incident room in our office. I'll get Bannerman to run it. He's good with getting things done. We have a name now. We can run Joshua Shalom Cohen through hotels, bed and breakfast, banks, credit card companies, hire car, whatever and wherever it takes to find him. My professional problem is that I've never dealt with water supply terrorism before. I've no experience of such events, Toni.'

'It's the intentional sabotage of a water supply system,' explained Toni. 'Chemical or biological warfare are the preferred weapons for a terrorist in this case. Top of the head, Boyd?'

'Go on,' replied Boyd.

'Top of the head I know of a religious cult who contaminated a city water supply tank in Oregon. 1984, if I remember correctly. They used salmonella to infect the water.'

'Nasty,' winced Boyd.

'Then there's the obvious copycat for you. In 1992, our man's organisation, the PKK, put lethal concentrations of potassium cyanide in the water tanks of a Turkish Air Force compound in Istanbul. I can go on if you want.'

'You get that off the Ticker system?' asked Boyd.

'Correct! Look, it's time we got back and pushed the boat out,' suggested Toni.

Boyd's mobile rang and he and he answered it with, 'Boyd!'

'Guvnor, it's Anthea,' came the reply. 'We got lucky in Manchester. A man fitting the description of the suspect, White Eagle, booked into a hotel in central Manchester on the same day as the Heaton Park Reservoir murders. We have CCTV footage of the suspect booking into the hotel at the reception desk, his signature on the register, and…'

'What name did he use?' quizzed Boyd.

'Joshua Shalom Cohen,' replied Anthea. 'Address in Tel Aviv.'

'That's our man,' snapped Boyd jubilantly. 'It's a long story but we've just learnt our man is travelling on an Israeli passport in that name. Now we're talking.'

'There's more, guvnor,' reported Anthea. 'We've traced his hotel room and secured it for a forensic team. I want his fingerprints and DNA if possible. You see, he went out for the day but didn't return. Where did he go?'

'The reservoir where he was disturbed,' replied Boyd.

'Exactly,' confirmed Anthea. 'He gets to Heaton Park, is disturbed, and decides it's too dangerous to return to the hotel. He really needs to leave the area as quickly as possible. After all, he didn't go to the reservoir to murder those people. He went to contaminate a small part of the water and it all went wrong for him. Maybe he was testing how much strychnine he needed to corrupt that particular reservoir. I don't know but we do know that he didn't return to the hotel to pay. There's a debt outstanding.'

Nodding, taking it all in, Boyd replied, 'Seek out Bob Smith, Anthea. I want the name Joshua Shalom Cohen circulated to all police forces in the UK – with a description – and a message indicating he's wanted for making off without paying from a hotel in Manchester. If traced, do not approach, but contact you immediately. Understood?'

'Already drafted,' replied Anthea. 'Bob and Martin are standing beside me now. This way we can circulate him without panicking the population about terrorism.'

'Well done, all of you,' responded Boyd.

'I haven't finished yet,' insisted Anthea. 'We've got two main exhibits from the letter poisoning. We've yet to trace the jiffy bag source but we've traced the purchase of a large supply of thin perfume bottles to a department store in Trafford, Manchester. Martin got in touch with the bottle manufacturer. They gave a list of where the bottles of perfume were on sale in the UK. It's a promotional supply and there was only one shipment to Manchester.'

'Tell me Joshua Shalom Cohen paid for the goods by a credit card?' ventured Boyd.

'No, a woman did the deal and she paid with cash. That's all we're likely to get on that one but it proves he has an accomplice,' offered Anthea.

'A Placer,' remarked Boyd. 'Okay, top work. Potentially, we have a female Placer to find. Follow all the leads you have and tie the evidence up on paper.'

'We're on it,' confirmed Anthea. 'Catch you later.'

Boyd stepped out smartly and offered, 'You hear that, Toni? Let's find this Darius man.'

'What do you have on your mind, Boyd?' enquired Toni. 'Something is going on. I can hear your brain ticking.'

Punching numbers into his mobile, Boyd contacted Ricky French and said, 'Hi, Ricky, do you remember we were discussing that new piece of kit recently?'

Toni frowned and looked at Boyd quizzically.

'That's the one,' said Boyd. 'Put it together and test it please. I'm planning to use it soon… Yes, thanks.'

'Mystery man?' offered Toni. 'What's the secret?'

'No secret,' replied Boyd. 'But a valuable weapon perhaps. Be honest, Toni, the reality is that Darius Yasin is the real mystery man here.'

'Darius Yasin from the Quandil Mountains,' replied Toni. 'He's out there somewhere. I wonder who the Israelis have got on his tail?'

\*

## Chapter Fourteen
~

Three Kings' Yard, Mayfair,
Central London,
Later

Giuseppe Mouretti opened the taxi door, swung his suitcase out first, and then stepped onto the footpath. He paid the driver and set off along Mayfair searching for the lane that would lead him to the Italian Embassy.

He negotiated Three Kings Yard, entered the embassy, and shook hands with a consulate assistant before introducing himself.

The assistant looked quizzically at Mouretti who then produced his credentials and said, 'You should have received a diplomatic bag addressed to me at the embassy. Can you confirm possession please?'

Studying Mouretti's credentials, the assistant immediately adopted a subservient attitude and declared, 'This way, sir. Please be careful of the steps. I would hate it if you fell and injured yourself. Goodness, we'd all be in trouble, wouldn't we?'

Mouretti smiled graciously and replied, 'And that would never do, particularly as I am just calling for the mail.'

Allowing the assistant to escort him through the marble concourse and down some steps, Mouretti quickly found himself in the heart of the building.

'The article arrived this morning by diplomatic courier and was secured in our diplomatic mail area earlier today,' explained the assistant. 'The courier had no problems in the transition of your mail and, as you appreciate, your mail was not subject to customs inspection.'

'Good,' acknowledged Mouretti.

Carrying his suitcase, the man from NATO followed the assistant to a secure area of the embassy where he was admitted to the diplomatic mailing section.

The assistant sorted through the mail delivery, found a briefcase secured tagged with Mouretti's name, and handed it to him.

'Thank you,' replied Mouretti. 'A private moment please?'

'Of course, sir,' replied the assistant who immediately withdrew from the room. 'Can I get you a light beverage, sir? Tea or coffee, perhaps?'

'No, thank you,' replied Mouretti courteously.

'Perhaps something a little stronger, sir?' persisted the assistant.

Turning promptly, Mouretti stared directly into the man's eyes and replied, 'Like I said, no thank you.'

Bowing slightly, the assistant withdrew.

Mouretti opened his diplomatic mail – the briefcase – and studied the design of one of the finest handguns ever made. It was a Remington pistol with a John Browning 1911 design.

He seized the single-action, semi-automatic, magazine-fed, recoil-operated pistol and weighed it carefully in his right hand. Swinging it up from his hip, Mouretti pointed it at an imaginary target. Then he removed the shoulder holster from the briefcase and tried it on. Carefully, he chambered a magazine of .45 cartridges, felt the smooth barrel, admired the wooden handle insert, and marvelled at its perfection. Lastly, he considered his ankle holster, which fit snugly into the briefcase lid. The holster held a Mustang Mini Browning 1911, which weighed eleven ounces. With a barrel length, slightly under three inches long, the pistol carried a magazine of .380 cartridges. It wasn't the most modern of covert weapons in the market place but it was his undoubted favourite.

Mouretti replaced the weaponry and locked the briefcase. He swung his suitcase onto the table and then placed the briefcase inside the suitcase.

Satisfied, Mouretti vacated the diplomatic mail section and returned to the reception area of the embassy where he was met by the assistant.

'To your satisfaction, sir?' ventured the assistant.

'Indeed, thank you,' replied Mouretti.

Without further ado, Mouretti left the embassy, hailed a taxi, and headed for a car rental in north London.

Later that day, Mouretti waited beside a telephone box at the appointed time and watched the traffic trundle along the M1 on its journey into the heart of England.

The phone rang and Mouretti stepped inside and answered it.

'Mouretti,' he said.

An Israeli voice sounded in his ear and the NATO investigator listened carefully before replacing the telephone.

Walking away from the kiosk, Mouretti returned to his car and fired the engine.

It paid to work with people from other agencies, he decided. To all intents and purposes the voice on the telephone belonged to a highly-paid source working inside Mossad on behalf of NATO. Yet he knew his man in Mossad only told him what he wanted him to know. It was evident to Mouretti that the Israeli Security Agency - responsible for intelligence collection, covert operations, and counter terrorism, as well as protecting Jewish communities - would point the way in the expectation that Mouretti would do their job at the end of the day.

259

It was as if Mouretti was running a clandestine undercover source into Mossad on behalf of NATO. Equally, it could be argued that Mossad were running a double agent into the high echelons of NATO. Such was the complex relationships between intelligence agencies the world over. Either way, there was an air of mutuality and unspoken respect between the two. Both parties knew they had their eyes on the same target. What was the problem with sharing a little bit of information here and there?

Yet it was much more complicated than that. A web of deceit and lies were apparent with the possibility that someone had turned turtle on White Eagle. Someone somewhere appeared to have sold White Eagle to the Israelis. Despite Mouretti holding the NATO post of Commander-in-Chief, Special Investigations, he could not fathom out who or why. There was someone else in the game but Mouretti didn't know who.

Mouretti shook his head and tried to dismiss the mystery from his mind. Right now, he sought vengeance for the murder of his father in Paris. It wasn't professional. It was personal. Deeply personal, and he was determined to have his day!

'British intelligence is onto White Eagle,' the voice on the phone had conveyed. 'They have his photograph and his passport details. The Placer tells us he's in the North of England. Yesterday he was in a coastal town called Silloth. Find and eliminate the individual. His car is a blue Vauxhall, registration number…'

Five hours later, Mouretti arrived in Silloth, parked near Christ Church, opposite the green, and took a stroll to get some exercise.

Breathing in the Solway air, Mouretti took a left at the crossroads and walked along Eden Street passing the police station.

Mouretti did not call at the police station. He had no need of their services. Walking by, he considered the future and how he would deal with the matter in hand. It was his business, his own private affair.

Giuseppe Mouretti was on a mission and murder was on his mind.

In the corridors of power, in Whitehall, the Foreign Secretary, the Home Secretary, the Director General of the Security Services, Commander Maxwell, Superintendent Sandra Peel, and the Metropolitan Police Commissioner, were in a meeting.

'How many now?' asked Maude Black, the Home Secretary.

Neil Atkinson, the Commissioner, glanced sideways at Commander Maxwell and gestured that he should reply on his behalf.

The Commander cleared his throat and announced, 'The Special Crime Unit is aware of a dozen first wave strychnine attacks using the UK postal services. Since the first day there have been twenty more similar attacks on members of parliament for Cumbria and the North West, various dignitaries in the South of Scotland, and senior employees of several companies involved in maintaining the nation's water supply. This makes a total of thirty-two attacks. I can also tell you that post office staff have intercepted a further ten packages containing strychnine phials bound for domestic targets.'

'Domestic targets?' scorned Maude. 'You mean real people, Commander.'

'Yes, of course,' replied Commander Maxwell.

'How many arrests have been made?' Maude enquired.

'None so far,' replied Maxwell. 'Our suspect has gone to ground although we have a huge manhunt taking place.'

The Home Secretary did not seem at all happy at the lack of progress and announced, 'DA-Notice 05 is still currently in force in respect of the United Kingdom Security and Intelligence Special Services. I issued the notice as government advice to the media informing them that such matters should not be reported on to preserve national security. I have listened carefully to your comments and observations over recent days and understand your desire to let this man – White Eagle – run free. You told me that you have more chance of catching him if his photograph is not on the front page of every newspaper and television. I say that ploy hasn't worked, Commander.'

'Our enquiries are ongoing,' insisted Neil, the Commissioner.

'And have been for far too long,' insisted Sir Henry: The Foreign Secretary. 'Our contacts in Europe require an update. More importantly, they want the matter resolved. The man is on an island, for god's sake – Our island. Surely it is simply a matter of promoting his facial appearance to the world, finding him, and arresting him.'

'This is the kind of man who will not come quietly, sir,' suggested Commander Maxwell. 'His focus is on destroying as many people as possible. One photograph we have of him reveals that he has a beard. Sandy…'

Detective Superintendent Peel accepted Maxwell's invitation to join the discussion and added, 'Our enquires took us to Manchester airport where an image of a man using a passport in the name Joshua Shalom Cohen leads us to believe that the man we are looking for is actually called Darius Yasin. We know that he booked into a hotel in Manchester and used a credit card in the name Joshua Shalom Cohen to cover services. There's no doubt he shaved his beard off because the photograph we have of him at Manchester airport shows that he is clean-shaven. He could have grown a moustache or a beard by now. Putting his face into the national media might cause him to change his appearance again but that is the Commander's decision at this stage. Remember, the suspect had ginger hair in the American Embassy attack in Vienna. He used a car bomb. Our suspect is a master of disguise and able to turn his hand to multiple attack syndromes.'

'Suspect!' ventured Sir Henry. 'You used the word suspect. Does this mean you really don't have a clue who committed these offences?'

'We'll find him,' replied Commander Maxwell. 'Despite what Sandy has told you, and all your various opinions, I have authorised the televising of his image in 'Crimewatch' tonight. The appeal is one of many in the schedule and will reveal that the man is wanted for a hotel fraud since he left without paying having given false details. We're hoping to find him without causing panic amongst the population whilst simultaneously preventing the media from potentially causing widespread panic.'

'Do you know his vehicle yet?' asked the Home Secretary.

'No, we think someone provided a vehicle for him. We call such a person The Placer – someone in the background who has helped organise these attacks and given shelter to the man we're looking for.'

'Who is leading the investigation?' enquired Sir Henry.

'Boyd,' replied the Commissioner. 'He's in the north where we think the suspect is. Sandy, here, is looking after London and the south putting safety procedures into place and driving enquiries and initiatives to unearth our man.'

'Is that a fact?' replied Sir Henry. 'Maude,' he pleaded. 'I really do think it's time you stepped in and ordered the Commissioner to replace the senior investigating officer and put someone much more dynamic in.'

Maude Black studied Sir Henry for a moment and then glanced around the gathering before saying, 'Commissioner?'

'Well, it may well be time to do exactly that, Ma'am,' replied Neil.

'What do you say, Commander Maxwell?' enquired Sir Phillip.

'I'm with Boyd,' replied Maxwell. 'More importantly, what is your opinion, Sir Phillip?'

The Director General rarely got himself embroiled in the nitty gritty of politics at this level. Particularly when arguments filled the air and reputations were at stake.

Nevertheless, Sir Phillip glared at the Commissioner, glanced at Maude, and replied, 'Boyd is a unique individual and, at times like this, history dictates it is those who step forward and grasp the nettle that are usually successful. Our detective is different from many. He thinks outside the box and has a remarkable imagination. More importantly, he understands what drives terrorists, what makes them tick, and what makes them the most dangerous and difficult of criminals to catch. It's not my decision. It's a policing decision but good detectives can think like criminals whether they are bank robbers, burglars, or shoplifters. On the other hand, politicians tend to be very good at criticising others whilst failing to produce alternatives based on evidence or proven experience. I suggest you stick with the man in the field. He'll do his best.'

'But will it be enough?' enquired the Foreign Secretary.

'Time will tell,' gasped Sir Phillip. 'Boyd correctly adduced that the offender seeks to blackmail the government by attacking the nation's water system. His demands include the release of several 'political' prisoners across Europe as well the payment of millions of pounds to the PKK, and the setting up of an independent Kurdistan.'

'We're never going to accept that,' stated the Home Secretary.

'Of course, we're not. It's terrorism – plain and simple - designed to terrify the population in order to achieve goals that are political, religious, or ideological in nature.'

'Yes, I think we all know that,' suggested the Commissioner.

'Yes, but people like Boyd understand terrorism a little bit better than most of us,' explained Sir Phillip. 'Boyd told me once that what we perceive as terrorism is not necessarily seen as terrorism in other places. An organisation on a banned list here may not be on a banned list elsewhere. Herein lies Boyd's understanding of the man he is chasing. White Eagle has not travelled to our country before. There are policing methods used here that are not used elsewhere. The unit that leads this investigation knows its way around terrorism and terrorists, and knows how to talk to those who have legitimate concerns that may not be replicated in this country.'

'I don't understand,' revealed the Foreign Secretary.

'But then you've never met a terrorist,' declared Sir Phillip.

There was a slight pause in proceedings before Maude suggested, 'I wish Boyd were here now. I think we could all do with a shot of Bushmills.'

There were one or two polite chuckles before Edwin Maxwell pursed his lips, looked disdainfully at the Commissioner, the Home Secretary, and the Foreign Secretary, and declared, 'Ladies and gentlemen, I think you should remember that your DA-O5 notice to the media is advice, not law. You cannot make the media comply with your advice. They usually comply but there is nothing in law to say they must. In similar vein, the Home Secretary cannot order either a chief constable or London's police commissioner to do their bidding. In this case the Commissioner is responsible for the operational control of the police, not a government minister. You rely on the press to toe the line. My advice would be to rely on Boyd and my unit to do the job in the way we have planned.'

Maude nodded and glanced at Sir Henry who in turn gestured to Neil, the Commissioner, to respond.

'If not,' continued Commander Maxwell. 'You can have my resignation right here and right now. I can easily walk out of the door.'

Silence prevailed for only a moment before Sandy added, 'And mine too. I'm with the Commander.'

'I agree,' added Sir Phillip.

'Mmm…' responded the Home Secretary. 'Well, you've made your position clear. What about you, Neil? You are the Commissioner and the person who is apparently in control of the policing operation.'

'I think I'd like more time to assess the investigation,' replied the Commissioner.

'Agreed!' stated the Home Secretary reluctantly. 'Commander Maxwell, whilst I have the utmost respect for your unit there must come a time when the question is asked is the right man in the right place doing the right job? My compliments but you have twenty-four hours to produce results otherwise I will insist that different personnel are considered for this enquiry. Yes, it is a political decision — as it the appointment of all Commissioners of the Metropolitan Police, I might add - but I do know that the Prime Minister supports this line of action if the matter cannot be put to bed soon.'

Maxwell nodded and heard Maude add, 'Boyd, Commander? Where is he now?'

Commander Maxwell checked his watch and revealed, 'By now, he should be half way up a mountain in Cumbria by all accounts. We have a second stage plan which is being actioned as we speak.'

Dressed in hiking gear, Boyd, Anthea and Ricky French were climbing the Lakeland Fells and striding out towards the summit.

Anthea paused, took breath, and looked down on the lake below.

'It's beautiful,' she offered. 'But can we please slow down. I can't keep up with you two.'

'Sorry,' replied Boyd. 'I want this done before nightfall. Dig in, Anthea. You'll get there. Ricky, can you manage that equipment okay?'

'Fine,' revealed Ricky. 'But tell me again why we couldn't use a helicopter. This pack is killing my back.'

'Helicopter!' remarked Boyd. 'No, we need to do this without attracting any attention. Come on. Onwards and upwards.'

Anthea took a deep breath and another step forward as the lake below remained serene, undaunted, and locked in an unforgiving time warp.

In North West Cumbria, the tide turned on the Solway Firth and brought a harsh wind inland which whipped across the green and swirled litter around the pavement outside Christ Church.

Mouretti found the caravan site he was looking for, stepped down the bank towards the location, and crept towards the caravan. Cautiously, he slid a hand inside his jacket and felt the handle of the Browning.

The door of a caravan nearby opened, startled Mouretti, and then closed shut again when a woman stepped onto the ground.

Middle-aged, dressed in jeans, a sweater, and a light-coloured raincoat, she asked, 'Hi! Can I help you?'

Mouretti's eyes darted from the woman to the target caravan and back again when he replied, 'Just looking for a friend.'

'Number six?' offered the woman. 'He left last night. You missed him.'

'Oh! Thank you,' replied Mouretti.

'Stay dry,' the woman advised. 'It's going to rain tonight.'

The woman left her caravan and was walking down the street with a shopping bag in one hand and an umbrella in the other.

Mouretti watched her go, looked over his shoulder, and then peered through the caravan windows. It was empty. Removing a pocket knife from his back pocket, Mouretti forced the door and entered the caravan.

The caravan looked bare as if no-one had lived there for a while. It had been wiped clean.

Mouretti systematically searched the caravan by rummaging through all the cupboards, drawers, and hidey-holes that you expect to find in a holiday site's caravan. He even checked the shower unit, cooker and bed before looking beneath the table.

Beside the table leg, on the floor, Mouretti found two ordnance survey maps of the Lake District. He unfolded the first map across the table and studied the detail. Then he unfolded the other map and saw several ink marks that had been deliberately written on the map. The ink marks were all red dashes and ran from Thirlmere east towards Ullswater and the Shap Fells where the map ended.

'Thirlmere,' said Mouretti aloud. 'Why of course. That's where he's gone. A lake that is a reservoir between Keswick and Ambleside in the shadow of Helvellyn in the middle of the Lake District. The killing ground!'

Mouretti threw the map on the floor and stepped out of the caravan leaving the door swinging on its broken hinges.

A car engine fired. Mouretti selected a gear and set of for the Lake District.

Sitting at a bar close to the harbour in Maryport, Eddie Tallentire downed his third pint of the night and turned his attention to the latest programme on the television.

'Another pint when you're ready, marra,' yelled Eddie. 'One more then I'm off. Got the early turn tomorrow.'

'Where to this time?' enquired the barman. 'London, New York or Paris?'

'Silloth, Allonby, Wigton and everything in the vicinity,' replied Eddie. 'I just love this courier job but the international travel is getting me down.'

'Lucky you,' chuckled the barman.

It was on the television.

The face of a customer Eddie had recently delivered a package to in Silloth suddenly appeared on the screen.

'That's him,' snapped Eddie. 'I know him. Turn it up, marra.'

Moments later, Eddie was at the end of the bar using the telephone.

'Aye, that's reet, marra,' revealed Eddie. 'A caravan in Silloth. It was definitely him. He's not from around here. Funny lad, didn't like me but then I couldn't understand him. Weird accent, he had. I'd say he was a Southerner…'

The barman began collecting empty glasses as Eddie continued his phone call to the police.

'Turkish? Nah, no idea really. Could be a foreigner though. He had a darkish skin, you see. A bit like an olive, marra. Now then, the reward! Is there a reward for this like, marra?'

## Chapter Fifteen

~

Cumbria
Dawn
The next day

'The Silloth caravan,' announced Boyd. 'We'll hit it hard and fast if we need to. The witness, Eddie Tallentire, has identified the caravan. It's number six here...'

Boyd pointed at a map on the wall of the briefing room and continued, 'Janice and Terry will take the lead car and have control. The rest of us will form up in convoy. On arrival at the scene, adopt stand by positions before you move in. Red Alpha three, four and five to surround the caravan and strike when Janice and Terry give the word. I'll be in Red Alpha One looking for a break out from the target should he take one of you down. I am your back up. Our target will be surrounded but give yourselves plenty of time to climb over some garden fences and crawl through some rose gardens.'

There was a chuckle or two from the assembly.

'Get as close as you can,' advised Boyd. 'Watch your backgrounds and don't get caught in the crossfire. We must get close and neutralise the subject. Any questions?'

There were none.

'Mount up! Let's go.'

The drive from Carlisle to Silloth took a little over forty minutes. When the team drove across the cobbled road near the green, the tide was turning on the Solway Firth and dawn was creeping over the hills of Dumfries to the north.

Terry turned into Eden Street, took a further left, and pulled up close to the caravan site.

'Am in stand by position,' he radioed. 'Units report in.'

Within minutes, the team were ready, had surrounded the caravan, and were waiting at various vantage points for the order to raid the caravan.

'I have control, stand by,' radioed Terry. 'Reconnaissance in progress.'

As the team responded, Terry glanced at Janice and asked, 'Ready?'

'Wait one,' replied Janice lifting night vision binoculars to her eyes. 'Let's have a look before we do it.'

Quietly, Janice slid out of the squad car and crept towards the caravan with a double-barrelled shotgun in one hand, a radio transmitter in the other, and binoculars slung around her neck.

Using a hedgerow for cover, Janice used her night vision binoculars to locate caravan six. She scanned the approach, the neighbouring caravans, and the windows. Then she crawled on her belly until she was about thirty yards from the caravan.

'Janice, come back,' radioed Terry. 'It's dangerous on your own.'

'I have control, stand by,' replied Janice.

A cat leapt from the roof a neighbouring caravan, frightened the life out of Janice, and scurried off beneath another caravan.

Zeroing in on the caravan door, Janice saw the broken hinges and realised the structure was empty.

'No, it's not dangerous,' radioed Janice. 'Come and join me, Terry. The cupboard is bare.'

Standing up, Janice allowed her shotgun to droop by her side as she strolled towards the caravan. Using the barrel of the gun, she opened the door and stepped inside.

'All Red Alpha units, stand down,' radioed Janice. 'The caravan is abandoned. Guvnor!'

'Attending,' replied Boyd.

The Porsche Cayenne swung into the site. Boyd stepped out of the vehicle with Anthea and shone a torch inside the caravan.

'Oh, yes, it's well and truly empty,' agreed Boyd. 'We'll secure it for forensics but what's that smell?'

'Almonds,' suggested Anthea. 'It's the same smell as the house in Lytham St Annes where one of those poison letters was delivered.'

'You mean the smell is strychnine?' enquired Terry.

'All I know is that strychnine smells like almonds,' disclosed Anthea walking closer to the table in the middle of the caravan. 'It's very faint and certainly not strong enough to harm anyone. Can you smell it, Janice?'

'Och, no, Anthea,' explained the Scot. 'But then I've a wee cold.'

Studying the table top, Boyd then cast his eyes on the floor and recovered an ordnance survey map which he unfolded.

'What do you make of this?' he asked.

'True or false?' enquired Janice. 'Has it been left here for a reason – to throw us of the scent for example?'

'Could be,' agreed Anthea. 'You can never tell with people like this.'

Sniffing again, Boyd suggested, 'Let's suppose our courier friend delivered a parcel from the Placer to Darius whilst he was living here. The parcel contained the bottles of strychnine posing as perfume, possibly even the jiffy bags.'

'You can buy those envelopes in a Spa shop or at the post office,' ventured Anthea. 'But the smell of almonds here does suggest Darius could have used this as a base from which to prepare and send his strychnine-laced letters.'

'Terry, brief two officers to visit the local shops with Darius's photograph,' instructed Boyd. 'Ask them to do the post office and Spa shop first. Let's confirm our thought patterns.'

'Will do, guvnor,' replied Terry withdrawing from the caravan.

'What about those red marks on the ordnance survey map?' enquired Janice. 'Do they mean anything?'

Boyd studied the map and said, 'The markings suggest a route to Thirlmere and then onward to Haweswater. If I remember the plaques on the wall at Heaton Park Reservoir, then that is the route of the water channel from Thirlmere to Haweswater and down to Manchester.'

'Water channel?' queried Janice.

'Aqueducts!' answered Boyd. 'Some over ground, others in tunnels below the ground, but would you believe they are all gravity driven. The level just drops a fraction of an inch every now and again until it reaches Manchester.'

'I didn't know that,' remarked Janice.

'It doesn't matter, Janice,' replied Boyd stepping out of the caravan. 'This man is so very professional at times but then sometimes he's just so careless.'

'Or is he just being clever?' enquired Anthea.

'Either way, it's a game to him,' remarked Boyd. 'And he wants us to know that he's ahead in the game.'

'What else is he thinking?' asked Anthea.

Boyd paused, deep in thought, before replying, 'I need to believe in what we do. If I allow this man to lead we will spend our days chasing him. It's time to lead not follow. Anthea, he's expecting us to chase him all the way to Thirlmere, that's what, and that's why he deliberately left the map behind.'

'Why would he do that if he wants to escape detection and get back to wherever it is that he came from?' asked Janice.

'Because he's a signature killer as well as a terrorist, Janice,' explained Boyd. 'Darius is a megalomaniac. He's obsessed with power. The man has to control everything he touches and everyone he comes into contact with. From people to …Yes, yes, of course, even animals.'

'Do you mean the eagle thing too, guvnor?' enquired Anthea.

'I suppose it's possible,' replied Boyd. 'It might explain the white eagle feathers although I don't for one moment think Darius wanders around the streets with an eagle perched on his arm. No, he just has access to the feathers from his homeland. He could carry them with him. You see, Anthea, Darius needs an audience to prove to his inner self that he is the greatest and the most powerful. Even his name – Darius - sends a powerful message. There was once such a King in Persia. Centuries ago, King Darius led the Persians and invaded Greece. Don't you see? We're his audience and his mind is locked in the past. Can you comprehend his mind and second guess him even though his mind is warped and broken?'

Anthea gradually nodded her understanding and replied, 'We can't disappoint him. Thirlmere, it is.'

'No,' ventured Boyd. 'Not Thirlmere. Haweswater! He's expecting us at Thirlmere. I'll bet he's lining up Thirlmere today.'

'Dear god,' remarked Anthea. 'I hope not but then you had Haweswater on your mind the other day when you took us mountain climbing.'

'Yeah, you see I've gradually began thinking like this man,' declared Boyd. 'It's just taken me a while to get right under his skin and inside his veins. He's one hell of character to fathom out, I can tell you. Look, this is what I propose. You, me and Janice will go to Haweswater – back to the mountain where we took Ricky's kit. Send the rest of the team to Thirlmere. Put Terry in charge there.'

'Are you sure?' pleaded Anthea. 'London won't like it if something goes wrong at Thirlmere and the DCI and DI are not there.'

'I'll inform the Commander. It's my responsibility,' remarked Boyd. 'It goes against the book but I know we need to be at Haweswater.'

'Are you sure Commander Maxwell will support you?' enquired Anthea.

'Yes, I'm sure but I would prefer you two to be with me at Haweswater,' explained Boyd. 'It will do Terry no harm to take command at Thirlmere and I have every confidence in his abilities. But what's done at Thirlmere is done and can't be changed. This Darius is always ahead of the game. Running off to Thirlmere to try and catch him will be a waste of time. He's already left there and moved on to plan the next attack.'

'We're with you, guvnor,' declared Janice. 'We're both with you, aren't we, Anthea.'

'Yes,' announced Anthea. 'I feel it too. I'll brief the team.'

'I'll brief Commander Maxwell on my reasoning and decision,' revealed Boyd. 'Thank you.'

Boyd made the call, checked that his firearm was fully loaded, and thought quietly of Thirlmere.

Simultaneously, at that very moment, dawn was also breaking over Armbroth Fell and the Helvellyn range.

Glass!

Thirlmere resembled a glass mirror which truly captured the calm serenity of the area. It was just so peaceful, so detached from the rest of the world, and so awesomely beautiful and tranquil as it nestled quietly in the shadow of the Helvellyn ridge.

The sun examined the lake, spread its glorious tentacles across the surface, and awakened it once more. The sun found places where it might have been forgiven for thinking that the lake was held in some kind of medieval time warp. Such was the unspoilt beauty to be seen. There were places where you could stand on the lakeside and, whichever way you looked, you would be hard pressed to find evidence of mankind and the modern day.

That dawn, the sun sprinkled its rays on the surface of the water and endowed it with a magical presence that had to be experienced to be believed.

Thirlmere was so still that the stands of trees on the Armbroth Fell side of the lake reflected on the lake's surface.

The time warp was broken when a mini bus travelled south down the A591 at a steady speed. Half way down the lakeside, the driver reached what appeared to be a miniature castle overlooking Thirlmere.

'First time here?' ventured Reg Smith, the driver.

'Yes,' replied Donald, the front seat passenger. 'Why are we stopping at this castle? It looks like one of those old Victorian follies you hear about every now and again. Reminds me of that gardening programme about Capability Brown. They always find a folly somewhere.'

'It's exactly that,' explained Reg. 'This is a folly designed to disguise a pumping station and that's where we're working today. The station is connected to the dam which is connected to the aqueduct which is connected to…'

'The thigh bone?' chuckled his colleague interrupting.

'Come on,' laughed Reg.

They parked up and the maintenance crew filed out of the vehicle to make their way towards the entrance.

'Damn! I forgot the keys for the station,' explained Reg who stopped suddenly, and turned towards the van.

Three seconds later, a bomb exploded.

Two blocks of orange Semtex, and an American M112 charge containing C4 plastic explosives linked to a timing device, ripped away the front door of the building. The blast took away the entire surrounding brickwork, the ageing concrete roof, three tons of surrounding vegetation, one quarter of an acre of tarmac hard standing, and the castle battlements.

Blown off their feet, the four maintenance men were hurled backwards towards the main road where each slammed into a dry-stone wall bordering the highway.

Reg slid to the ground bleeding heavily from a bang on the head where his skull was fractured.

Vegetation and debris crashed down onto the tarmac. Stonework and slabs of concrete splashed into the lake causing an explosion of water that rose into the air, reached a pinnacle, and then splashed down once more. Scores of birds took flight reaching a crescendo of screeching, squealing, and shrieking as peace and tranquillity transformed into shock and horror.

Three other maintenance men suffered back, shoulder, and head injuries as a result of the blast.

Forensic examination and on scene investigations, subsequently led by Detective Sergeant Terry Anwhari of the Special Crime Unit, led to an understanding that if the bus driver had not forgotten his door keys for the pumping station, the likelihood existed that he would have led the team forward and he, and possibly others, would have been killed instantly.

One minute after the explosion occurred at the pumping station, a secondary device detonated at the dam at the northern end of the lake – about a mile away.

Another two blocks of Semtex were used to detonate a device that immediately breached the dam.

The explosion destroyed the two-metre aqueduct at its starting point, tore away brick work, and annihilated the very existence of the barrier between the lake and St John's.

Rising to forty metres, the brick work reached a pinnacle, bore down on the surface of the lake, and fractured the mirror image of the lake. Serenity destroyed, the surface of the water buckled under pressure, protested its innocence, and then rushed to its newest outlet.

Within seconds, water breached the masonry, plummeted over the remains of the Victorian brickwork, and began to ravage the lands towards Keswick, north of the lake.

Half an hour later, St John's beck overflowed and its waters overlapped the banking and began to invade various cottages and holiday homes in the area. Fields were water-logged, roads flooded, campsites destroyed, and the Lake District badly bruised by its newest enemy – terrorism.

Five minutes after the explosions, Giuseppe Mouretti arrived in his hire car at the pumping station. Parking at the side of the road, he took stock of the pumping station, wondered at the damage caused, and ignored the casualties. Stepping around the maintenance team's van, he realised that some of the debris had landed on the vehicle and smashed its windscreen.

Removing binoculars from a case, he scanned the immediate area and then clambered onto a flat piece of dry stone wall where he zoomed in on the area near the dam.

Mouretti shook his head, folded his binoculars, and returned to the car.

A whispered cry for help from Donald was met only by the bite of a Vauxhall car engine igniting when Mouretti drove off. Suddenly, Mouretti braked, slammed the car into reverse, and spun the vehicle around to face Kendal.

Ignoring the injured, Mouretti put his foot down and began to ascend Dunmail Rise as he sped towards Kendal and the south Lakes.

Swearing under his breath, Donald pulled a pen from his overall pocket, removed a battered notebook from another, and scrawled Mouretti's car number on the cover.

Exhausted with the effort, Donald dropped pen and paper on the ground as he fell into semi-consciousness to the sound of Mouretti' car accelerating along the lakeside road.

The Special Crime Unit were soon at the scene where Terry Anwhari took command and requested medical assistance at the scene as well as police from the local area. He quickly spoke to the maintenance team to try and establish what had happened.

'Was there anyone around when you got here?' he asked.

'No,' replied Donald. 'We were heading for the building when Reg realised he'd left his keys in the van. He went back for him and we waited. Then the explosion occurred. What was it? Is there a problem with the pumps down below or is it something else?'

'I'm pretty sure it was a bomb,' revealed Terry. 'I think you're all lucky to be alive. We'll get you off to hospital as soon as possible and come to see you when you are better. But before we do that I just have to ask you a couple of questions.'

'Go on,' replied Donald. 'I'll try and answer them but I feel like I've been dragged through a hedge backwards. Reg is the boss but he's out of it at the moment.'

A glance across at Reg revealed Mark cradling the maintenance team supervisor's head in his arms as they gently moved him away from the dry-stone wall.

'Careful,' remarked Mark. 'Sorry, old son. I know it's hurting but the wall is going to collapse any minute and you don't need another crack on the head.'

A murmured incoherent reply escaped Reg's lips.

'That bastard on the wall didn't help much either,' stated Donald angrily.

'What are you talking about?' enquired Terry.

'Some idiot turned up here minutes after the explosion,' revealed Donald as he tried to ease himself into a more comfortable position. 'He stepped across me, ignored us all, and used his binoculars to look up the lake. What a first-class bastard he was. I would have punched his lights out if I could have got onto my feet.'

'Just lie still,' suggested Terry. 'I can hear a helicopter. The medics are on their way. 'Was he on foot?'

'No,' explained Donald. 'I got his car number though. Can you find out who the driver was? I'd like to give him a piece of my mind.'

Donald pointed to a notebook lying on the ground.

Terry stooped to recover the book, read the number, and replied, 'Me too! That's not the normal thing to do. Yes, my friend, I'll find out who the driver was. Don't you worry about that.'

'Good,' replied Donald.

'The main thing is you're all alive,' commented Terry. 'Here's the Air ambulance helicopters to evacuate you.'

With the road closed in both directions, two helicopters landed and their medics attended to the casualties.

Activating bomb scene management procedures, Terry set up an incident room at the King's Head public house in Thirlspot and began investigating both incidents.

Terry contacted London and asked for more assistance from surrounding forces and various partnership agencies.

Flooding severely hampered the investigation which quickly turned into the emergency evacuation of many residents in the area. Water continued to breach the broken dam, fill the lowland below, and wreak carnage on the county of Cumbria.

London responded by deploying Detective Superintendent Sandy Peel to the county. On arrival, she took over from Sergeant Anwhari.

Two hours after the bombs had exploded, Darius entered a telephone kiosk, made a call, and dropped the correct coinage into the machine.

'This is White Eagle.'

The news reporter immediately recognised his voice and replied, 'You rang the other day.'

'I did,' voiced Darius. 'I have a message for you and your government. You will be aware by now that there has been an attack on the water pumping station at Thirlmere. There has also been an attack on Thirlmere dam.'

'Yeah, we know. You did it, didn't you?'

Ignoring the question, Darius continued, 'You will inform your government that the sum of fifty million pounds will be paid into the following bank account by twelve noon tomorrow…'

As the reporter made a note of the bank account details, he replied, 'That's the same account you mentioned the last time you rang.'

'Correct!' barked Darius. 'Let me repeat that for you – fifty million pounds by twelve noon tomorrow. You will inform the government and the people of the United Kingdom that the destruction of Thirlmere reservoir is merely the start. It is a warning that we mean business. We shall not be defeated. Failure to deposit the money on this occasion will result in members of the White Eagle terrorist group attacking the following reservoirs throughout the United Kingdom…'

'Wait, wait while I get a pencil,' responded the reporter trying to elongate the conversation.

'Windermere,' continued Darius. 'Castle Carrock, Ulverston, Killington, Rutland Water, Kielder Water, Lake Bala, Lake Vyrnwy, Chew Valley, Bristol, the Queen Mother Reservoir in London, Grimouth, Yorkshire, Stocks, Lancashire…'

As Darius continued his list of reservoirs threatened with attack, the reporter beckoned his editor over.

When the call ended, the editor looked at the list and replied, 'To hell with the D notice. Publish and be damned.'

'Turning to the news room, the editor shouted, 'Listen up! Hold the front page. We're going national! In fact, we're going global! Reservoirs! Where the hell are they? Here's the list. I want to know where they are and I want the writing team in my office in two minutes. Let's roll them presses.'

Replacing the phone on its cradle, Darius stepped out of the kiosk, walked into Carlisle railway station, and withdrew a package from the 'left luggage' facility.

A newspaper billboard nearby read, 'Lake District Hunt for terrorists as region's water supply threatened…'

Darius ignored the headlines, placed the package inside a haversack, and hoisted it over his shoulders. Deep within his mind, vengeance fed his heart, neutralised his brain, and drove him onwards.

Darius was on the move again.

*

## Chapter Sixteen

~

Cabinet Office Briefing Room A
Whitehall, London
That night

COBRA is an emergency response committee, which consists of a gathering of ministers, civil servants, police, intelligence officers, emergency service workers, and any others who have an appropriate skill or professionalism that can contribute to whatever problem the committee is considering.

On this day, an emergency relative to the nation's water supply had been identified and COBRA were considering the 'White Eagle Terrorist Group'.

'Have you seen the Standard?' queried Sir Henry Fielding, the Foreign Secretary.

'Briefly,' replied Maude Black, the Home Secretary. 'More importantly, have you been seen the evening's edition? They've completely ignored my advice.'

'Haven't they just,' agreed Neil, the Commissioner. 'What good is a D notice when no-one plays the game. I've brought a selection of journals with me. Look at these…'

Holding the newspapers for all to see, the Commissioner of the Metropolitan Police read aloud, 'Panic in government circles… Call in the army… White Eagle terrorist group destroys Cumbria infrastructure… Manchester water supply at risk… Four seriously injured in Thirlmere bomb explosion… Where will they strike next…? And I could go on.'

'But you won't,' ventured Sir Henry waving more newspaper headlines. 'But I will because some of them put you right on the spot, Commissioner. For example…

Thirlmere aqueduct destroyed… Keswick braces for flooding… St John's Vale takes emergency measures… Arab Sergeant in charge of investigation into White Eagle terrorist attack in Cumbria… White Eagle terrorist group to launch attack on British infrastructure… Now I think that requires input from yourself, Neil.'

'Of course, I should say…'

'Calls for the Home Secretary's resignation,' continued Sir Henry cutting off the Commissioner… 'D Notice ignored by Press and Media…. And finally, this one… Where are all the missing police leaders? Maude, I really do think this committee needs to adduce a reply to the last one from the police officers here. Just where – precisely – is the police command system at a time of national emergency?'

There was an uncomfortable silence, the shuffling of nervous feet, and a slight cough before Maude looked sternly at the Commissioner and barked, 'Neil! You oversee the police and have the lead on terrorism and national security. Your response is required. It's late and we could do with wrapping this one up. We're short on sleep and not much better in temper. Now, if you please.'

'We have learnt some obvious things from these newspaper reports,' announced Neil. 'Firstly, I can confirm that a Sergeant Anwhari was made Bomb Scene Commander at Thirlmere and initially took charge of the investigation. Of course, once I learnt of this, he was replaced by Detective Superintendent Peel who has international experience of major terrorist attacks. Things are now progressing nicely. As Commissioner for the Metropolitan Police, let me remind you once more that I have consistently argued that the term White Eagle applies to a group – not an individual. These newspaper reports clearly support my argument.'

'Newspaper reports are not evidence,' declared Commander Maxwell interrupting. 'There is a fine line between reporting the news and writing articles that capture the public's imagination sufficiently to make people want to buy the paper so that advertising revenue can be accrued. Furthermore, I would add that Detective Sergeant Anwhari is a first-class officer of Pakistani parentage. He, however, was born and bred in England. The West Midlands, to be precise. Hardly an Arab, if you don't mind me saying.'

The Commander reached out and poured himself a glass of water before continuing, 'I'm sure none of you need to be reminded that the same officer was responsible for the recruitment of the source codenamed Patient Lamb who led us onto the trail of White Eagle. For the record, I, and not the Commissioner, deployed Superintendent Peel to the scene. She took more officers with her in order to enhance the capability of the enquiry team. Her international experience, by the way, appears to have been a week-long jolly to Istanbul at the request of the Foreign Secretary.'

Leaning back, the Commander heard no response and continued, 'And if I might add - There is no firm intelligence to suggest there is a White Eagle Terrorist Group. I have steered this investigation, with my colleagues, on the premise that there is one primary suspect who is aided and abetted by at least one accomplice. These horrific attacks are carried out by one individual supported by Placers who provide the wherewithal to accomplish the task whilst they, themselves, are not present. Nothing has happened recently to change my mind and any ideas that you have of some kind of mass group attack by an armed militia need to be banished forthwith.'

Taking a sip of water, Commander Maxwell then finished with, 'Unless anyone here convinces me otherwise.'

There was no reply.

'In which case,' remarked the Commander. 'I will continue our investigation in the manner in which it is presently being conducted.'

Sir Henry raised a hand and enquired, 'Boyd, Commander! As I understand it from your briefing papers this Anwhari chap was sent to look after a major incident whilst Boyd deployed the mainstay of his team elsewhere. That is not acceptable. The man is an imbecile and ought to know better. He is a liability to us and should be removed from office.'

'Commissioner?' remarked Maude. 'Despite what Commander Maxwell has said I do believe there is substance in Sir Henry's argument. Major emergencies should not be left in the hands of the minor ranks of the police service. People like Boyd should know that and accept their responsibilities.'

'The team has been trained to the highest degree possible,' intervened Commander Maxwell. 'You've also poured millions into the Special Crime Unit and its technological expertise. It is bad practice to train officers to a high degree of capability and then criticise them half way through an extremely complex investigation. There is a defined need to progress the investigation in tandem with how those on the ground see it.'

Ignoring the Commander's remarks, Maude barked, 'Sir Phillip! On which bench do you sit tonight?'

Sir Phillip did not hesitate in his response when he replied, 'As Director General of the Security Service I recommend we continue as planned. My analysis is that there is no terrorist group and Boyd and his people are best placed to catch our man. Politically, that is difficult for some of you here to comprehend because you have little or no experience of chasing megalomaniacs. Boyd has adopted the concept of 'the Greater Good' and he is correct in that assertion.'

'But we do have experience in managing impending disasters,' growled Sir Henry. 'I recommend we deploy the army to provide a security presence at every reservoir mentioned in the target list presented to us by the media.'

'Would it not be cheaper to pay the ransom?' enquired General McAdam from the Ministry of Defence.

'No, of course not,' announced the Home Secretary. 'We do not pay ransoms. But I am in favour of military deployment at a time of national crisis. In the absence of the Prime Minister - with whom I have recently consulted and who is currently in America visiting their recently installed new President - I intend to pursue that course of action. General McAdam, avail yourself of the target list detailed by White Eagle and deploy the military to guard each establishment.'

'When?' asked the General.

'Now,' replied Maude. 'I understand the pros and cons but politically I cannot be seen to be doing nothing. I'd appreciate the early execution of my request, General. Please note, with the Prime Minister's approval, an emergency meeting of JTAC – the Joint Terrorism Analysis Centre – has raised the threat level to threat level one. We are now at critical.'

'Of course, Home Secretary. Immediate deployment!'

Commander Maxwell glanced at Sir Phillip who added, 'Closing the door after the horse has bolted?'

'Not at all,' responded Maude. 'I'm covering all the bases. Commissioner! I'll ask you again – Boyd – it's time, is it not?'

Nodding, the Commissioner replied, 'I'll instigate disciplinary proceedings immediately.'

'How ridiculous,' responded Commander Maxwell angrily. 'What for? He's done nothing wrong.'

'And nothing right,' contended the Commissioner.

'May I?' suggested Sir Phillip. 'It is not my place to make such decisions but the purpose of COBRA is surely to take the correct steps forward. I suggest we leave things exactly as they are and wait for Boyd and his team to execute the final stages of their plan.'

'No,' replied the Commissioner. 'I have the final say in respect of operational police matters. Commander Maxwell, I hereby inform you that Detective Chief Inspector William Miller Boyd is immediately suspended from duty.'

'On what charges?' growled Commander Maxwell.

'Boyd is suspended pending enquiries into his gross incompetence,' announced the Commissioner. 'I see a serious inability to perform the duties of the role and rank that he currently undertakes. He is below the satisfactory standard to the extent that his dismissal would be justified.'

Commander Maxwell stood up, set his chair back, and replied, 'One day you will all cease to play your futile games of political one-upmanship and learn the true meaning of leadership. I will inform the officer accordingly, oh ye of little faith. It is a scapegoat you seek, not an answer to the crisis before you.'

The hinge of the door closing was the only sound in the room when Commander Maxwell walked out of the COBRA meeting.

'More time!' exclaimed Sir Phillip. 'You could have granted Boyd's team more time.'

'We have no time,' barked the Home Secretary.

Pursing his lips, Sir Phillip considered the Home Secretary's eyes and replied, 'Some of us will use every second we have to win.'

'Why?' enquired Maude. 'It's over for him. His time has run out. If Boyd has any sense he will step aside and let someone else take the reins.'

Sir Henry stroked his chin and then asked, 'What exactly is Boyd doing, Sir Phillip? Do you know at all? Or have you thrown your toys out of the pram because we did not support your comments?'

'Boyd? Of course, I know what he's doing,' replied Sir Phillip glancing at the Commissioner. 'He's playing with his new toys.'

'Toys!' ventured the Home Secretary. 'Toys have to be tested and approved before use.'

Nodding, Sir Phillip chuckled and said, 'That's Boyd. He didn't read the instructions on the box but he'll always find time to play with his toys.'

'But they're not yet approved or even tested for viability,' argued the Home Secretary disapprovingly. 'We don't even know if they work properly.'

'What toys?' enquired the Commissioner.

'You would do well to fully understand the working capabilities of the Special Crime Unit, Commissioner,' suggested Sir Phillip. 'But then you are new in post and have not yet grasped the importance of listening to those in the ranks below you. It's usually where most effective police work is done.'

The Commissioner was lost for a reply.

'The toys that you speak of,' suggested Maude. 'Are actually dangerous in their present state.'

'Well, they are being tested now,' revealed Sir Phillip looking at his wristwatch. 'Right now.'

Mouretti braked, slipped down a gear, and brought the car to a standstill. He was in a hotel car park but the premises appeared to be closed. Presuming there was a lack of holidaymakers in the area due to recent events, Mouretti checked his surroundings before reversing the car into a space. He switched the engine off and waited.

'How long will I be here?' he wondered. Then, inspired by the need for revenge burning deep within his soul, he told himself, 'As long as it takes. The trap is set.'

Removing binoculars from the glove compartment, Mouretti approached the lakeside where he scanned the draw off tower before turning his attention to the dam.

'Another circular folly,' he thought. 'Another strange castle at the side of the lake. A circular castle that is rooted in the lake yet climbs to a height of twenty yards or so and meets a jetty made of brickwork and a path which is decorated with battlements. No matter, the man will come soon.'

Terry Anwhari pulled into a lay-by on the outskirts of Ambleside, withdrew his mobile phone, and prepared a text message to be sent to Boyd. The text contained the registration number of a car driven by a stranger who was one of the first at the scene of the Thirlmere attack.

'It's a hire car,' added Terry as he tapped the digits. 'The hirer gave a false name and address. Circulated to all patrols, but for your information.'

In capitals, Terry added, 'SUGGEST TREAT WITH CAUTION. DRIVER NOT KNOWN...'

Exhaling, Terry pressed 'send', and then immediately answered a call from Superintendent Peel.

'Terry, a state of emergency still exists throughout the county due to flooding, potential loss of water supply to the region, and a mountain of enquiries and actions still to be undertaken.'

'I'm on way, Ma'am. I'll be with you shortly.'

'No, Terry,' replied Sandy. 'I've linked up with the local Cumbrian commanders and they are now in charge of the humanitarian crisis. This leaves us free to concentrate on what we do best – investigation, analysis, and response. I've already spoken to Boyd. I want you to travel north over Kirkstone Pass and meet up with Martin and myself in the Penrith area. We're on channel 316 encrypt. Get a move on. We're back in the game.'

'Will do,' smiled Terry. 'I'm on my way.'

Terry Anwhari fired the engine and headed north for Ambleside. Within a couple of miles, he found Hayes Garden Centre, filtered into the one-way system, and negotiated the town centre.

At the mini roundabout, Terry swung the car to the right and began his ascent up Kirkstone Pass.

Driving up the slipway from the motorway, Darius negotiated the roundabout and headed south. In the distance, he marvelled at the high mountains rising from the grasslands below. To some extent, the scenery reminded him of home but then thinking of his past only drove him further and intensified his calling.

Darius Yasin was fuelled by revenge as he gunned the vehicle along the country lane towards his destiny.

Elsewhere in Cumbria, a newsagent stripped away last night's advertisement from an A board outside his shop and replaced it with the latest headline.

Standing back, he read the headlines.

'Mass tourist exodus in aftermath of terrorist attack…Lake District closes for business as the Home Secretary raises the nation's threat level to Threat Level One…. 'critical'…'

*

## Chapter Seventeen
~

Mardale Head
Haweswater,
Dawn, the next day

The car park at Mardale Head, at the most southerly part of Haweswater, was deserted except for a couple of unsigned squad cars and a motorhome in which Ricky French, Boyd, Anthea and Janice were busy setting up operations for the day.

Ricky, and his colleagues, had adapted much of the vehicle for use by the Special Crime Unit but it had never been used operationally before. Now, Ricky – the gizmo man, as they called him – was in his element as he switched the technology suite on and brought the system to life via a row of switches.

Moments later, a covert external camera beamed images to a television screen inside the vehicle.

Serving mugs of coffee, Janice enquired, 'How long?'

'Soon,' replied Ricky. 'Let's hope the activation system works otherwise we're doomed.'

'Have faith,' replied Boyd. 'We didn't drop it.'

'Oh, you've taken stuff up there before have you?' asked Anthea.

'I once dragged a canoe up to Kidsty Pike and camped for a week at Blea Water,' announced Boyd. 'Mind you, I was a lot younger then. Our problem is the system is new and it needs the height to begin with otherwise it's a non-starter.'

Janice stirred milk and sugar into her drink and asked, 'I take it the road stops here and there's only one way in and one way out?'

'That's right,' confirmed Boyd. 'Of all the lakes in the county, you won't find one more remote than this.'

'At this time of the morning, we won't find anyone out there,' suggested Janice. 'And that's good. We're first here and ahead of the game at last.'

'I hope so,' remarked Boyd glancing at his wristwatch. 'I sure hope Sandy and the rest of the team are lined up too. If I'm wrong then we're in the wrong place again.'

'I'm ready,' interrupted Ricky. 'Just say when.'

'Now,' replied Boyd. 'Let's do it.'

Ricky nodded and turned his attention to the control unit.

Four miles north, close to Haweswater Beck, in Frith Wood, Darius climbed out of his bivouac.

He checked the immediate area and then folded the improvised canvas shelter tightly into his rucksack. Removing some dried meat and nuts from one of the pockets, Darius ate a quick breakfast before taking a few slugs of water from a leather canteen. Standing, he hoisted the rucksack onto his shoulders and used the cover of Frith wood to walk down to the dam near Burnbanks.

At Mardale, on the crags overlooking the lake, the bird stumbled at first but eventually flew from its nest on Eagle Crag.

Initially, it swept low over Heron Crag, Swinside Crag, and the Rigg, before the bird circled Mardale Head car park. The eagle swooped low over the motorhome then began to climb following the course of Riggindale Beck. Gradually, the bird climbed a little higher until it reached Kidsty Pike before turning back towards Birks Crag and the Haweswater Reservoir draw off tower. As the bird reached the midway point across the stretch of water, it failed for a second or two, dipped low suddenly, found new wings, and rose again.

On waste ground, at the side of Haweswater Hotel, Mouretti yawned, checked the time, and then removed a handgun from his shoulder holster. Checking it was fully loaded, Mouretti then reached down to his ankle holster and did likewise. Finally, he reached into the rear passenger seat and examined a holdall. Selecting a Heckler and Koch MP-5 submachine gun, he assured himself of its readiness and then replaced the German designed masterpiece.

Giuseppe Mouretti reminded himself of why he had spent the night in this remote area of the Lake District. He thought of his father – General Tomaso Mouretti – and vowed again that he would avenge his death.

Ravaged by sorrow and with an inability to forgive, Mouretti looked at himself in the driver's mirror. He was a shadow of his former self. His eyes seemed dull and his skin was drawn tight across his face. Stress riddled his inner soul, destroyed him, and made him unaccountable for the actions he intended.

Shaking himself free, Mouretti cursed the image before him and pushed the mirror to one side.

'I've overslept,' he chided himself. 'The dam or the draw off tower – which?'

Twelve miles away, Sandy Peel and Terry Anwhari drove off closely followed by Martin Duffy on his motorbike. At the roundabout, they took the A6 south, turned off at Eamont Bridge, and headed into the Lake District.

The car park at Mardale remained uncluttered and free from early morning walkers or tourists.

'Nearly lost it there,' ventured Ricky wrestling with the controls. 'New-fangled, that's all.'

'Will it make a thousand feet?' enquired Janice.

'It should reach fifteen hundred metres according to these instructions,' replied Ricky. 'We don't need it that high today.'

'It looks small up there.'

'It's six feet in diameter,' replied Ricky. 'And a handful of weight for one man to handle.'

'How long do the batteries last?' asked Anthea.

'Seventy-two hours,' replied Boyd. 'Our eagle is top of the range apparently.'

'I thought it was going to crash,' suggested Janice. 'And if you dinae mind me saying, that surveillance drone looks more like a hawk than an eagle.'

'It's supposed to look like a bird,' stated Ricky. 'I spent weeks disguising it so that you can't easily see the propeller units and stuff. It's not brilliant but when it gets that high I don't really care what it looks like as long as it does its job. People below will see a bird if they look up, nothing else.'

'Made by a Sassenach?' suggested Janice.

'Not according to the paperwork,' revealed Boyd. 'A company from Motherwell have the contract. Ricky just added a few feathers and a beak.'

'Och, it'll work then,' chuckled Janice.

'I think you're biased,' suggested Boyd with a smile.

'Does the video link work, Ricky?'

'I think so,' replied Ricky. 'There's a slight time lapse, I understand, but once Bannerman confirms reception we'll be good to go.'

'Good,' smiled Boyd. 'Come on, ladies, let's get kitted up.'

Darius emerged from the wood, bent low on his haunches, and took stock of the land ahead.

He took a deep breath and tried to distinguish the odour of his surroundings. Everything was fresh. Darius couldn't detect the hint of an exhaust fume, the smell of tobacco on the wind, or the tell-tale odour of human sweat. His nostrils filled with the presence of the wood and the surrounding countryside.

Removing a slender monocle from its trouser belt holding, he scanned the land before him. All he could see was the mirror image of dawn over Haweswater. It was nothing less than a unique sheen portrayal of undiluted elegance.

Then a deer filled the circular image of his monocle. Proud, unashamed, perhaps a few hundred yards away on the edge of the lake, the deer chewed remorselessly whilst looking in the direction of the hunter.

Darius smiled, wanted to reach out and stroke the animal, but then holstered the monocle and moved forward.

Boyd's mobile phone rang and he answered it. The caller was Commander Edwin Maxwell speaking from his office in the Operations Centre of the Special Crime Unit.

'Bannerman asked me to tell you that he has live video coverage from the eagle, William. Please pass my congratulations to Ricky.'

'I will, sir,' replied Boyd. 'But what brings you out so early in the morning? Surely dawn hasn't broken over the Thames yet?'

'I'll come to that shortly, William,' replied the Commander. 'This might sound a little unusual, but I'll explain in a moment. I'd like you to confirm your field of vision for Operational Command please.'

Darius approached the dam with all the stealth his mind and body could muster.

'I'll be proud and unashamed like the deer,' he thought. 'Here for a moment and then gone on the wind. Or shall I slither through the grass like the unseen snake?'

Clinging to the wall, Darius crept low and out of sight, and found his footing on the old brickwork. In the middle of the dam, he unfastened his haversack and removed the C-4 plastic explosives, a fuse cap, a length of detonator cord, and that part of a smartphone which incorporates the timer. Using the oldest and simplest type of fuse cap, he inserted a fuse into the open end of the cap where there was a space. He then added a small amount of pyrotechnic ignition mix before crimping the cap. Linking the fuse cap to the detonating cord, Darius then crimped the detonating cord slightly and connected it to a tiny mobile phone USB. He then connected the USB to the mobile phone. The whole system depended on the mobile phone detonation device. All Darius had to do now was ring the mobile phone number from his own phone. This would cause an electronic pulse to rush down the detonating cord and ignite the C-4. The explosion would be instantaneous.

Checking his watch, he knew it would take less than a second to detonate the plastic explosives and rip the dam apart. Two pounds of plastic explosives was all he needed to blow a hole the size of a dustbin in the dam wall. The pressure of the water against the dam wall would do the rest.

Checking his watch, glancing over his shoulder, he realised he was alone in his world of hatred and revenge.

'I will always remember. I will never forget,' he murmured as he checked the system.

'Basic, but you will do the job well without much fuss,' he muttered to himself. 'The valley will flood and backwater because of the high land ahead, but the draw off tower! That is where we will enter the pipeline and tunnels to destroy their water.'

Simultaneously, at that very moment, Boyd heard alarm bells ringing in his brain and knew something wasn't quite right.

'That's not like the Commander,' he thought.

'William! An Operational Command Briefing, if you please.'

Boyd switched the phone call to public mode so that others present in the vehicle could hear the conversation.

'William!' pleaded the Commander.

Glancing at the television screen inside the motorhome, Boyd took a deep breath and replied, 'Commander, the eagle is a quadcopter drone fitted with four cameras and four mini propellers. Two to the front and two to the rear. All four cameras operate independently, produce colour imagery as well infra-red night-time images, and have zoom capability.'

With two more explosive packages now inserted into the dam's brickwork, Darius took another slug of water and returned to the woodland. On route, he paused at each station, checked that all three USBs were properly connected, and then moved on.

A shadow crossed his path and Darius glanced upwards to capture the image of a bird in the sky.

'An eagle,' he chuckled. 'I have heard about the golden eagle of the Lake District. What kind of country only has one eagle? All this way from home and an eagle decides to watch over me. Maybe Malik is right. There really is an Allah somewhere and today is my lucky day. It is the day of the White Eagle'

In the motorhome, Boyd continued, 'The eagle is programed to complete a figure of eight tour of the reservoir at a height of five hundred feet above the level of the water. The circuit takes about twelve minutes to accomplish at an average speed of twenty miles an hour. There is a hover capability and a speed control if required. Like an eagle, the quadcopter can reach speeds more than thirty miles an hour on a level plane, and much more in a dive. During the twelve minutes' circuit, the eagle will provide live coverage of the dam at the north end of the lake, the car park at the south end, and the draw off tower towards the south-east. At any specific time, a quadcopter camera will be focused on a target. The eagle can be controlled either on site from the technology suite in the motorhome or the operations centre where Bannerman is controller. The latter option will be utilised today because we want to make the lake look as if it is totally devoid of people. Hopefully, a sighting of the suspect by the eagle should trigger a response from ourselves and we will take steps to counter any threat uncovered.

'You mean White Eagle,' remarked the Commander.

'Correct, sir. I'm pulling Ricky out of the car park and sending him north to the village of Askham. There's not a vehicle to be seen here. I have one problem though.'

'Which is?' quizzed Commander Maxwell.

'That was the eagle's maiden flight,' explained Boyd. 'It's the first time we've used it and the damn thing nearly crashed.'

Mouretti drove casually along the side of the lake, worked out his proximity to the draw off tower, and parked the Vauxhall on the roadside.

Leaving the vehicle, he noticed how isolated the area was. There was no sign of a living mortal anywhere.

Mouretti crossed the road and crept towards the draw off tower.

Meanwhile, fifty yards' way, walking parallel in the dense undergrowth, Darius skirted the lakeside and eased the contents of his rucksack as he made his way towards the draw off tower. The ground was flat where he walked but it was also steep to his left-hand side. His versatile bearing and physical upbringing had equipped him with the wherewithal to defeat the uneven terrain.

Head down, determined, he ploughed on. To the casual observer, he would pass for a tourist walking. Except today, there were no tourists on the area and Darius Yasin was bent on revenge.

'And your reasoning for the operation, William?' demanded the Commander.

'The operation is designed to draw out the suspect and lull him into a feeling of supreme confidence because of the lack of people in the area, and its isolation from the rest of the world. There is an option to deploy large numbers of police or military to defend this and other areas but I have decided that course of action will merely extend the period of the threat to the nation indefinitely. It will also add untold expenditure to the nation's law enforcement budget and is likely to stretch personnel beyond their capabilities. Since this unit is briefed to defend the realm it is intended to neutralise the threat at the earliest opportunity and therefore reduce the threat level from critical to a less severe level.'

'And your armoury?'

'Standard operational briefing applies. Team Red Alpha are covertly deployed to the operation each carrying handguns and pump action shotguns.'

'Anything else command should know?'

'No, sir,' replied Boyd.

'Thank you, William. I accept your command briefing and hereby authorise the operation. However, Inspector Bannerman has just handed me a formal document which arrived last night. It is from the Commissioner.'

'I see,' replied Boyd. 'What does it say, sir?'

Bannerman winked at Commander Maxwell when the Commander announced, 'It says that you have been suspended from duty on the orders of the Commissioner of the Metropolitan Police, William. You are hereby ordered to stand down and abort the operation forthwith. That's why I wanted you to do an Operational Command Briefing, Boyd. For the record, and a good explanation of your reasoning should the matter go to disciplinary proceedings.'

Spellbound, Boyd held the phone for a moment, engaged the gathering inside the motorhome, and said, 'Did I hear that right? I'm suspended!'

'That's what the man said,' confirmed Anthea.

'Confirmed,' remarked the Commander. 'You are hereby ordered to abort the operation.'

Studying his screen, Bannerman took remote control of the eagle drone. He manipulated the controls and said, 'Commander!'

In the motorhome, Boyd looked at his phone and remarked, 'We're all ready to go, Commander. You know what will happen if we just drive away and leave it like it is. You can't suspend me. I mean, it's just not right.'

'Commander! Look at this,' suggested Bannerman pointing at the eagle's screen coverage.

'Are you telling me, William,' suggested Commander Maxwell. 'That there are occasions when protocol and bureaucracy ought to be abandoned in the name of 'the Greater Good' as they say?'

Janice nodded and whispered, 'Och, you told me aboot that when we were on with Patient Lamb that time. Do you remember, guvnor?'

'The boss is giving you a lifeline,' suggested Anthea quietly.

Lost in his thoughts for a moment, Boyd suddenly kick-started himself and replied, 'Yes, yes, of course.' Then louder, Boyd added, 'Yes! Yes, Commander, I am.'

'Then that sounds about right to me but…'

Boyd cut the Commander off when he declared, 'I'll do this on my own. Those here needn't put their neck on the line. If it all goes wrong the Commissioner and his cronies will hang them out to dry whatever the circumstances are.'

'It is their choice,' recommended Commander Maxwell. 'I will support you all in whatever decisions you make.'

'One thing, sir,' ventured Boyd. 'Has Bannerman got the car registration number from Terry?'

Bannerman turned to the Commander and said, 'I've got more than the car number, Commander. I had an image of a man with a haversack on the dam wall. He's gone now but that could be our man. I'm checking the dam wall at the moment.'

The eagle drone hovered above the lake and swivelled slightly. One of the cameras focused on the dam wall whilst another scanned the area.

Spinning on his heel, Commander Maxwell eyed the images and replied, 'Can you zoom in closer?'

'I'll try,' replied Bannerman. 'I'll need to bring the eagle around once more to get closer.'

There was the almost inaudible sound of Bannerman moving the control dials when the Commander returned to his phone call and said to Boyd, 'William, we've had a sighting of a man on the dam at the other end of the lake. It might be a local walking the dog, poaching, fishing, or who knows what. Bannerman is bringing the drone around once more for a better look. By the way, yes, he's got the car number. Patrols may well intercept the vehicle before it reaches you.'

'In that case, Operation Eagle is go,' revealed Boyd.

'Good luck,' replied Commander Maxwell.

'Sir,' remarked Boyd. 'Thank you.'

'For the Greater Good, William. The Greater Good!

The call ended.

Turning to the group, Boyd asked, 'Who's with me?'

'You'll need auxiliary power and an extraction vehicle,' suggested Ricky. 'I'll stay close but out of sight.'

Looking at the two ladies, Boyd heard Janice say, 'Och, aye. The show is about to start. I didnae join this mob to swop knitting patterns and drink tea in the garden.'

'Always with you, guvnor,' suggested Anthea. 'We are who we are and we stand for what we are. Whatever others say.'

Nodding, smiling, Boyd declared, 'Let's get on with it then. Throat microphones only. Bannerman,' he radioed, 'Test signal and image focus.'

'Audio visual is good all round,' replied Bannerman. 'I take it you are failing to obey a lawful order?'

'Yes, are you with us?'

'Of course,' replied Bannerman. 'I've nothing better to do today.'

'In that case.... Deploy!' demanded Boyd.

Bannerman piped back, 'You have it but I have a vehicle travelling from the hotel car park towards you. Stand by... I'm zooming in... Yes, it's the same car number. Confirmed... It's the Vauxhall that was at Thirlmere yesterday. There's one occupant. It's a male driver and I'm wondering if it's the same man I saw on the wall at the dam.'

'The draw off tower,' announced Boyd. 'Let's go.'

Ricky fired the engine and set off towards the draw off tower. Within seconds, Anthea, Boyd, and Janice overtook the motorhome on the climb out of Mardale towards the tower.

In the Operations Centre of the Special Crime Unit, Bannerman manipulated more dials and watched the image of Haweswater change on his control screen.

'Red Alpha One,' radioed Bannerman.

'Go ahead,' replied Boyd.

'The eagle has spotted what appears to be three packages inserted into the dam wall. I can see some wires coming out of the brickwork. In addition, your suspect vehicle is still moving towards the draw off tower. It's the Vauxhall and it's coming your way.

'I have that,' replied Boyd. 'Red Alpha One to all Red Alpha units, close in. Close the road at Burnbanks. Exercise caution. Suspect may be armed.'

'I have that,' acknowledged Sandy. 'We are deploying. All units… all units, support Red Alpha One. Lock the area down.'

Mouretti swung the Vauxhall down the road, glanced to his offside, and saw Darius in the distance walking on a narrow gravel beach near the lakeside. A second later, Mouretti slipped the clutch and turned the Vauxhall's engine off.

Coasting downhill, Mouretti allowed the downhill gradient from Haweswater Hotel to carry the vehicle gently towards the draw off tower.

Silently, and out of Darius's sight, Mouretti guided the Vauxhall along the lake road.

Separated by the dry-stone wall, a steep bank down to the lakeside, and a narrow gravel path, Darius continued to head in the same direction as Mouretti. He was completely oblivious to the vehicle and driver passing him.

'Come into my web said the spider to the fly,' murmured Mouretti as he made plans for the arrival of Darius at the draw off tower. He would be there before him.

Meanwhile, a few miles away, the rest of Boyd's team were preparing.

'Road fully closed at this location,' radioed Sandy from Burnbanks to the north. 'There's no way out. We are in lock down.'

'I have that,' replied Boyd.

'Red Alpha One,' radioed Martin. 'I have a Ford parked on wasteland near Thornthwaite Hall, just north of the lake at Burnbanks. A check on the police national computer reveals no suspicious trace. It's a rental and it's locked and secure. More interestingly, there's an automated machine car park ticket on the side window.'

'Where from?' queried Boyd. '

'Guvnor,' radioed Martin. 'The car park ticket is from Silloth and it's fairly recent.'

'Disable the vehicle,' radioed Boyd. 'Tyres!'

'I have that,' replied Martin.

Moments later, Martin Duffy dismounted his motor cycle and inserted a device into the front offside tyre.

There was a long slow hiss when the Ford's tyre deflated.

'Two cars but only one suspect,' remarked Boyd. 'What's going on?'

'Maybe we were wrong,' suggested Janice. 'Two cars might carry eight people or two people. It could be a gang of terrorists after all. We just mucked up, guvnor.'

Nodding, Boyd replied, 'It's too late now, Janice. Let's get on with it.'

'Aye,' agreed Janice. 'For the greater bloody good it is then.'

Mouretti, the NATO investigator, mounted the grass verge to the nearside and got of his vehicle. Reaching into the rear passenger area, he armed himself with a Heckler and Koch MP-5 submachine gun.

Checking the magazine, Mouretti walked forward.

Bannerman studied the screen image from the eagle and announced, 'Red Alpha One, I have a close-up image of one of the packages at the dam. Scanning the wall, I can tell you we have three potential bombs linked to timing devices at the dam.'

'What time is it now?' radioed Boyd.

'Coming up to half seven,' replied Bannerman. 'The time limit for the payment is twelve noon.'

'We have time,' replied Boyd.

'I can deploy Sandy and her team to the dam,' suggested Bannerman.

'No!' ordered Boyd. 'They are briefed to seal the area. No-one gets out of the valley today and I want that Ford Martin has his eye on bottomed out. Who owns it? Who drives it? What was the mileage when it was hired? The works please!'

'I'll find out,' replied Commander Maxwell standing behind Bannerman.

'We're on it,' radioed Bannerman.

Anthea radioed, 'I'll take the dam. Bannerman, can you see any anti-handling devices?'

'Nope,' replied Bannerman. 'Look before you touch when you get there, Anthea. You know the drill. It looks like a detonator plugged into the explosives via a tiny black box which may be a timer.'

'It's mine,' volunteered Anthea. 'I have the knowledge. Boyd?'

'I have that,' radioed Boyd. 'Janice and I will engage.'

Bannerman slapped his desk angrily when the eagle's image went down. 'Damn it! Not now!'

'Oh, not now! Please not now!' roared Commander Maxwell.

'The eagle is down,' radioed Bannerman. 'I'm fighting to get the images back… Stand by. I say again, the eagle is down. We have no images.'

With no other mortal in sight, Mouretti crossed the road and crept towards the path to the draw off tower as Darius approached the outer wall from the lakeside.

Here, the lake was shallow due to the lack of recent rain. Darius made out the pebbles that covered the lake bed, stepped gingerly onto them, and eyed the battlements towering above him.

The distance between the two men was about fifty yards but it began to close when Mouretti climbed over the dry-stone wall and made the path.

There was a crunch on the gravel when Mouretti's shoe scraped the surface.

A vehicle accelerated hard past the draw off tower when Anthea journeyed north in the squad car and snatched a lower gear to maximise performance on the empty road.

Darius heard both sounds, glanced to the roadside, and stood still for a moment. Looking over his left shoulder, he saw the rear of Anthea's car disappearing around an offside bend as it headed towards Haweswater Hotel. Then he listened and simultaneously reached for a handgun in his shoulder holster.

Aiming his handgun towards the top of the tower, Darius scoured the area he could see near the roadway and the dry-stone wall. His vision was limited but he wasn't going anywhere until he was sure.

'There's one unidentified male just entered the path at the draw off tower,' radioed Anthea. 'He's yours. I'm making for the dam.'

'Got that,' replied Boyd. 'We are closing. Control... Contact... Contact.... Contact!'

In the Operations Centre, Commander Maxwell nodded and whispered, 'I wish I was twenty years younger at times. Good luck!'

'I have your contact with the target,' radioed Bannerman.

Darius considered his next step. It was then that the eagle reappeared in the skies above him.

'There's no-one there. I worry too much. An eagle would not approach if there were people about. Not an English eagle with no other eagles in the area. Thank you, my friend.'

Reaching inside the rucksack, Darius removed a grappling iron. There was a medium sized anchor hook on the end and he began to weigh the rope and anchor in his hands as he looked at the tower above him.

The eagle flew over the tower and continued towards the dam as Darius began to measure the sway need to hoist the grappling iron over the battlements and climb the wall.

There was a soft clunk when the rope soared over the battlements and the anchor snagged on the brickwork. Darius tugged the rope and felt satisfied that the rope would hold him for the climb ahead. It was only twenty feet or so above him but he had reached the target without using the road and without being seen by anyone.

The only sound Darius could hear was the soft creaking of the rope as he began his climb in the morning breeze.

Mouretti knew Darius was climbing the wall and would eventually arrive on the battlements but he couldn't see him for the circular tower. Somewhere on the tower there was a door which led down into the pipeline and tunnel network that was part of the route to Manchester and the north west of England.

Dropping to the ground, Mouretti crawled on his belly, slithered into a gully by the path and waited to take his first shot.

With time on his side, he tightened the weapon into his shoulder and took aim at the tower's door.

'That's where he's headed,' thought Mouretti. 'But he'll never make the other side.'

Mouretti heard a foot fall on the outer brickwork and knew Darius was climbing again.

'Where are you, my friend,' thought Mouretti. 'I have a bullet with your name written on it.'

Boyd and Janice abandoned their squad cars and approached on foot. Using the dry-stone wall for cover, they noticed Mouretti's abandoned Ford and then reached the path to the tower.

'No sign,' whispered Boyd. 'The path is clear.'

'Watch my back, guvnor,' replied Janice as she dropped to her knees and began to crawl towards the path.

'Approaching the dam,' radioed Anthea.

'I have that,' acknowledged Bannerman in the Operations centre.

Boyd took cover behind the dry-stone wall as Janice belly crawled along the path towards the tower. Wanting to present the smallest target possible to any would-be killer, she moved slowly but accurately as Boyd shrunk behind the wall and took in the scene as he covered her movements.

The circular draw off tower and battlements were clear to Boyd but he could not see a door. The path was clear save for Janice crawling towards uncertainty.

Deep inside that complex brain, Boyd sensed something wasn't quite right.

'I'm on the dam wall,' radioed Anthea. 'I confirm the presence of at least one device. Engaging!'

'We all have that,' radioed Bannerman. 'Go easy, Anthea.'

Darius climbed over the battlements, left the rope hanging in the breeze, and removed plastic explosive from the rucksack. Approaching the draw off tower, he found it to be a circular building. He located the door. It was secured by a digital code mechanism that demanded a code prior to opening. He began to rig the entrance with a device for immediate explosion.

Fifty yards away, Mouretti lay in wait.

Janice belly crawled towards the draw off tower with her heart thumping and blood racing through her veins.

She made another five yards before the cold barrel of a gun touched her temple and a voice demanded, 'And who the hell are you?'

Janice froze on the spot.

'I said who the hell are you?'

'I'm wildfowling,' offered Janice. 'Why? What's it to you?'

Mouretti pressed the gun harder into her temple and asked, 'I'm not asking again. You've got three seconds or I'll blow you to kingdom come.'

Turning her head slightly to face Mouretti, Janice snapped, 'Police! Your time is up whatever you do.'

Chuckling, Mouretti replied, 'Young lady, you've no idea who you are talking to. Goodbye!'

'Freeze!' barked Boyd levelling his gun at Mouretti. 'You're under arrest, Darius. Drop your weapon.'

Surprised at the intrusion, and the comment, Mouretti turned to face Boyd and asked, 'What did you just call me?'

Janice remained motionless as Boyd's mouth dropped open when he declared, 'Darius! You're not Darius. You're…'

'Someone you'll never know. Are you with her?'

'Hands!' growled Boyd. 'Drop the gun. Now!'

'No way,' replied Mouretti. 'I'd put your gun down because I'll happily send this young lady to kingdom come. Back off and drop your weapon or she'll get it first.'

'And you'll get it second,' barked Boyd.

There was an impasse with Boyd's gun inches from Mouretti's head and Mouretti's weapon pressed against Janice's temple.

'I'm going to try and make these bombs safe,' radioed Anthea. 'Stand by.'

'I have that,' replied Bannerman.

Hearing the low murmur of a radio, Mouretti ventured, 'Police?'

'Yes,' replied Boyd. 'One of my team dismantling a bomb at the dam, Mister Mouretti.'

'You know me?' puzzled Mouretti.

'Not personally,' reported Boyd. 'But our paths have crossed before. Let her go.'

Shaking his head, Mouretti said, 'Any minute now Darius is going to appear on the battlements and I'm going to shoot him dead. Stand in my way and you can join him.'

At the dam, Anthea's eyes worked overtime as she scanned the first device. Reaching into her jacket, she withdrew a knife and inserted it into the plastic explosives.

'How did you get the information that led you here?' enquired Boyd.

'Yes, I know you. You're the one they call Boyd. I've seen your photograph in the files.'

'Mister Mouretti,' repeated Boyd. 'I want to know how you found out the man was here.'

'From your ticker system,' replied Mouretti unmoved.

'No, you didn't,' proposed Boyd. 'NATO only has partial access at the present moment. Political reasons, nothing personal.'

311

'Enough, this is my man,' remarked Mouretti. 'Walk away now.'

'No, we're going nowhere. We can look down each other's gun barrels all day but we're stuck here with a job to do.'

Mouretti pushed his gun further into Janice's temple and said, 'You wouldn't shoot me. I'm a law enforcement officer.'

'And I got the sack an hour ago,' replied Boyd. 'Officially, I'm not even here.'

'I don't believe that,' offered Mouretti.

'You'll know when I pull the trigger,' replied Boyd. 'Listen, I ran a cyber security check on you. There's nothing on Ticker saying who Darius is.'

'I have friends,' revealed Mouretti.

The point of Anthea's knife made a circle in the plastic explosives. Then she dug the knife deeper and began to ease the end of the detonator out. The end of the detonator, and the fuse cap, still clung to the plastic explosive.

With plastic explosives packed around one of the hinges at the entrance to the draw off tower, Darius inserted a quick burn device and turned his attention to the bottom hinge. As he changed position, Darius moved a yard to his right and heard voices.

Stunned, he stopped what he was doing and reached for the gun in his shoulder holster.

'Let me think,' suggested Boyd. 'Your friends aren't likely to be American or Turkish. The Yanks aren't that much involved and the Turks want to put him on trial. It could be the Russians but their interest is minimal. That leaves the Germans and Israel. Of course, Tel Aviv. The Israelis told you, didn't they? You did a deal with the Israelis, didn't you?'

Mouretti did not reply.

Darius switched the safety catch off his sidearm.

Anthea unpacked the detonator from the explosives and threw it into the lake. She began work on the second device fully aware that the device she had just disposed of would explode when activated. The difference was that she had reduced the blast potential significantly.

The sound of a motor bike invaded her ears as she dug her knife into the second block of explosives.

'What did you trade with them?' asked Boyd.

'I didn't,' revealed Mouretti. 'They told me where he was because the Placer told them. I agreed to do their work for them. Revenge! You won't understand.'

'How much did they give you for the contract?'

'Nothing,' replied Mouretti.

Darius, gun in hand, crept closer as he listened to the men talking. Inches later, he saw Janice lying on her belly with a shotgun pointed towards him but a gun pressed into her temple by an unseen individual.

Retracing his steps, Darius finished his work on the door and sought his mobile phone.

At the dam, a second device ended up in the lake and Anthea began digging out the third. A motor bike engine revved and the rider snatched first gear.

'White Eagle murdered my father in Paris,' volunteered Mouretti. 'He was one of the NATO generals killed by this megalomaniac.'

'And that gives you the right to take his life?' asked Boyd.

A finger pressed a button on a mobile phone and sent a wireless signal to a timer on the dam at Haweswater.

Martin roared down the wall of the dam, braked hard and slewed the bike around to retrace his steps.

'Hop on!' he yelled.

Anthea clambered onto the back of Martin's motor bike and he twisted the throttle for all he was worth. With the back tyre slithering from left to right and snatching what purchase it could find on the brick surface, Martin accelerated to safety with Anthea hanging on for grim death and three devices suddenly exploding in the lake nearby.

Huge mountains of water ascended into the sky, reached a pinnacle, and crashed down on the surface.

At the draw off tower, a match lit the end of a detonating cord. The flame rushed down the cord, collided with the ignition device, and exploded. The hinges blew from the tower door at the same time that Darius showed himself.

Standing away from the tower, he pulled the trigger and let of a round of bullets that penetrated Mouretti's chest as he screamed, 'He will never forget and neither will I.'

Janice rolled to her right and returned fire blasting a slug towards Darius.

Mouretti toppled backwards and was dead before he hit the brickwork.

Boyd flattened to the ground and let off a stream of bullets.

Moments later, Darius was out of sight with Janice shouting on the radio, 'Shots fired. One down at scene. Shots fired.'

'The tower!' yelled Boyd. 'He's trying to get inside to destroy the tunnel system.'

'I have him,' screamed Janice as she rushed to the doorway.

In the Operations Centre, Bannerman ordered, 'Shots fired at the draw off tower. One down. All units attend. I have control. Repeat, I have control.'

Once inside the tunnel complex, Darius lugged his rucksack further into the darkness but only to find a huge metal gate which was fitted with a padlock.

He let off a salvo of bullets at the lock but to little effect. The gate held.

Turning, Darius dropped the rucksack, rammed another magazine into his firearm, and climbed the steps that would take him to the top of the tower.

Approaching the open door of the tower, Boyd snatched a view inside, saw only darkness, and threw a stun grenade into the void.

Covering his ears, Boyd waited for the silence to follow as Janice reloaded and dropped low and to the left of the doorway.

'Left and low,' queried Janice.

'High and right,' indicated Boyd. 'Shoot before entry! Ninety-degree arc of fire.'

'On three,' responded Janice. 'One… Two…'

There was a barrage of shooting as Boyd and Janice fired into the darkness from the entrance of the draw off tower.

Out of ammunition, they both took a step back into the daylight to reload.

There was the unmistakable scrape of a manhole cover when Darius reached the top of the steps and climbed out of the tunnel complex.

Standing on the roof of the draw off tower, a manhole cover leading to the steps behind him, he looked down on Boyd and Anthea and shouted, 'Your turn.'

A hand pushed a dial. An eagle soared, paused, then dived headlong into the roof of the tower and collided with Darius.

There was an almighty clatter when a six-foot diameter quadcopter drone, disguised as an eagle, smashed into Darius.

Losing his footing instantly, Darius's finger pulled the trigger and let of a salvo of shots that fired into the air as the force of the impact knocked him from the tower and sent him reeling backwards.

There was a sickening crunch of skull and backbone when the body of Darius Yasin struck the rock-strewn bed of Haweswater.

Rushing to the battlements, Boyd and Janice ignored the grappling iron and rope, and peered down on the man below.

It was as if Darius was alive, beckoning them to come and join him. Then, graciously, the body surrendered to the waters and turned over. Head down, the body of the boy from the Quandil Mountains lay uncomfortably in its final fatal posture.

'Job done,' remarked Boyd.

A shower of feathers sprinkled to the ground when the eagle drone lost its electronic connection again and plunged into the lake beside the body.

Bending, Boyd picked up a handful of feathers and offered them to Janice saying, 'How lucky were we today?'

'Luckier than these two,' replied Janice. 'Should we check the tunnel below? I don't think he had time but…'

'Yes, yes of course,' agreed Boyd.

As the two detectives made their way to the tunnel entrance, Boyd radioed, 'Red Alpha One reports two down at this location.'

'Are you injured?' enquired Commander Maxwell.

'No casualties at this location,' replied Boyd. 'White Eagle is neutralised and we have a law enforcement officer from another organisation dead at the scene. Anthea? What happened at the dam?'

Bannerman replied, 'She kept the bombs together, cut them out of the main explosive packages, and threw them in the lake. When they detonated, only the primer exploded. The dam is intact and so is Anthea.'

Janice smiled and Boyd replied, 'Good! This is Red Alpha One requesting Senior Command to attend the crime scene. Also, request full forensic and search team plus explosives ordnance disposal. Contact is over. We have weapons to surrender.'

Bannerman replied, 'I think my weapon has already surrendered. The eagle is down again.'

'Did you break it, Bannerman?' enquired Ricky on the radio.

'Whoops!' came the reply.

Chuckling, Commander Maxwell took the radio and said, 'William, I take it your Operational Command Briefing is now over?'

'All except the feathers, sir,' replied Boyd. 'We're covered in white feathers.'

From the sky above, the feathers of the eagle continued to flutter down on the scene below.

. . .    . . .    . . .

One Month Later

Whilst sitting at a desk in the Israeli Embassy, Benjamin hoisted his feet onto the edge and waited for a voice on the other end of the telephone to respond.

Eventually, Toni answered and Benjamin began the conversation with, 'Shalom, Miss Harston-Browne.'

'Shalom, Benjamin Shakira,' replied Toni. 'It seems we both have names now.'

Chuckling, the diplomat enquired, 'It is time to have that lunch we once talked about. I wondered if you were free soon?'

'Possibly, I'm rather busy at the moment,' replied Toni. 'Any particular reason you have decided to proposition me today?'

'I am always interested in discussing matters of a mutual interest, Miss Harston-Browne,' chuckled Benjamin. 'Indeed, we are both in pursuit of a peaceful world are we not?'

'We surely are,' replied Toni.

'By the way,' explained the man from Israel. 'Would you like to know who the Placer is?'

There was a slight pause before Toni replied, 'Lunch! Yes, I can do lunch tomorrow if that's convenient?'

On the streets of Paris, Miryam walked alone taking in the sights and sounds of that wonderful city. Miryam was happy.

The sister of Malik had stalked the streets of many capital cities, taken the phones calls, made the arrangements, and placed the articles required for the job to be done by whomever and wherever. Miryam had remained undetected for over a decade.

She was still placing and still important in the scheme of things.

Only Miryam, and a man from the Israeli Embassy, knew that she had traded the identity and location of Darius Yasin in return for an agreement that her brother's home in the Quandil Mountains would never be bombed again.

Such was the complexity of global political relationships that she truly believed that the Israelis would be able to use leverage on their western allies and do a deal in return for regular and accurate information.

In Miryam's mind, she would continue life as the Placer and occasionally feed the Israelis with information they could use as bartering power. Never again, would the mountains of her home be bombed and obliterated. She was now a double agent.

In return, there would be no more jets over the Quandil Mountains. Miryam was happy, so very happy.

A weekend arrived and four friends took to the Lake District for a fell walking expedition.

Boyd, Toni, Meg, and Phillip stood on Eagle Crag overlooking Haweswater.

Ten yards away, the Boyd twins - Issy (named after Doctor Ismail Farooqi who had delivered them) and James (named after Boyd's first Commander, James Herbert) sat on a rock eating crisps and drinking pop.

'So this is where it happened?' queried Phillip.

'Yes,' replied Boyd. 'We set up a drone camera system here to cover the entire lake and then ran the product via a satellite link to a covert motorhome there on the car park. There was a remote override that linked to the Operations Centre in London.'

'Which is being reassessed because it didn't work correctly,' declared Phillip.

'First time out,' replied Boyd. 'One day in the future maybe but it worked when we needed it to work.'

Sir Phillip nodded agreement and offered, 'I spoke on the phone briefly with the Home Secretary this morning.'

'What about?' probed Boyd.

'Oh, I just expressed private pleasure in the knowledge that you had been reinstated and there was no question of discipline proceedings being taken against anyone in the unit.'

'Yes,' nodded Boyd. 'She rang to tell me that the Commissioner had lifted the suspension and officially commended everyone in the Red Alpha team on a job well done.'

'The Home Secretary rang you?' queried Phillip.

'Yes,' confirmed Boyd. 'Then the Commissioner rang me. He was quietly apologetic, that's all I say.'

'Don't forget the medals, Billy,' remarked Meg. 'Billy, Janice, and Anthea have been awarded the Queen's Gallantry Medal.'

'Don't forget the locals in Cumbria,' remarked Boyd. 'Quite a few have been commended for their work on the floods in Thirlmere and Keswick.'

'Brilliant,' acknowledged Toni. 'I'd have brought champagne if I'd known that.'

Meg giggled and replied, 'We'd have smashed it on the rocks by now.' Then she shouted, 'Issy! James! Are you alright?'

The twins waved back and yelled,' Fine, mum!'

Phillip congratulated Boyd and then said, 'You deserved it but the Home Secretary did tell me you have upset the apple cart again. What did you tell her this time?'

'That it doesn't matter how much you put into intelligence and technology, the systems are only as good as the people using them.'

'And loyalty?' suggested Phillip. 'You mentioned loyalty apparently.'

'Yes, I did,' confirmed Boyd. 'I suggested loyalty must precede the use of intelligence otherwise…'

'We end up with people like Mouretti,' remarked Phillip. 'Well-meaning and understandable but in the scheme of things…'

'Lacking,' declared Boyd. 'And self-promoted above the legal system he chose to serve. That makes people like Giuseppe Mouretti bigger criminals than the people they chase. On one hand, you have the signature killer and megalomaniac Darius, and in the other you have Mouretti who believed he was above the law – a tyrant in waiting. If Mouretti had lived, he would have been charged with espionage.'

'Perhaps his death has prevented a problem with our NATO colleagues,' offered Phillip.

'I think so too,' replied Boyd.

'It's beautiful, so calm, so peaceful here,' announced Meg. 'Haweswater is a glorious diamond, a hidden gem in one of the most isolated parts of the lakes. Somewhere everyone forgets to visit when they tour the lake district.'

'Isn't it just,' agreed Boyd.

They surveyed the area and took in the glory of it all.

'Makes you think what might have happened after the First World War,' suggested Boyd.

'What do you mean?' enquired Phillip.

'The victors decided to enjoy the spoils of war by destroying the old Ottoman Empire – the Persian Empire,' ventured Boyd. 'Turkey was created, the region was shared out, and the Kurds got nothing. How easy would it have been to nestle Kurdistan in that cradle between Turkey, Iraq and Iran? It might have prevented places like the Quandil Mountains from becoming a centre of criminality, and a centre of terrorism. They could have embraced the area, improved the infrastructure, and made it better. Instead, they left it, denied the Kurds, and it turned out the way it did.'

'Reminds you of the creation of the State of Israel in 1948,' suggested Phillip. 'Immediately after the Second World War when they carved up the Middle East.'

'To deny Palestine to the Arabs and agitate the problem still further by not reaching an agreement at that time,' offered Boyd.

'Will mankind ever learn?' asked Toni.

'The world is still flat, isn't it?' suggested Meg.

'We'd have no Placers or Collectors to worry about if it was,' offered Boyd.

'It's all over now,' declared Toni.

'No, it's not – for me but not for you,' revealed Boyd.

'What do you mean?' enquired Toni.

'You know what I mean,' proposed Boyd. 'The Placer, and the Placer of Placers.'

No one responded.

Boyd removed white feathers from his pocket and said, 'We'll never be sure of his real name. Was it Darrius or something else?'

'He was never identified properly,' confirmed Toni.

'The man with no name,' suggested Phillip.

'Phillip,' insisted Boyd. 'The Placers…When?'

Checking his watch, Phillip replied, 'About now…'

In Paris, a motor bike drove down a road and approached a woman walking along the pavement. The woman was Miryam: The brother of Malik.

The pillion passenger withdrew a Uzi submachine gun from beneath his jacket and rattled half a dozen shots into her chest. Then he dismounted the bike and drilled another half dozen shots into her head.

The rider twisted the throttle. The killer jumped back on the pillion seat and they rode off.

The Placer was dead.

A squadron of jets overflew the village.

They flew very low and very fast hugging the ground and making it difficult for the guards to see them approach.

From a NATO base in Turkey, they held their formation and listened to the Squadron Leader give his commands.

'On my mark, three, two, one… Strike… Missiles away… Contact… Contact … Contact… Away… Away… Away.'

Totally surprised, Malik looked skywards when the first missiles rained down on the village and destroyed the drugs laboratory. A succession of explosions followed when dozens of bombs, missiles and bullets, laid down their wrath across the village floor.

Within moments, Malik – the Placer of Placers – was killed in the bombing raid.

Elsewhere in the village, a youngster ran away from the bombs, and tried to hide. He'd lost his home and his family.

The youngster wept and wept.

'Why?' he shouted.

'What have I done to you? This is my home.'

'Why? Why? 'Why?'

In the stillness that followed, a Persian leopard stalked the valley floor.

A tap dripped water in the village.

A white eagle flew in the skies looking for its prey below.

Calling!

An eagle was calling for its parents, looking for its future, searching for the way out.

The white eagle soared above the mountains, extended its wings, and flew north to a valley unknown on its search for its destiny.

The White Eagle of the Quandil Mountains lived supreme.

*

## Notes from the Author

~

## The Eagles of the Quandil Mountains, and the Reservoirs of Cumbria.

~

## Thirlmere

~

Thirlmere is situated in Cumbria's Lake District. It runs from Wythburn in the south to High Bridge End Farm in the north. The reservoir, or lake as the locals like to call it, is bordered on the eastern side by the A591 road and on the western side by a minor road.

Before the construction of the reservoir there was a smaller natural lake, known by various names including Leathes Water, Wythburn Water, Thirle Water, and Thirlmere. The Ordnance Survey six-inch map of 1862 shows a single lake with its narrowest point at Wath Bridge roughly level with Armboth.

In 1863, it was urged that Thirlmere and Haweswater should be made reservoirs. It was proposed that their water should be conveyed via Ullswater, which was to be used as a distributing reservoir, 240 miles to London to supply it with two hundred million gallons a day of clean water. The cost of the project was put at ten million pounds.

By 1876, the scheme had grown to include a branch feeder from Bala Lake, in Wales. The cost rose to £13.5 million. Nothing came of this, but both Manchester and Liverpool became concerned that their existing water supplies would be rendered inadequate by their growth. Accordingly, they sought supplies from further afield.

In 1877, Manchester Corporation proposed, instead, to supply Manchester with water from a Thirlmere reservoir.

There was strong local opposition to the construction of the lake and the Thirlmere Defence Association was formed to oppose the parliamentary act which was required before work could begin. The Association opposed on the basis that raising the water level by 50 feet would submerge the dramatic cliffs which then surrounded the lake and a receding shoreline in summer would expose the smelly and unsightly lake bed. The organisation managed to stall the Bill in Parliament in 1878, but the Act was passed in 1879.

In 1890-91, the Corporation constructed a dam at the northern end of Thirlmere, raising the water level, flooding the valley bottom, which included the village of Wythburn and the hamlet of Armboth. A school, vicarage, inns, farms and houses were also lost forever. Only the hamlet of Steel End, at the south end of the present Thirlmere, and Wythburn Church remained. New housing was created at Fisher End and Stanah.

The reservoir provided the growing industrial city of Manchester with water supplies via the 96 mile-long Thirlmere Aqueduct.

A tunnelled section under Dunmail Raise was dug by two teams mining towards each other.

The dam at Thirlmere rises 64 feet above the old stream bed, and the reservoir, when full, has a surface area of 814 acres and a holding capacity of 8,235,000,000 imperial gallons.

The aqueduct stretches all the way to Heaton Park Reservoir, Prestwich. Its most common form of construction is cut-and-cover, which consists of a concrete covered channel, approximately 7.1 feet wide and between 7.1 feet and 7.9 feet high. There are 37 miles of cut and cover that are made up of concrete horseshoe-shaped sections 12 inches thick. Typically, the conduit has 3 feet of cover and traverses the contours of hillsides.

It is the longest gravity-fed aqueduct in the country, with no pumps along its route. The water flows at a speed of 4 miles per hour and takes just over a day to reach the city. The level of the aqueduct drops by approximately 20 inches per mile of its length

## Haweswater

~

Haweswater is also a reservoir built in the valley of Mardale in the county of Cumbria. The controversial construction of the Haweswater dam started in 1929, after parliament passed an Act giving Manchester Corporation permission to build the reservoir to supply water for Manchester. The decision caused public outcry, since the farming villages of Measand and Mardale Green would be flooded, with their inhabitants needing to be relocated. Also, many desired to maintain the picturesque valley in its existing state.

Originally, Haweswater was a natural lake about two and a half miles long. The building of the dam raised the water level by 95 feet and created a reservoir four miles long and almost half a mile wide.

Before the valley was flooded, in 1935, all the farms and dwellings of the villages of Mardale Green and Measand were demolished, as well as the centuries-old Dun Bull Inn at Mardale Green. The village church was dismantled and the stone used in constructing the dam. All the bodies in the churchyard were exhumed and re-buried at Shap.

At the time of construction, it was considered to be cutting-edge technology as it was the world's first hollow buttress dam, using 44 separate buttressed units joined by flexible joints. A parapet, 56 inches wide, runs the length of the dam and from this, tunnelled supplies can be seen entering the reservoir from the adjoining valleys of Heltondale and Swindale. When the reservoir is full, it holds 18.6 billion gallons of water. The reservoir is now owned by United Utilities PLC. It supplies about 25% of the North West's water supply.

Today, when the water in the reservoir is low, the remains of the submerged village of Mardale Green can still be seen, including stone walls and the village bridge.

Manchester Corporation built a new road along the eastern side of the lake to replace the flooded highway lower in the valley, and the Haweswater Hotel was constructed midway down the length of the reservoir as a replacement for the Dun Bull. The road continues to the western end of Haweswater, to a car park, a popular starting point for a path to the surrounding fells of Harter Fell, Branstree and High Street.

There is a population of schelly fish in the lake, believed to have lived there since the last Ice Age.

The Royal Society for the Protection of Birds first became involved in Haweswater because of the presence of golden eagles. The organisation currently manages two farms in the area.

Until 2015, Haweswater was the only place in England where a golden eagle was resident. A pair of eagles first nested in the valley of Riggindale in 1969. The male and female of the pairing changed several times over the years, during which sixteen chicks were produced. The female bird disappeared in April 2004, leaving the male alone. There was an RSPB observation post in the valley for people wishing to see the eagle: the last sighting was in November 2015. It was reported that the 20-year old bird may have died of natural causes.

The Golden Eagle of the Lake District has never been seen since.

In the area of Mardale Head car park, mentioned in the book you have just read, Dudderwick dominates the opposing side of the lake above Mardale Beck. The crags here ascend from the lakeside, at the Rigg, and feature Swinside Crag, Heron Crag, Eagle Crag, and

Rough Crag before the ridge merges with Riggindale Crag and the High Street range.

There are no recent sightings of any eagles in this area.

\*

## Heaton Park Reservoir

~

Heaton Park Reservoir is a granite sided reservoir in the North-West of England on the border between the City of Manchester and Bury. It is owned by United Utilities and located within the grounds of Heaton Park, which is close to Junction 18 of the M60 motorway.

The water carried by aqueduct from Haweswater to Manchester terminates at Heaton Park Reservoir.

In 2008, a £3.5 million Ultra-Violet disinfection plant was installed at Heaton Park water treatment works to meet water quality requirements. The UV building was designed to nestle within the embankment of the existing service reservoir.

The reservoir is known for its wintering wildfowl. Amongst the most recorded are tufted duck, goldeneye, goosander and common teal. Other, less common sightings, include the lesser scaup, the ring-necked duck, the Slavonian grebe, the black-necked grebe, the long-tailed duck, the Leach's petrel and the European honey buzzard. Due to a nearby landfill site, the reservoir also plays host to a large gull population including yellow-legged gulls, Caspian gulls, Iceland gulls and Kumlien's gulls.

The reservoir is not part of Cumbria despite its obvious association. There are no reports of sightings of Golden Eagles in the Heaton Park area.

\*

# The Reservoirs of Cumbria
~

There are eighteen 'reservoirs of Cumbria.'
They are listed as follows: -

Borrans Reservoir, north of Windermere town
Castle Carrock Reservoir, near Brampton
Chapelhouse Reservoir, south-east of Uldale
Cow Green Reservoir, east of Dufton Fell
Dubbs Reservoir, north of Windermere town
Ennerdale Water, Copeland, West Cumbria
Fisher Tarn, east of Kendal
Harlock Reservoir, Ulverston
Pennington Reservoir, Ulverston
Poaka Beck Reservoir, west of Ulverston
Haweswater Reservoir, Mardale, Askham
Hayeswater, Hartsop, Patterdale valley
Kentmere Reservoir, Kentmere, north-east Windermere
Killington Reservoir, Howgill, Sedbergh
Meadley Reservoir, by Flat Fell, Ennerdale, Cumbria
Simpson Ground Reservoir, east of Newby Bridge
Thirlmere, Allerdale, Dunmail
Wet Sleddale Reservoir, Shap

*

### The Eagles of the Quandil Mountains

~

Despite this being a fictional novel, I can tell you that the Quandil Mountains really do exist. They are known by intelligence services the world over as the headquarters of various factions, and offshoots, of the Kurdistan Workers' Party. They are also regarded as part of the Golden Crescent of heroin supply and a base of international criminality.

Yet this area is also renown for the eagles that dominate the high peaks of the Zagros Mountains. Over the centuries, the eagles and mankind, in this region of our amazing planet, have formed an obvious and special bond that defies the normal relationships existing between man and beast. There is little doubt that eagles here have accepted the presence of human beings in what is a far-flung outpost of modern day society. Cut off from the rest of the world by virtue of its topography and culture, the mountains are riddled with tiny villages and hamlets where the sparse population live out a seemingly scant existence in the midst of an almost medieval background.

Not all the eagles here are white eagles. They are the exception and they have taken to their human neighbours in an amazing way.

They, amongst other things, have provided the basis and inspiration for this story….

….White Eagle…


\*

**The End…… Nearly….**

## About Paul Anthony

~

Paul Anthony is a retired Cumbrian detective who has extensive policing connections throughout the United Kingdom and elsewhere. In the past, he has been published by a Vanity House and a Traditional Publishing House but is currently an independent publisher with his own publishing imprint and editorial services business. Paul has written both television and film scripts either on his own, or with the award-winning screenwriter Nick Gordon.

Paul Anthony is a pseudonym. Born in Southport, Lancashire, he is the son of a soldier whose family settled in Carlisle before he joined Cumbria police at the age of 19. As a detective, Paul served in Cumbria CID, the Regional Crime Squad in Manchester, the Special Branch, (Counter Terrorist Command) and other national agencies and consultancies in the UK. He has an Honours Degree in Economics and Social Sciences, a Diploma in Management, and a Diploma in Office Management.

When not writing, he enjoys reading a wide range of works and playing guitar badly. He likes Pilates, kettlebells, athletics, keeping fit, dining out and dining in, travelling, and following politics, economics and social sciences. Married, he and his wife have three adult children and five grandchildren.

Paul is a former winner of the Independent Authors Network Featured Author Contest and was a Featured Author at the 'Books without Borders' Event in Yonkers, New York, 2012.

He has also been a Featured Author at the Frankfurt Book Fair, Germany. This is his amazon page....

Paul Anthony
Reviews
~

'One of the best thriller and mystery writers in the United Kingdom today'....

Caleb Pirtle 111, International Best Selling Author of over 60 novels, journalist, travel writer, screenplay writer, and Founder and Editorial Director at Venture Galleries.

\*

'Paul Anthony is one of the best Thriller Mystery Writers of our times!'...

Dennis Sheehan, International Best Selling Author of 'Purchased Power', former United Sates Marine Corps.

\*

'When it comes to fiction and poetry you will want to check out this outstanding author. Paul has travelled the journey of publication and is now a proud writer who is well worth discovery.' ... Janet Beasley, Epic Fantasy Author, theatre producer and director - Scenic Nature Photographer, JLB Creatives. Also Founder/co-author at Journey to Publication

\*

'Paul Anthony is a brilliant writer and an outstanding gentleman who goes out of his way to help and look out for others. In his writing, Paul does a wonderful job of portraying the era in which we live with its known and unknown fears. I highly recommend this intelligent and kind gentleman to all.' ...

Jeannie Walker, author of the True Crime Story 'Fighting the Devil', 2011 National Indie Excellence Awards (True Crime Finalist) and 2010 winner of the Silver Medal for Book of the Year True Crime Awards.

\*

'To put it simply, Paul tells a bloody good tale. I have all his works and particularly enjoy his narrative style. His characters are totally believable and draw you in. Read. Enjoy'....

John White, Reader and Director at Baldwins Restructuring and Insolvency

*

'Paul Anthony's skills as a writer are paramount. His novels are well-balanced throughout, all of which hold the reader with both dynamic and creative plots and edge-of-your-seat action alike.

His ability to create realistic and true-to-life characters are a strength lacking in many novelists that pen stories based on true events or real life experience. He is a fantastic novelist that will have you craving for more! Get his books now...a must have for all serious readers!'

Nicolas Gordon, Screenwriter - 'Hunted: The enemy within'.

*

'Paul Anthony has been working with the Dyslexia Foundation to develop and digital audio Library, he has been very generous in giving his time and expertise for free. As a long-time fan of Pauls work, it was very altruistic of Paul to allow us to use one of his excellent books. We have recently turned 'The Fragile Peace' into our first audio book, to be used in an exciting project to engage non-readers into the world of literacy. The foundation has an audio book club that will be running in Liverpool and Manchester and Paul again has been very generous with his time in agreeing to come and talk to the audio book club about his book The Fragile Peace. The Foundation and clients are very appreciative of the support of the author Paul Anthony.

Steve O'Brien, C.E.O. Dyslexia Foundation,

This guy not only walks the talk, he writes it as well. Thrillers don't get any better than this....

Paul Tobin, Author, novelist and poet.

### The UK ANTI-TERRORIST HOTLINE

~

If you see or hear something that doesn't sound quite right, don't hesitate. You may feel it's nothing to get excited about but trust in your instincts and let the police know.

~

Remember, no piece of information is considered too small or insignificant.

~

If you see something suspicious – tell the police.

~

'Suspicious activity could include someone:
… Who has bought or stored large amounts of chemicals, fertilisers or gas cylinders for no obvious reason…
… Who has bought or hired a vehicle in suspicious circumstances…
… Who holds passports or other documents in different names for no obvious reason…
… Who travels for long periods of time, but is vague about where they're going…

~

It's probably nothing but… if you see or hear anything that could be terrorist-related trust your instincts and call
the Anti-Terrorist Hotline on 0800 789 321.

~

The UK Anti-Terrorist Hotline
0800 789 321

~

THE END

Printed in Great Britain
by Amazon